A CHOSEN PATH

A CHOSEN PATH

From Moccasin Flats
to Parliament Hill

Frank Oberle

Heritage
House

Heritage House Publishing Company Ltd.
#108 – 17665 66A Avenue
Surrey, BC V3S 2A7
www.heritagehouse.ca

Library and Archives Canada Cataloguing in Publication

Oberle, Frank, 1932–
    A chosen path: from Moccasin Flats to Parliament Hill / Frank Oberle.

ISBN 1-894384-83-0

    1. Oberle, Frank, –   2. Cabinet ministers—Canada—Biography.
3. Canada—Politics and government—1984-1993. 4. Peace River Region (B.C. and Alta.)—Biography. I. Title.

FC601.O24A3 2005   971.064'7'092   C2005-902696-0

Edited by Laurel Bernard.
Book design by Darlene Nickull.
Cover design by Frances Hunter.
Cover photos by Chris Cheadle/BritishColumbiaPhotos.com (bottom front and back); top front photo © NCC/CCN.
All interior photos courtesy of Frank Oberle.

Printed in Canada

Heritage House acknowledges the financial support for its publishing program from the Government of Canada through the Book Publishing Industry Development Program (BPIDP), Canada Council for the Arts, and the British Columbia Arts Council.

The Canada Council | Le Conseil des Arts
for the Arts | du Canada

BRITISH
COLUMBIA
ARTS COUNCIL
We acknowledge the support of the Province of British Columbia
through the British Columbia Arts Council

This book has been produced on 100% post-consumer recycled paper, processed chlorine free and printed with vegetable-based inks.

Dedication

I have no one to blame but myself for reawakening the painful memories of my childhood and early youth, during which a cloud of darkness descended over the European continent and mankind's actions were guided by its most primitive instincts.

I am overwhelmed by the response that *Finding Home*, the first volume of my memoirs, has generated—not only from hundreds of my compatriots, people of my own generation for whom the book recalled memories similar to my own, but many others as well who served with the allied forces, bearing witness to the horrors of the Second World War from a different perspective, and whose scars are just as deep. I feel a strong sense of guilt for having caused all of them renewed suffering, and I hope to relieve my own conscience by dedicating this book to them.

Acknowledgements

Any attempt to list all the people whose love, friendship, and trust helped to enrich our lives in so many ways and whose dedication to the causes we shared and the exemplary service they have given during my many years in public life, would render this book entirely too voluminous.

But I would be remiss were I not to offer an acknowledgement of a special debt of gratitude at least to some of the people who invited us into their homes, who worked in the various constituency and Parliament Hill offices, my personal and special research assistants, and some of the many volunteers who gave so generously of their time and resources not only during elections, but throughout my tenure in parliament.

Lee and Bob Acott, Barb Bale, Bernard Barrett, Lynn Belsey, Joanne Bott, John Bracken, Lee and Ernie Bodin, Reinelle Boudrias, Gudrun and George Boyce, Ruth and Garry Callison, Peter and Diane Christie, Nancy Chiulli, Ken Cook, Lorne Dalke, Joanne Doerges, Hilary and Floyd Crowley, Jan and Don Edwards, Warren Everson, Orville and Maureen Endicott, Jack and Ella Fraser, Pam Glass, Thorine and Graham Goodall, Arna and Gary Halderson, Louise Hayes, Gail and Jim Henderson, Robin and Irene Heather, Frank and Lotte Hinteregger, Bob Hunter, Henry and Etta Hryciw, Maureen Keibel, Marry Humphries, Hemi and Stan Klemik, Linda Klone, Valerie Kordyban, Tom Lazenby, Larry and Pat Lewin, Angus Laidlaw, Shirley and Don Marshall, Fred and Anne Marie Maides, Rod Maides, Bunty Mercier, Don and Alayne McFedridge, Lorne and Dorothy McCuish, Denise McCullough, Richard Prokopanko, Kirk Rustad, Annemone and Martin Schliessler, Kim Seguin, Norm and Bev Stirling, Denise Stromberg, Noreen Stubley, Donna Spear, Bobby and Richard Suen, Jeannine Tracy, Ian Urquart, and Geri and Gordon Webb. To all those who most assuredly have been missed, I offer my sincere apology.

I offer a special thanks to my wife, Joan, for giving me the freedom to pursue my dreams, for her steadfast support, for offering encouragement when I was in doubt, and for sustaining me with her love.

A special thanks also goes to Laurel Bernard, my editor, for her infinite patience and valuable professional advice.

Contents

Minister of State for Science and Technology and Minister of Forestry: 1985–1993
Aftermath: 1993–2005

Publisher's Note

The first volume of Frank Oberle's memoirs, *Finding Home: A War Child's Journey to Peace*, recorded his childhood in Forchheim, Germany, and his terrible wartime years as a young witness to the horrors of the Second World War. It followed him to Canada, where he carved out a living in British Columbia as a logger, gold miner, and entrepreneur. By the time he was 30, he and his wife, Joan, had founded a successful business, a family, and the beginnings of a political career.

But now he faced a new challenge: life in the public eye. After war and frontier living, Frank Oberle thought he was ready for anything life could throw at him—only to discover that nothing had prepared him for Ottawa or the realities of small-town politics.

This second volume of Frank Oberle's memoirs continues his remarkable story, tracing his path from mayor of Chetwynd and member of Parliament for Prince George–Peace River to an eminence beyond his wildest dreams: Minister of State for Science and Technology and Minister of Forestry in the Queen's Privy Council of Canada.

Introduction

As life is action and passion, it is required of a man that he should share the passion and action of his time, at peril of being judged not to have lived.

—Oliver Wendell Holmes Jr.

From a European perspective, it's strange to think of a town in which every one of its citizens is older than the place itself. Even our youngest son, Peter, born in March of 1962, was three months old when Chetwynd received its charter. Chetwynd did have an earlier incarnation as Little Prairie, a name dating back to the early 1930s, when the first settlers of European origin, mostly farmers escaping drought on the prairies, came to northwestern British Columbia in search of greener pastures. It was a small, isolated farm community with little prospect for growth until permanent crossings were built to bridge both the Pine River to the east and the Parsnip River to the west, linking the area to the rest of British Columbia.

With the construction of the Hart Highway through the Rocky Mountains from Prince George to Dawson Creek in 1952, and the railway's arrival in 1958, the settlement evolved as the gateway to the resource-rich Peace River area. Almost overnight, Chetwynd became a centre of rapid growth and enough new, sufficiently diversified development to afford it the permanence to escape the fate of such places as Pioneer, the boom town of my gold-mining years that is now a ghost town.

For Joan and me, our arrival in Chetwynd was the end of a long, onerous, eventful, and, at times, torturous journey—30 years that are recorded in my first book, *Finding Home: A War Child's Journey to Peace.* This second volume of our memoirs, which follows our story from 1962 to the present day, is meant to be a tribute to Canada, the greatest place on earth, and to her people, among them the many friends and supporters who have helped us along the way and to whom we are so deeply indebted.

I also hope to offer my grandchildren a glimpse into our past and inspire them and others of their generation to believe that there are no limits to what they can accomplish and be—if only they have the courage and conviction to pursue their dreams. As well, it is my hope that our fellow Canadians not fortunate enough to inherit citizenship by birth will find reinforcement for their belief that as long as they are committed to Canada, there are no limits to the status to which they may aspire as full members of our society.

I bear no malice toward any of the characters described in these pages. In fact, I have changed the names of certain people or have introduced them in the abstract in an effort not to offend their friends and families. I am also relying on memory for those parts of this account not in the public record, and I have no doubt that with the passage of time, other people's recollections of certain events will be at odds with my own. If so, I offer my sincere apologies to anyone whom I may have offended.

Finding Home: A War Child's Journey to Peace starts with that far-off place of my birth, Forchheim, on the edge of the Black Forest in southwestern Germany. There I spent my early childhood working on the land in a society little changed since the Middle Ages—until the war came and disrupted all our lives. I was only eight years old when, in 1940, my family was forced to relocate from our ancestral home on the Rhine to Poznań, Poland, where Hitler had set up much of his secret war production and manufacturing operations to put them beyond the range of Allied bombing.

Under the auspices of the *Kinderlandverschickung* [relocating children to the country] program, established by the Nazis to indoctrinate the nation's children at the earliest possible age, I was enrolled in a residential school far enough away from the city to prevent any but the most essential contact with my family. Since the school's pupils had not been sent back to be reunited with their parents before Germany's inevitable defeat on the eastern front, they joined thousands of refugees and defeated troops fleeing westward ahead of the Soviet advance. After enduring the fear, the hunger, the cold, and the sheer horror of this epic journey, we arrived in Dresden on February 13, 1945, in time to witness the firestorm that turned one of Germany's historic cities and cultural icons into a living hell that claimed the lives of between 35,000 and 135,000 innocent people.

When the war finally came to an end, one of my classmates and I—both of us just 13—struck out on a 500-kilometre journey in search of my parents and our families. In the famine and chaos of a beaten postwar nation, it was a trip that tested our will and endurance and for which our only sustenance was our raw instinct for survival. On reaching home, instead of finding either my parents or a welcome, I was rejected by my own grandfather, shunted from place to place, and separated from the friend who had shared all the sufferings of my journey.

Miraculously, all my family did survive the war, and all of us—my parents, Rösel and Adolf, my two brothers, Ludwig and Erich, and my sister, Lina—eventually found our way back to where we started at the beginning of the war. But things would never be the same. The emotional scars we all had acquired were much too deep, and the lack of essentials to sustain us as a family soon forced us to strike out on our own and pursue our separate ways. Now 14, I was placed in an apprenticeship position offering room and board at a bakery in Karlsruhe, and I worked in that trade until the age of 19, when I decided to break with my troubled past and seek my fortune in another part of the world: Canada.

Meanwhile, Joan's childhood was no less troubled than my own. Joan and I had met for the first time on the altar of Forchheim's St. Martin's church, where we were both being baptized, and later, in 1938, we started school together. Her father, Emil Kistner, was drafted in the early days of the war and survived the torture of a Siberian prisoner-of-war camp, returning nine years later a human wreck.

When I returned after the war, Joan's mother, Berta, though a total stranger, saw it as her Christian duty to offer me a home, setting the seal of my lifelong bond to Joan. We swore to one another then that we would commit to any compromise, any sacrifice, so as never to be hungry again—and to escape to the farthest corner of the earth, if necessary, to avoid the horror of future wars and provide our children with a better life.

Penniless and without any English-language skills, I landed in Halifax, Nova Scotia, in 1951, where I soon discovered my trade was of little use in pursuing the ambitious goals Joan and I had. Instead, I opted for the much more demanding but more lucrative jobs in the logging camps along British Columbia's coast, and in the Pioneer gold mine high in the Coast mountain range of B.C.'s interior. Joan joined me 18 months after

I had left Germany, and we began our true life as a family—a family that was to be blessed with four children: Ursula, Isabell, Frank Jr., and Peter.

From Pioneer, after a brief stopover in 100 Mile House and abortive attempts at ranching and insurance sales, we finally reached the home of our dreams. Resisting the lure of the province's cities, we chose to pursue a crazy scheme to operate a gas station in the middle of nowhere, and so arrived in Little Prairie in October of 1958.

Over the next three years, bursting with energy and youthful enthusiasm, we made our Standard Oil service-station franchise into a thriving enterprise that soon yielded the necessary resources, self-confidence, and courage we needed to pursue other opportunities. We expanded—first into real estate, and later into an integrated automotive sales-and-service facility in which only the bank shared ownership.

Not unlike the settlers who had preceded us there, we came to Chetwynd in search of a new home. Haunted by our past and deeply scarred by the horror and dislocation of our childhoods, we felt we had found a place that offered just enough distance between ourselves and the ghosts that kept denying us the peace and security we so desperately sought. We discovered in the various clubs and organizations we joined a way to replace the social contacts we had left behind in Germany. We felt comfortable attaching our hopes for the future to the community. In Chetwynd, we had finally found a place where the horizon's limits stretched as far as our own commitment to hard work and our dreams dared them to go.

It wasn't long before we found ourselves in the position of wanting to give something back to our adoptive homeland. We wanted to be part of nurturing the growth and development of our new community. Right from the beginning, we chose to actively participate and contribute to its social development, so that it would keep pace with the industrial and economic progress sweeping it. The early settlers had built a community hall that served as the focal point for a myriad of social activities, and it was soon complemented by a curling rink, a Legion hall, a modest library, and the Elks Hall. All of these were built with volunteer labour and generous donations from the business community.

But we also saw injustices in Chetwynd, particularly in the way a large component of the local residents were treated. Inevitably, we found ourselves wanting to redress some of these inequities. So, with Joan's unceasing support, I took my first steps along the road to a full-blown career in politics. It turned out to be a long and arduous journey, often rewarding and successful beyond my wildest dreams, but also frequently disillusioning in its astonishing revelations of political reality. My newly chosen path, destined to lead away from our home in the heart of northern British Columbia, started small—with the fight over Chetwynd's name.

Historic Milestones During Frank Oberle's Career

1962–1972 Chetwynd Village Councillor and Mayor

1962   On June 18, Progressive Conservatives and John Diefenbaker win a minority government

1963   On April 8, Liberals and Lester B. Pearson win a minority government
On November 22, John F. Kennedy assassinated

1965   On November 8, Pearson and Liberals win a minority government again

1967   On September 9, Diefenbaker is replaced by Robert Stanfield

1968   On June 25, Pierre Elliott Trudeau and the Liberals win election against Stanfield

1969   On July 20, Neil Armstrong walks on the moon

1970   On October 16, Trudeau invokes War Measures Act during the October Crisis

1972   Terrorists assassinate 11 Israelis at Munich Olympics
On August 30, Dave Barrett and the NDP defeat W.A.C. Bennett and the Social Credit Party in a B.C. election
On October 30, the federal Liberals win a minority government

1972–1985 Member of Parliament for Prince George–Peace River

1973   U.S. launches its first space station, Skylab
Watergate and the energy crisis in the U.S.

1974   On July 8, Trudeau and Liberals win a majority government
On July 30, Bill 22, making French the official language in Quebec, is passed

1975   On December 11, Bill Bennett and the Social Credit Party win a B.C. election

1976   In February, Joe Clark replaces Stanfield as Conservative leader
On July 17, the Summer Olympics start in Montreal
On November 15, René Lévesque and the Parti Québécois win the provincial election in Quebec

1978   Commonwealth Games held in Edmonton

1979   On May 10, Bennett and the Social Credit Party are re-elected in B.C. with another majority
On May 22, Clark and the Conservatives win a minority government
On August 16, Diefenbaker dies
In November Trudeau announces resignation as Liberal leader
On December 13, the Conservative government falls

1980   On January 28, Ambassador Ken Taylor helps Americans escape from Iran
On February 8, Trudeau and the Liberals return with a majority government
On May 20, the Quebec referendum on separation is won by the federalist side

1981   On July 17, the B.C. government names a mountain peak after Terry Fox
On November 13, the Canadarm is first deployed

1982   On April 17, Queen Elizabeth II proclaims the new Constitution Act, and the Canadian Charter of Rights and Freedoms comes into effect
On August 26 Anik D is launched

1983   On May 5, Bill Bennett's Social Credit government wins another election
On June 11, Brian Mulroney replaces Joe Clark as Conservative leader

1984   On February 29, Trudeau announces resignation and John Turner becomes Liberal leader in June
On September 4, Mulroney and the PCs win election with the largest majority ever
On October 5, Marc Garneau becomes the first Canadian in space

1985–1993 Minister of State for Science and Technology and Minister of Forestry

1985   On March 17, the "Shamrock Summit" between Mulroney and U.S. President Ronald Reagan takes place
On June 23, Air India flight 182 explodes between Toronto and London
1986   On January 28, the space shuttle *Challenger* blows up seconds after launch
On February 20, the Soviet Union launches the Mir space station
On April 26, a leak in the Chernobyl nuclear reactor causes a release of radioactive isotopes
On August 6, Bill Vander Zalm is sworn in as B.C. premier
1987   The Meech Lake Accord is negotiated by Mulroney and the provincial premiers
In October the Canada–U.S. Free Trade Agreement is signed
October 19 is "Black Monday" on world stock markets
1988   On January 28, Canada's abortion laws are struck down by the Supreme Court
On February 13, Calgary opens the Winter Olympics
On March 19, Jacques Parizeau becomes leader of the Parti Québécois
On August 9, Wayne Gretzky is traded to Los Angeles Kings by the Edmonton Oilers
On September 26, sprinter Ben Johnson is stripped of his Olympic gold medal
On September 29, NASA resumes space shuttle flights after the Challenger disaster
On November 21, the Conservatives win a second majority government
On December 21, Pan Am Flight 103 is blown up over Lockerbie, Scotland
1989   On January 1, the Canada–U.S. Free Trade Agreement comes into effect
On January 20, George Herbert Bush becomes U.S. president
On March 1, the Canadian Space Agency is created
On March 24, the *Exxon Valdez* oil spill causes a pollution catastrophe
On June 4, Chinese authorities crush Tiananmen Square protest
On December 6, Marc Lepine massacres 14 women in Montreal
1990   On June 15, the Bloc Québécois is formed, led by Lucien Bouchard
In June Jean Chrétien becomes leader of Liberals
1991   On January 1, the Goods and Services Tax comes into force
On January 15, Canadian Forces start participation in the Persian Gulf War
On October 17, Mike Harcourt and the NDP win the B.C. election
1992   On January 22, Roberta Bondar becomes the first Canadian woman in space
1992   On May 9, 26 miners are killed in the Westray mine accident
On August 22, the final draft of Charlottetown Accord is released
On October 26, a national referendum rejects the Charlottetown Accord
On December 17, Mulroney signs the North American Free Trade Agreement
1993   On February 24, Mulroney resigns as prime minister
On March 16, Canadian soldiers in Somalia kill teenager Shidane Arone
On June 25, Kim Campbell becomes the Conservative leader
On October 25, the Liberals win a majority; the Conservatives are left with two seats

CHETWYND VILLAGE

COUNCILLOR AND MAYOR

1962–1972

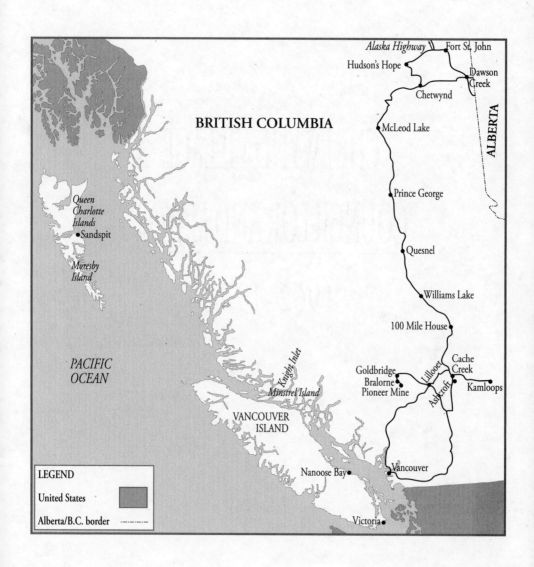

Alaska Highway · Fort St. John
Hudson's Hope
Dawson Creek
Chetwynd

BRITISH COLUMBIA

McLeod Lake

ALBERTA

Queen Charlotte Islands
• Sandspit

Moresby Island

Prince George

Quesnel

Williams Lake

100 Mile House

PACIFIC OCEAN

Knight Inlet

Minstrel Island

VANCOUVER ISLAND

Goldbridge
Bralorne
Pioneer Mine

Lillooet
Cache Creek
Ashcroft
Kamloops

Nanoose Bay

Vancouver

Victoria

LEGEND

United States

Alberta/B.C. border

CHAPTER 1

A Town Is Born

Nothing astonishes men so much as common sense and plain dealing.
—Ralph Waldo Emerson

In 1962 Chetwynd was born.

That was the year the little community in northern British Columbia, 650 kilometres north of 100 Mile House on the way to the Peace River country and Alaska, was officially incorporated as the Village of Chetwynd. The earlier settlers, wanting to stay connected to their roots, had called it Little Prairie, but in 1958 the first train on the Pacific Great Eastern Railway's northern extension arrived and the seeds of a name change were planted.

Presumably for technical reasons, the new name could be no longer than two syllables. It was chosen to honour Ralph Chetwynd, a former B.C. Minister of Railways who had played a prominent role in promoting the province's transportation infrastructure. It took some time for the idea to gain acceptance; in fact, right to the end, a faction in town remained steadfastly opposed not only to the new name of their little town, but to the convulsive changes in the economy that the railway brought with it.

The PGE line quickly became the lifeline of the community. It meant that Chetwynd was now the staging point for transport of the area's rich resources. Given the existing provincial climate at the time, everything seemed to be in place for the town to benefit from the promise of new growth and prosperity.

In 1962 B.C. was under the sway of Premier W.A.C. "Wacky" Bennett's Social Credit government, and the sky was the limit when it came to such grandiose development schemes as the great hydroelectric projects and the expansion of rail and road networks to facilitate and service the massive new hydrocarbon, mineral, and timber resource industries.

On the national scene, the Progressive Conservatives and Prime Minister John Diefenbaker were in power. They too believed in development of the north. Like Sir E.B. Lytton, the head of the Colonial Office a hundred years earlier, who could "with the eye of genius pierce the veil that shrouded the northern horizons and see the vision of the world, and all the wonder that would be," Diefenbaker could see a vast storehouse of resources in the north. He commissioned the Canadian National Railway to build the 700-kilometre Great Slave Lake Railway all the way to Hay River in the Northwest Territories, with an extension to Pine Point, to access the mineral deposits at the south shore of the lake.

Bert Leboe, a devout Baptist first elected in 1953, was the federal member for Prince George–Peace River and one of my predecessors in Parliament. Before entering politics, he had been a lumberman and had served as the president of the Northern Interior Lumbermen's Association, headquartered in Prince George. Both Bert Leboe and Stan Carnell, who represented the area in the provincial legislature, were elected and served under the Social Credit banner.

The John Hart Highway opened in 1952, linking Prince George with Dawson Creek to the northeast, close to the Alberta border, and running through Little Prairie. It brought with it new opportunities for tourism and other industrial activities. Of course, one couldn't really call it a highway for at least another decade. Aside from a few kilometres just north of Prince George, it was a primitive trail covered with sizable boulders that were listed in the highway department's inventory as "rough gravel." Phil Gaglardi, Minister of Highways at the time, was fond of quipping, "We spread it. You crush it."

The new railway opened up several promising prospects for major industrial development, and soon boxcars were hauling lumber and grain and bringing back pipe for a new natural-gas line that would tap the vast reserves of hydrocarbon north of Fort St. John. Sixty miles to the north of Chetwynd, the massive Peace River hydroelectric project was about to start, and geologists and engineers from around the world started to assess potential mine sites for the rich coal deposits to the south.

Chetwynd was smack dab in the middle of it all.

The town itself was slowly acquiring everything a community needs. By 1962 it had a bank, a newspaper (*The Chetwynd Chinook*), schools, a post office, a library, a curling rink, a baseball diamond, and a Legion hall. But Chetwynd was still known as the place where you could stand up to your ankles in mud, yet still have dust blowing in your face. All the streets—basically one main street 15 buildings long and a couple of frontage roads to keep local traffic off the highway—were made of dirt. Of course, as one highway official in Victoria once told me, "that wouldn't matter since the place is covered in snow for six months of the year anyway." Much of the population consisted of seasonal workers, but there were perhaps a thousand or so permanent residents, not counting the dogs, who rendered the place inhospitable to the occasional moose meandering through the streets.

The day the town was christened Chetwynd in 1962 was a memorable one. The legendary Margaret "Ma" Murray—then publisher of the *Alaska Highway News* in Fort St. John—helped us mark the occasion with a rousing hour-long speech on the life and career of Ralph Chetwynd, who, in her words, "graduated from spreading manure on his fruit orchard in the Okanagan Valley to spreading bullshit as the Minister of Railways in Victoria."

A big parade started from the hotel parking lot and proceeded to the ballpark. Father Jungbluth, our local priest and another legendary character, was at the main intersection, directing traffic and elucidating on the message and meaning of various floats, using "God's voice," as it was affectionately known by the local Native people (a loudspeaker installed under the hood of his car). Postmaster Ernie Pfanner, among the most strident opponents of the name change, had mounted a coffin on top of his car adorned with a sign that read "Little Prairie Rest in Peace." It was a nice thought, but I didn't think his heart was really in it.

The new volunteer fire department was on hand with its freshly painted truck equipped with 200 feet of firehose that had been discarded and donated by the forestry office, and a new Briggs and Stratton pump mounted on the end of the 500-gallon tank. The initial pump had fallen victim to severe frost on its first response to active duty and had failed to yield even a drop of water to douse the flames that had consumed the Gerwin home, at the east end of town.

Two recently retired outhouses had been skidded to the ballpark where, as one of the main features of the festivities, an active fire demonstration

The fire truck and its brave band of volunteers headed by Chief Norm Stirling.

was to take place. The event was planned and rehearsed with split-second precision. Enough gasoline and diesel fuel had been spilled inside the doomed structures to cause a minor explosion. So much, in fact, that one of the doors was blown off its hinges, landing among the curious spectators after the designated fireman had set off the blaze, sacrificing his moustache and eyelashes to the cause.

No sooner were people over this first shock than, from a distance, they could faintly discern a siren, one that had previously been mounted on top of the old police car. A full complement of brave volunteers clung to the side of the fire truck for dear life as it left the highway on its heroic mission, outside wheels just barely touching the ground. But the velocity of the 500-gallon load of water was too great for the hydraulic brakes, which fought unsuccessfully to bring the show to a halt before the truck skidded much too close to the now towering inferno.

The driver, however, skilfully backed the contraption out of harm's way just in time to prevent a much more serious calamity. Even before the truck came to a complete halt, the hoses were being attached to the pump and expertly flung toward the flames. An arm was raised to signal the attachment of the nozzle, prompting Chief Norm Stirling to bellow out the command: "Water, march!"

Two men firmly gripped the nozzle, bravely bracing themselves against the anticipated force, but they needn't have worried. The hose had obviously seen better days. It did discharge the water, but none of it toward its intended target. Instead, along its entire length, it produced a fascinating array of small fountains shooting high up into the air and in all directions. The outhouses, now totally at the mercy of the flames, had witnessed more pressure from the orifices of their patrons than what the fire nozzle was able to produce.

Finally, for the pleasure and entertainment of everyone in attendance, the hose ruptured completely, treating spectators to a special encore. It became an angry serpent, whipping itself in all directions, venting its anger and spewing its venom at everything within a 200-foot radius, defying even the most gallant and heroic efforts by the firemen to arrest and slay the monster.

Mercifully, someone among the spectators had the presence of mind to shut down the pump, bringing the situation under control—although not before everyone in the vicinity was drenched with water and splattered with mud.

This wasn't the last of the volunteer brigade's adventures. Actually, Chetwynd's early firemen seemed to have an extra-special flair for drama. The first mention of the new town in the Vancouver newspapers featured the brigade and the headline "After the Ball—Up Goes the Hall." The story involved the annual Firemen's Ball and the building in which the old fire truck and sundry equipment were stored.

The Firemen's Ball was among the most prominent features in the village's social calendar. It served not only to relieve some of the stress of the daily grind, but also as a means to raise much-needed funds for more and better equipment. It goes without saying that, at this time, a firehose topped the wish list.

After one such particularly successful celebration, some brigade members felt the urge to top off the festivities with a little more serious drinking in the company of the old truck—their pride and joy and the object of their affection—in the comfort of the den it was kept in. The storage building, its walls insulated with sawdust, had an attic outfitted with some well-used furniture. The building had been donated by the telephone company, but this had been more an act of frugality than charity, in that it saved the company from having to dispose of the dilapidated structure in some other way.

There would have been little point in attempting an inquiry into the cause of the fire that broke out after everyone had finally retired for the night. The chief opined that a cigarette, carelessly discarded, might have been the culprit. In any event, all that was found the following morning was a pile of still-smouldering rubble. Not a single person had actually seen what must have been a spectacular blaze competing with the northern lights in the night sky.

It was just as well. Why spoil a perfect evening with such a sad ending? Apart from the piles of snow that had melted off the roof of the structure, there would have been no means to attack the fire anyway.

By this time in 1962, Joan and I were still operating the Chevron service station we had opened in 1958. We had built a two-storey commercial structure that housed a grocery store, which was leased to Lee Phillips, an M & M store franchisee, and our own living quarters on the second floor. This was also the year the building housing both the office and living quarters of Chetwynd's first permanent RCMP detachment—our second major real-estate venture—was commissioned. In 1964, buoyed by our earlier business success and with the support of a somewhat uncharacteristically

Chetwynd: The Chevron station and the Chamber of Commerce, circa 1958.

friendly banker, we built another, much more ambitious, automotive-service facility. It operated under the Esso banner and had a modest car dealership associated with it.

For a time we managed both these enterprises, which were referred to by our customers as "his and hers" gas stations, with Joan retaining the bulk of the local trade, while I enjoyed the better part of the business generated by the highway traffic. Over time, two competing, more modern service stations were established. But as we soon discovered, competition is not only essential to a free-market economy; it also relieves much of the stress of having to cater to customers who have no other choice but to deal with you. Thanks to the proceeds from our two businesses, in 1965 we were able to build our first family home at the base of Baldy Mountain, overlooking the town that had become our home.

By partway through 1962, we had all of our four children. That was the year Peter, the youngest member of the family, was born, when Isabell and Frank were seven and five years old respectively. Ursula, just 10, assumed the role of surrogate mother and contributed most of her spare time to looking after household chores as well. Our dreams for them and our family life became attached to a 2,000-acre ranch property we had acquired. Situated west of Chetwynd, it was nestled idyllically beside the Pine River, which carves its way through the rugged terrain of the divide high up in the Rocky Mountains to join with the Peace River on its timeless journey to the Arctic Ocean.

Having convinced ourselves that the letters ESSO on the sign towering over our new business were an abbreviation for "every second Sunday off," we had also built a cabin on Moberly Lake, 15 kilometres north of town on the way to Hudson's Hope. The cabin was a special place, with lots of fond memories of the precious moments we spent together as a family.

We were thus well established, secure, and supported by a cadre of good friends who shared our enthusiasm and commitment to the town and could be called upon in times of crisis. Among them were Gordon and Helen Moore, the owners of the Chetwynd Hotel and the Fort St. John Lumber Company (the major employer in the area), and their daughter and son-in-law, Beverly and Norm Stirling—as well as most of the business-and-industry movers and shakers associated with the Chamber of Commerce, of which I had been president during its formative period.

There was never any shortage of things to do or of pressing matters begging for solutions through political activism—not the least of which was the lack of medical or health services within a hundred kilometres of Chetwynd. Many wasted and anxious trips were made to the emergency ward in Dawson Creek to get help or seek reassurance that a high fever or a stubborn cold were not signs of something more serious.

Every small town at this stage of development has its heroes who respond to critical, often disastrous, situations at great risk to their own comfort and safety. In 100 Mile House, where we used to live, it was Jerry Brown, the local druggist, on whom everyone relied—not only to dispense just the right remedy for a common ailment, but also to diagnose more serious afflictions and to be available 24 hours a day for every medical emergency within a radius of 30 miles. I would not like to contemplate the consequences of one of Isabell's frequent brushes with disaster without Jerry Brown's timely intervention.

During one of her special dance performances put on for the entertainment of her siblings, she stumbled backward into a tub of boiling hot water—Joan's substitute for the washing machine that was not yet on any list of priorities as an essential household asset. The whole of Isabell's backside began to blister instantly, throwing her audience into a state of panic. Jerry was there in minutes, calmly applying salves and administering medication to soothe the pain.

"I wouldn't worry," he told us the following morning when he stopped by on his way to the store. "It looks like she is responding well, and unless we discover any infection, there is no need to torture her by dragging her into a car for a drive to a hospital."

Chetwynd did not yet have a drugstore, putting the onus on the lumber company's first-aid attendant, Nelson "Wink" Wheeler, to fill the void. Wink was a reserved, slight, soft-spoken man whose wisdom-greyed hair reflected his age. He, like Jerry Brown and other heroes everywhere in small-town Canada, are infinitely more deserving of being honoured with an Order of Canada than some of the pompous specimens whose only claim to fame is the proximity of their address to the viceregal mansion in Ottawa's Rockcliffe Park.

As both the occasional driver and one-time passenger of the first makeshift ambulance (a 1958 Ford station wagon), I had first-hand exposure to the selfless heroic acts that Wink performed on a routine basis—including one occasion when I nearly bled to death.

The rule around the pump island at the service station was that every move had to be "on the double." Customers didn't like to be kept waiting, least of all to pay their bills. During one particularly busy period, I stumbled in my haste over a small ledge at the front entrance and smashed my left arm through a heavy, double-glazed front window, cutting the main artery and severing most of the tendons to my hand. My fascination with the rhythmic thrusts of the fountain of blood escaping from my wrist turned to panic as everything in the vicinity became splattered with my vital juices.

Luckily one of the customers, obviously trained in first-aid procedures, produced a tourniquet from a first-aid kit and stopped the hemorrhage—but not before I started feeling its effects.

"This man has to be taken to a hospital now," he declared, probably unaware that the trip would take at least an hour. Joan was already on the phone to Wink Wheeler, who arrived just as Ted Hauck, our head mechanic, was manoeuvring the "ambulance" into position at the front door. Adding to the adventure, the road we had to take was still unpaved in places and produced blinding clouds of dust that rose to obscure the driver's vision any time we caught up to another vehicle. Every 20 minutes Wink released the tourniquet to allow the blood to flow again, at least to the point of the injury.

In Dawson Creek, Dr. Erwin, no stranger to these kinds of emergencies, was ready and waiting in the operating room when we arrived. After my earlier experience at the hospital, when the treatment of Frank Jr.'s broken hip left much to be desired, I had nothing but praise this time for the masterful job Dr. Erwin performed to restore all movement in my hand and fingers. Apart from the scare and some dead nerves in the little finger, there were no after-effects.

I was in the driver's seat of the ambulance on another such emergency. The driver of the regular Greyhound bus, which had just pulled into the terminal at the hotel, came running across the highway, obviously in a panic, explaining that a passenger was about to deliver her baby in the back of his bus. The "doctor," he told us, had already been summoned, but he would probably need an ambulance.

Wink and I arrived on the scene at the same time. Eleanor, the wife of our friend and sometime employee Rudi Krass, was being helped off the bus as she delivered herself of a blue streak of obscenities that would have made union president Pat Miller, from my Pioneer mining days, proud. Just the day before, Rudi had taken her to the hospital, from which she had been discharged that morning on the doctor's assurance that it was a false alarm.

With Eleanor resting comfortably on the makeshift stretcher in the back, Wink positioned himself next to me in the passenger seat. At first reluctant, he finally let himself be persuaded to come along. He didn't relish the prospect of having to deliver a baby, but he was reasonably sure that we had enough time to get to the hospital. Nevertheless, I wasted little of it getting the operation into high gear.

Apart from the moans and groans inspired by Eleanor's labour pains at very short intervals, I thought that all seemed well and even quite normal—judging from my experience in 100 Mile House when, just in the nick of time, I delivered Joan and our third child-to-be, Frank Jr., to the hospital in Ashcroft.

But as we were pulling up the hill in East Pine, the situation became critical.

Unlike Joan when she was in much the same condition, Eleanor was much more assertive in her demands to stop the car. She demonstrated a proficiency in Canada's unofficial third language far beyond what we would have expected from such an otherwise refined lady. Every bump on the road produced a primeval response from the back that could easily have shattered windows. And the louder she screamed for me to stop the car, the more urgent were Wink's pleadings to keep the pedal pressed to the floor. Worried that the poor woman would choke herself, Wink finally climbed over the seat to lend whatever assistance he could.

Then I caught up to a delivery truck that was sending huge clouds of dust into the air and spraying rocks in all directions, making it impossible for its driver to either see the red light flashing or hear the siren I had activated in my desperation. After several minutes of driving in his wake, I had no choice but to make an attempt at Canadian roulette.

The rules of this game are basic. With absolutely no visibility ahead, the driver who wants to pass fixes his eyes on the left shoulder of the road, steps on the gas, and leaves the rest up to the angels. As people who have experience driving in such situations know, the results of meeting oncoming traffic during the crucial seconds it takes to pass are almost always fatal. On this occasion, the angels were on our side.

By the time I pulled up to the emergency entrance of the hospital at Dawson Creek, things appeared relatively stable. However, when a nurse and an orderly, attracted by the siren I had forgotten to turn off, rushed out to meet us and began extracting not one, but two passengers from the back of the ambulance, I discovered, to my horror, that the baby had arrived.

I just sat there, my knees shaking uncontrollably, not realizing until Wink returned to suggest we go for coffee that I was still holding Eleanor's false teeth in my hand. Even the trip home, with a pile of blood-soaked blankets emitting noxious odours from the back, is indelibly carved in my memory.

Rudi, the proud father, was waiting for us to deliver the good news—he had been driving the school bus at the time. Mother and son were just fine, Wink offered in his always polite and reserved manner. Rudi was not at all surprised at the rapid advance in Eleanor's condition.

"No bloody wonder," he opined. "These goddamned roads would shake the nuts off a brass donkey."

Unfortunately, not all the incidents had such satisfactory outcomes. On more than one occasion, it was Wink Wheeler's gentle hand that closed the eyes of some unfortunate victim of a heart attack or serious accident for the last time. It was hardly surprising, then, that the Chamber of Commerce and later the village council concentrated much of their efforts on attracting a doctor and other qualified health professionals to settle in Chetwynd. Dr. Christensen was one of several, no doubt highly motivated, individuals who responded to our pleas. But even with the best intentions, these medical staff could not sustain themselves without a pharmacy or a health clinic to back them up, so we began in earnest to promote the idea of a hospital for Chetwynd.

Meanwhile, other major building blocks had been added to the foundation of our confidence in the future. The new school was commissioned in 1960, major improvements were made to the John Hart Highway and the village streets, and a sanitary sewer system was installed.

Morley Kitchen and his wife, Carol, were the first tenants in the new police station Joan and I had built. They moved in just before Christmas and found a fully decorated Christmas tree perched in front of the office as a gesture of welcome—no doubt inspired by the season, Morley felt assured. How could he have known that so early in his tenure he had earned the affection of local pranksters who had appropriated the festive display from some other location?

Suspicion must undoubtedly have been aroused when Emil Breitkreitz presented himself at the station the following morning to report the theft of a Christmas tree. He identified the tree in front of the station as almost identical to the one that had adorned the front entrance of his own establishment the night before. But Emil never quite had the courage to make a positive identification, and the constable was already facing a list of priorities much more pressing than a Christmas tree theft.

Emil and his industrious wife were well respected as hard-working, honest, civic-minded, and charitable businesspeople. Emil served on the first village commission and as alderman on the subsequent village councils, where he made a major contribution during the critical period of Chetwynd's development and deserved much praise for his sound judgement. But he did have a certain knack for drawing attention to himself.

Ray Rebagliati, superintendent of PGE's northern operations, had a story about an encounter with Emil Breitkreitz that had taken place when Ray tried to deposit a Kodak film for development at Emil's store.

"What size do you want the pictures to be?" said Emil.

"Just the normal, ordinary size."

"How many copies do you want?"

"One copy is all I need."

"You mean to say you want no copies at all?"

"Why the hell would I ask you to have this film developed if I didn't want a copy of the pictures I took?"

"That's not a copy. That's known as the original."

Rebagliati, by now somewhat impatient: "Whatever, just send out the goddamned film and get it developed."

"Okay, okay, you don't have to shout. How do you spell your name, anyway?"

"R-e-b-a-g-l-i-a-t-i."

Then, after several repeats: "Is that with two Ts?"

"If it was, I would have said so, for Christ's sake!"

Emil: "Jesus Christ, if I had a name like that I'd change it."

Ray: "Well, if you ever think about changing your own, 'asshole' would be a good choice."

In 1963, one of the major projects hinted at by Premier W.A.C. Bennett during his historic first visit to Chetwynd aboard the inaugural train in 1958 came to fruition. Survey crews had been working for some time to select the best site for a gigantic power project on the Peace River near Hudson's Hope. Whole armies of job seekers were now flooding into the area, hoping to land jobs with the contractors preparing the site. It proved to be a mixed blessing for established businesses such as ours. The wages offered, even for unskilled labourers, were at least three times those we could afford to pay, making it exceedingly difficult for us to recruit additional help to cater to the increased demand. Thankfully, our core staff—Marshall Peters, Ted Hauck, and Lorne Procter—not only remained loyal to us, but were always ready to work the extra hours necessary to get the most urgent jobs out on time.

At home, Ursula, mature far beyond her years, continued to play the ever-increasing role of surrogate parent, sacrificing many of the simple childhood pleasures enjoyed by her friends. Ursula also ranked among the brave pioneers of her gender to break into the gas-jockey fraternity. During the busy season, she and her high-school friends were pressed into service as soon as they were out for the summer. Her good looks and pleasant demeanour more than made up for her deficit in height, which necessitated a sizable extension to the handle of our car-window washing tool.

She deserved most of the credit as well for allowing Joan and me to participate in some of the social life in the community. Without the help of our children pitching in with the chores, both at home and in the business, we would have had to pass on many opportunities to enjoy our own leisure— and we would have had to scale down some of our ambitious goals for further growth and expansion of the business. We both managed to become active curlers and to participate in the social activities of the club. We even found some precious time to satisfy our passion for reading and enjoying a good book now and then. In later years, we derived great comfort and pleasure from sharing the sweet fruits of our labour with our children, but we have never quite been able to totally shed feelings of guilt over what we may have deprived them of during this critical time in our busy lives.

Joan, too, took on huge extra burdens. My frequent forays into the political arena often meant being away for several days at a time, and the extra burden invariably fell on her shoulders. She managed the office, manned the gas pumps, and even helped out in the repair shop, fixing the occasional tire. She did all that between making sure the kids had their breakfast, were well dressed (she knitted and sewed all their clothes), and sent safely off to school. Peter, not yet of school age, had ruled out kindergarten, like his father before him—"I am not staying here and that's final," he said after just a brief survey of the situation—so he accompanied his mother during the day, thus affording him an early introduction to the world of business. This experience may well have sparked a curiosity about his parents' psychological well-being that led him to pursue a career in the field of psychology, in which he later earned a master's degree from one of the more prestigious eastern universities.

For both Joan and me, apart from the fact that we continued to live at least two years ahead of our bankers, life during this period was progressing along a regular path, and it was anything but dull. Yet, having tasted a certain measure of success in business, I was always restless, constantly looking for new challenges and opportunities.

We invested whatever little spare time—and less spare money—we had available to us in making further improvements to the ranch, with the dream of developing it to the point where it might sustain us in later years. Often Joan and I would steal away for an hour or so just to stroll through the site we had selected for our home or to walk among our cattle. We felt sure that this was the place where we would finally find our inner peace.

Naturally, we needed help and expertise with such an ambitious project, so we entered into an arrangement with Ray Schreiber, a long-time local

The budding politician tries out his speeches on his Chetwynd ranch.

resident with roots in both Germany and the Canadian prairies, where his family had settled. Born and raised on a farm, he knew his way around livestock and offered to manage the place for us in exchange for earning some equity in the business and being allowed to keep his own livestock on the place.

I have never found anything more therapeutic, more stress-relieving, or of more recreational value than those times I spent with him, helping out with chores or putting up feed for the winter. Ray was a skilled horseman, too, and I fondly remember the hunting parties he organized for us in the fall and the times we spent on horseback exploring the backwoods.

However, my interest in the world around us and my penchant for getting involved in the affairs of the community—nourished and strengthened by my work with the Chetwynd Chamber of Commerce—brought me into frequent contact with municipal and provincial officials. My work with them started to encroach upon our lives more and more, leading naturally toward my own, more formal, involvement in public life and politics.

CHAPTER 2

God Helps Those
Who Help Themselves

Politics is the art of the possible.

—Otto von Bismarck

The incorporation of the village in 1962 brought with it a flurry of excitement and activity. The notoriety Joan and I had earned by that time was rewarded with my seat on the first village council. Formerly active as president of the Chamber of Commerce, I was now officially a village commissioner. Not that I needed to add to our workload, but there were only so many people willing and able to serve in what was seen by most as a thankless job.

My stint on the council turned out to be my first exposure to the adventure and challenge of small-town politics. I quickly learned that there is nothing more stimulating and exciting; it certainly is not recommended for the faint of heart. Very few people ever bother to get involved in the political process, but many more are immediately suspicious of anyone who does. It's the same in every sphere, of course, but nowhere more so than in small-town politics. If there's some minute detail of one's personal life, no matter how far in the past or how hard one tried to forget it, some people will, in the most generous and selfless fashion, make it their mission to ferret it out and assist in refreshing one's memory.

Any detail deemed too boring to capture the imagination of the public will be embellished and, in some cases, new facts will be invented and promoted as a true reflection of one's integrity and character. Outlandish rumours attributed me with the most fabulous riches, all acquired at the

Chetwynd village council: Seated, from left, the author as mayor, and Emil Breitkreitz; back, from left, Ernie Pfanner, Ron Tarr, and Morris Hayward.

expense of the public, and by the time my career in municipal politics came to an end, there were apparently very few beds in the little town under which my shoes had not been parked at one time or another.

Nonetheless, with the support of Emil Breitkreitz and one or two others, I managed to win most of the battles. Right from the start I locked horns with some of the other members over contracts that had to be negotiated and awarded for sewer installations and road improvements. Fred Sandy, one of Gordon Moore's partners at the hotel, was sponsoring one of the bidders by underwriting the customary performance guarantees. Frank Bonnetti had been operating a modest construction and excavating business in Dawson Creek and was willing to back his bid with a promise to move to Chetwynd permanently, providing he was given the contract. I insisted on structuring the sewer contract to favour his effort.

True to his word, Frank Bonnetti, his wife, Carol, and their two young children settled in Chetwynd and established what grew into a thriving construction business. He became one of my most trusted friends and confidants who, over the years, contributed in a major way to the progress and development of the town.

Not all of our close friends from the early days in Chetwynd shared an interest in the political and social causes to which Joan and I had become attached. Some just drifted away, letting us know politely that they couldn't afford to be associated with the issues we were promoting; others, no doubt, were simply offended by my style and the brazen manner with which I was prone to press my case. Still others, it pained us to discover, became strong adversaries, forcing us to choose between their continued friendship and the causes that had become central to our lives. But there were also people like Norm and Beverly Stirling, Henry Hryciw (the new police sergeant) and his wife, Etta, and many others who worked with us on different projects, who are among our dearest friends to this very day.

Beginning in the early '60s, the Chamber of Commerce embarked on a crusade to optimize the opportunities for Chetwynd promised by the massive hydroelectric project at Hudson's Hope. First we had to assure ourselves that Chetwynd would become the staging point. There were rumours of a road branching off much farther south and perhaps even a rail link that would cut us off from activities and benefits flowing from the project.

In the winter of 1959–60, Gordon Moore, who owned the new sawmill, and some local logging contractors were persuaded to donate the necessary equipment to punch a road through the bush in order to facilitate the journey of a cavalcade of cars and trucks, a publicity stunt meant to promote the construction of a road link to the site. Our counterparts in Hudson's Hope promised to build an ice bridge across the Peace River to complete the link.

On the appointed day, 80 cars and trucks participated in the adventure. Not all made it back in one piece. In places, a string of several vehicles would be hitched to a Caterpillar or some other heavy-duty piece of equipment and then pulled through muskeg or over one of many steep hills en route to our destination. Our spirits ran high; that is to say, everyone was "high" on the spirits of various kinds fuelling the operation. By some estimates, the liquor stores in Dawson Creek and Fort St. John (Chetwynd had not yet attained the status of having a liquor store) dispensed roughly the same volume of spirits as did the service stations that fuelled the mechanical components of the trip.

The day culminated with a banquet at the community hall in Hudson's Hope, where I made a rousing speech, leaving not a single dry eye in the house. So impressed were the mayors, council members, and other assembled dignitaries that I was chosen on the spot to act as the spokesman (the term "spokesperson" had not yet been coined) during another visit planned by Premier W.A.C. Bennett, this one to monitor the progress of the preliminary work toward the construction of the Peace River hydro dam, a monument that would eventually bear his name and stand in his honour. The only instruction I was given during a preparatory meeting was to refrain in my presentation from using the word "village," which to this day, I am told, I still can't pronounce.

As usual, "His Highness" arrived by train. The meeting in his private coach was scheduled for early morning on a bitterly cold Peace River day. The station master, Bill Williams, offended no doubt at being excluded from the delegation, refused to open the station premises to shelter us from the Arctic air that had blanketed the area. The premier was just finishing his breakfast, we were told as we awaited him at the appointed hour. When we were finally ushered into the coach, it took us several minutes to thaw out and find a space not already occupied by the larger-than-life persona and powerful aura of the great man.

At the outset we were all much too intimidated to present our petition, but fortunately the premier was so well briefed on our situation that he required little input from us. It came naturally to Bennett to adapt any public encounter to his own agenda, which luckily for us coincided with what was on our minds—at least on this occasion. He also had the exceptional talent of conversing with himself, posing and then answering certain pertinent questions, some of which we had not even thought of. Only rarely did he need to be prompted with a couple of words before launching himself into another 15-minute monologue.

"How will local businessmen benefit from the project?" he speculated.

"Well," he replied, "I have ordered that local enterprise is to be given preferential access to the procurement process during construction."

"Yes," I ventured timidly, taking advantage of a brief pause to allow the poor man time to replenish his breath before he went on. "Has any thought been given to assure some lasting benefits to the area?" he asked.

"Why," he said, pleased someone had asked the question, "among other things, arrangements are in place to allow the corporation to provide you with on-site power within a 50-mile radius of the dam, including the cities of Dawson Creek and Fort St. John, at some very low rates. With the whole

Excitement reigns in Chetwynd as the railway and Premier W.A.C. Bennett (second from right) arrive in 1958 to bless the new town.

world starving for energy, that measure alone will set off an industrial boom that will be without parallel anywhere."

He paused, briefly noting my existence. "In fact, if you have left your native Germany to seek wealth and fortune, you have come to the right place. Your own energy, your ambitions, ingenuity, and the sky are the only limits to your success. This is the place I would choose to raise my family if I were 20 years younger."

In just half an hour, W.A.C. Bennett, the most dynamic prophet ever installed in the premier's office by B.C.'s people, had generated so much hot air that none of us felt the sting of the cold as we stepped outside to huddle beside our cars for an initial debriefing. We were euphoric. It wasn't until the following morning that city officials in Dawson Creek pointed out to Mayor Trail that the city of Dawson Creek falls just outside any such 50-mile radius. Frantic phone calls between the mayors in the region resulted in the decision to urgently dispatch a delegation—including myself—to Victoria to lobby for an extension.

We were met by the premier's secretary, who told us that the premier would unfortunately be unable to meet with us. However, he had asked his senior northern minister, Ray Williston, to fill in for him.

Williston, during his lifetime, would later lend his name to a lake with 650 miles of shoreline. If ever there was a man deserving of such an honour, it was him. During his tenure as the Minister of Lands and Forests, he revolutionized the forestry industry, challenging some of the major companies with just the right kind of incentives to exploit the commercial value of the interior and northern forests. He single-handedly laid the foundation for the huge pulp mills in Prince George and the growth of the area's logging and solid-wood industries that have turned it into the most important forest region in Canada. I am sure that, had he been given his way, the flooding of the reservoir behind the Peace River dam would have been delayed long enough to allow for the removal of millions of cubic metres of valuable timber; instead it was flooded, resulting in navigational hazards and an environmental disaster.

On being informed of the premier's cheap-power proposition, Ray, honest politician that he was, readily confessed that he had never heard of it. However, a phone call to one of the aides confirmed what we had understood the premier to say. Ray promised that he would take the matter up with the senior planning committee of Cabinet during its next meeting, expressing little doubt that our request would find favour with his colleagues. In fact, he suggested, to avoid any discrimination, it would make sense to simply extend the benefitting area right to the Alberta border.

The incident was a testament to W.A.C. Bennett's far-sighted, visionary approach, characterized by "off-the-top-of-his-head" policy making. It was terribly unfortunate that it was also characteristic of the great man for his fertile mind to be cleansed of some of his great ideas in as little time as it took to conceive them. Consequently, the boundaries of the so-called benefitting area never did get extended past the perimeter of the actual site of the project, much less to the border with Alberta. To this day, the people in the Peace River area of British Columbia pay the same domestic and industrial rates that BC Hydro charges customers throughout its network, thus forcing them to share in the cost of transmitting power from its local generation point in Hudson's Hope all the way to Vancouver, over a thousand kilometres away.

Soon after W.A.C. Bennett blessed us with his presence, we had another landmark visit. In 1965 Emil and Berta, Joan's parents, followed my parents' lead—Adolf and Rösel had visited in 1962—and ventured across the great ocean to check up on the two black sheep who had left their fatherland for the new world, trying to escape their troublesome past and the rigid social order into which they had been born.

Emil and Berta stayed with us for several months. Back home, at first, Emil had hated the mere sight of me, let alone the thought of his daughter attaching herself to a vagabond whose father refused to attend regular church services. But given the fact that we were now legally married, ensconced in a moderately successful business career, and the parents of four adorable grandchildren, he had harboured the hope that we would find our way back to our ancestral home in the Black Forest. It didn't take him long at all to appreciate that having tasted the freedom, allure, and promise of our new homeland, it would be difficult for us to ever find happiness again in the stifling confinement of our birthplace. In fact, Emil fell in love with the ranch and could easily have been persuaded to stay.

But Berta had other ideas. She was keenly interested in the social work Joan was doing with Native children and her involvement in Father Jungbluth's charitable projects. Bursting with pride that not just one but two of her children had answered the call to serve God—her son Rudi had entered the priesthood three years earlier—she wanted to go home, if for no other reason than to share her adventures in Canada, some of which she had recorded on film and in a diary, with the ladies of St. Martin's parish and her many friends.

Not that there was any urgency. Her sister Anna, who during the war years had been Joan's surrogate mother and main employer as the operator of a modest neighbourhood grocery store, was keeping everyone well informed about Berta's adventures in the new world and her good fortune. As well, Joan's sister Cilli and her family were still living in and looking after the family home, which also housed her respectable photography shop and atelier.

Nevertheless, Berta and Emil left for home after four months, but before they did, we took them on a trip through Jasper and Banff national parks, places where, without question, God has chosen to display the greatest triumphs of his creation.

Tragically, Berta wasn't given much time to expend her still-enormous energy sharing her experiences and praising the Lord for the blessings he had bestowed upon her. Shortly after their return home, she suffered a massive stroke that confined her to bed for the rest of her life. Sadly, the woman who had shown such indefatigable courage and a strength that had carried her and her family through the ravages of war totally surrendered to her affliction. Perhaps she was impatient to be called home to receive her just reward for the sacrifices she had made and her service to the glory of God. For eight long years until her death in 1973, she only allowed herself on rare occasions to be taken outside in a wheelchair.

In 1968 I felt compelled to take a more active part in village politics. At the time, the contest between progress and development and the preservation of the old values was still going on between the old-timers and the newcomers. Life had been simple and good in the old days; the only stress had been having to decide which direction to take on the Sunday drive (there were only two, up or down the highway). Life, the old-timers feared, would become much too complex with all this activity.

The hydro project had become a magnet for tourists. There were all kinds of speculation about coal mining to the south of Chetwynd, and the oil and gas sector was beginning to show interest in the area. However, nobody in the municipal administration was making any effort to promote the town as the hub of all these activities by expanding the social infrastructure or by upgrading roads and other services.

This fact was brought home to me during my first trip to Victoria, where I'd gone to remind the premier and his ministers of their previous commitments. I was visiting the headquarters of BC Hydro in order to suggest that Chetwynd and the by-now impressive assets we had accumulated as a town be included in their promotional material, when I overheard someone giving directions to one of the engineers assigned to the Hudson's Hope project: "You fly to Prince George, where you rent a car that will take you in a northeasterly direction to the end of the world. Then you turn left to follow the road to Hudson's Hope."

I promptly offered to warn the curious traveller of the danger of venturing past the "end of the world," since we had not yet got around to bending the nails flat on the far side of the picket fence.

In Chetwynd's municipal administration, Bert Chatham, our former service-station partner, had served as chairman of the village commission and did an admirable job, but he was defeated in 1966 by our old friend the postmaster. Bert won the next election, in 1968, but had to resign to pursue his professional career. It was time for me to take up the fight and run for mayor myself.

The election turned out to be a cliff-hanger; Pfanner was back with a vengeance.

Ernie was a pleasant enough fellow and well respected among the original settlers. They had chosen him for the position of postmaster, at first only on a part-time basis that supplemented his income from the Campbell family's grocery and variety store and the little one-pump gasoline dispensary attached to it. Like me—an immigrant with big dreams and a willingness to fight for them—he had become accustomed to getting his way and found it exceedingly difficult to compromise or to accommodate any of the new ideas and plans we newcomers were promoting. He and his supporters used every trick in the book—adding several new chapters of their own—to gain control of the village office and prevent town affairs from evolving in too progressive a manner. After the polls closed it took the Ernie-friendly village clerk and the scrutineers several hours to count the 341 ballots that determined the outcome: Pfanner 170, Oberle 171.

Historically, close marginal votes have had significant impacts. In the tight U.S. federal election race of 1960, for example, if the vote count in states such as Illinois, Missouri, New Jersey, and Texas had been slightly different, Americans would have had Richard Nixon gracing the White House eight years earlier.

Well, the good burghers of Chetwynd flirted with danger as well, but in the end made the right decision. In fact, the village election of 1968 resulted in a mandate for which every municipal official should strive—the most successful of them are those who have 49 percent of the people against them and 51 percent in favour, giving them the support they need to get re-elected. Even though I worked very hard to maintain that balance, I missed it by six votes two years later, when six additional voters cast their ballot in my favour.

In fairness to the previous administration, the heavy burden of debt associated with the sewer and water installations would have made it sheer folly to even consider any new capital projects. It was clear to me from the outset that any additions or improvements to the town's capital assets would have to wait for the local tax base to expand through future growth or else be financed with money from another source. It boiled down to the proverbial chicken-and-egg situation: We couldn't expect substantial growth without improvement in the town's infrastructure, the expansion of which, on the other hand, could not be supported by the overburdened tax base. Certainly no one among the village council was in the mood to spend more money.

Initially this left us with very little room to manoeuvre. Had the situation stayed that way, I would have found little satisfaction from a job that was confined to tackling the huge intellectual exercise of deciding which service station in town should supply fuel for the single village truck next month, or to receiving weekly reports from Joe Embree, the village's public-works superintendent, on his latest adventures as the town bylaw-enforcement and animal-control officer.

Actually, Chetwynd's dog problem was not entirely devoid of entertainment value. For one thing, dogs seemed to outnumber their two-legged masters. The situation was not unlike that faced in larger cities, where certain criminal elements pose a serious threat to the peace and tranquillity of the general public as they compete with one another for dominance. In this case, the Chetwynd dogs, in the main peace-loving, were constantly attacked by their Native counterparts, which penetrated their domain from the fringes of town. So fierce were these street battles that on several occasions the leg of an innocent child walking home from school, or even the limb of a dog-catcher trying to mediate a dispute, got caught up in one of the combatants' jaws.

Joe Embree, a veteran of the Korean War, was a very patient man, but he had his limits. He was also ingenious at finding practical and lasting solutions to even the most complex problems. So at one point he decided that a somewhat radical, permanent solution was called for to deal with our four-legged compatriots. He calmly left the house while most of the town was still deep in slumber, and to each of the hind wheels of the village truck he tied a sturdy rag for the dogs to sink their teeth into. Then he took a leisurely drive through the streets. He had discovered, after diligent research, that only two things were sure to distract the local canines and divert their attention away from the fight: a female in heat or a noisy vehicle competing for space in the arena. Not inclined to pose as the former, he chose his trusty pickup truck to do the dirty deed and lure the canine population to their doom.

It required a special meeting of council to deal with the aftermath of Joe's early-morning adventure, which had resulted in an epidemic of the always-fatal "broken-neck disease" that a sizable number of dogs had contracted during the night.

At one point, Joe also proposed to council that, given all the time and effort he and his staff were required to invest in the dog problem, we might wish to consider including them in the census that determined the annual grant provided by the provincial government to help municipalities deliver essential services. In fact, Joe, never short of interesting ideas, suggested that the census might be conducted by simply counting the legs of the entire population, including the dogs, and dividing the number by two.

In my quest to discover other unconventional sources of funds for additional new development, I chose to try my hand at coercing the provincial government into sharing some of its wealth through a direct appeal to the provincial trinity. This entity, not to be confused with the Father, Son, and Holy Ghost, was equally respected and powerful and was referred to as God (Premier Bennett), Ginter (Ben Ginter, a notorious highway contractor), and Gaglardi (Phil Gaglardi, the Highways minister). I pioneered an early version of the frequent flyer program: Several times a year I travelled to the capital to subject myself to the monologues of either the premier or his Minister of Highways, as they extolled their latest vision for the future and the catalogue of recent accomplishments.

The time allocated by the deity to such meetings was based on the importance of the subject to be addressed and the prominence of the person presenting it. Since I was deemed a person with a friendly disposition toward the Social Credit Party and considerable influence among Peace River–area mayors, I could expect to be given an hour to present my case. On one such occasion early in my mandate as mayor, the Highways minister—as always, pressed for time—offered to deal with my request during a working lunch in the executive parliamentary dining room.

Like his boss, God himself, Phil Gaglardi was blessed with a degree of humility to match the Pope's in his ancestral homeland and considered himself blessed with the same infallible judgement. As usual, the dialogue was one-sided, with only momentary interruptions on Gaglardi's part to catch a breath and swallow some food, allowing me the opportunity to contribute a word or two in acquiescence or praise.

Halfway through my chocolate pudding, my host was interrupted by one of his aides reminding him that his next appointment was waiting in his office.

"They hardly give you any time to think around here anymore," Gaglardi said as he pushed back his chair and signalled to the waiter to bring the bill. Knowing my hopes of making my pitch were fading fast, I was sweating bullets. Finally, during our descent down the staircase from the dining room and the brief walk along the hallway back to his office, the minister inquired about the purpose of my mission.

Our concern had to do with the fact that the Highways department wanted Chetwynd to build and maintain a system of frontage roads on both sides of the highway in order to discourage local traffic on the highway itself. It was beyond our means to improve and cope with the additional maintenance of these roads, and it was equally unreasonable to expect us to put up with having the entire town shrouded in clouds of dust every time a car or truck made its way along them. An impending provincial election had spawned the idea of paving a major section of the Hart Highway; this, I argued, presented a unique opportunity to address the problem. Would it not make sense to modify the Highways contract already commissioned to include the paving of our frontage road system, at least around the village's centre in front of the hotel?

Gaglardi, blessed with a quick mind as bright as the coloured lights adorning the Parliament Buildings during the Christmas season, had no trouble at all recognizing the good sense in such a proposition—and a way to send me off in a happy state of mind.

"Look, would you mind fleshing out the details of what you have in mind with my deputy minister?" he asked, pushing open the door to the latter's office. "The mayor here has an idea we'd better not pass up," he said by way of an introduction. "Would you discuss it with him, please, and make the necessary arrangements to get it looked after."

That's the way business was done in the days before governments learned to opt for the convenience of committees that conduct environmental impact studies and cost-benefit analyses for the purpose of postponing decisions indefinitely. Not that politicians at that time could always be relied upon to follow through on the promises they had made during elections—Bennett's "on-site power" proposition serves as a reminder of that—but, with some delicately timed reminders, the debts inherent in the promises were usually paid.

Soon after my trip to Victoria, I had a visit from the paving contractor's engineers to inquire about the size of the area that the government had agreed to pave in front of the hotel and our service station. They were quite amazed when I told them that the commitment was to pave the entire stretch of road parallel to both sides of the highway, a distance of about two kilometres. The contractor, of course, had known nothing of our plans and pointed out that it would be a waste of money in any case to place pavement on a so-called road that had not yet been outfitted with a gravel base to support it.

I got on the phone at once to the deputy minister, telling him how reluctant I would be to bother his minister with an accusation that he was reneging on the promise he had made to me and the instructions the minister had given him to accommodate my request.

"Let me talk to the contractor," he requested. After some prolonged discussion, I was handed back the phone to hear the confession that the Highways department had not realized what was involved in the project. To outfit the road with an appropriate gravel base would be formidably expensive, since there was no ready source of aggregate within 50 miles. Would I be willing to help the deputy minister out of this embarrassing situation by scaling down the project somewhat to fall within more manageable costs? Being a reasonable man, I suggested that perhaps we could postpone some of the work on the south side of the highway, which had not yet been developed and where traffic was minimal.

"You must have a lot of pull down there," one of the engineers opined after he hung up the phone with his new instructions. "Or you must have caught the old man having his way with a sheep."

CHAPTER 3

The Chetwynd Housing Project

With stupidity the gods themselves struggle in vain.
—Friedrich von Schiller

The initial boundaries of the village extended far beyond the settlement in order to allow for the growth we had been forecasting. Attracted by the prospect of jobs in the lumber mill and the proximity to schools and shops, the Native population had also increased. However, none of them had the means or opportunity to obtain the necessary financing to make their houses conform to the new, ambitiously high standards and codes being established. Every time a new subdivision was developed, it first had to be cleared of the Native hovels and shacks that dotted the landscape, the homes of families squatting on the fringes of town. Joan and I, who couldn't reconcile the contrast between the abject poverty in which these people existed and the unbounded opportunities available, never found ourselves at peace with this situation. We felt that simply skidding these ramshackle buildings farther into the bush without regard to the extra hardship imposed on their occupants was no solution at all.

Joan became obsessed with the problem. With her friends in the Catholic Women's League, she organized bazaars and bake sales to raise money for programs to involve the children in the town's activities. They organized a kindergarten and spent much of their time promoting it among the Natives by picking the kids up at home and supervising them during the day. At Christmas they bought mountains of toys, baked cookies and gingerbread, and had armies of high-school students wrap and address parcels with each of the children's names. Weather permitting, Santa Claus

Frank and Joan's children in 1965: From left: Peter, Frank, Isabell, and Ursula.

would arrive by snowmobile at the site of a big bonfire in front of the hotel, where hot chocolate and cookies were served. Volunteers with snowmobiles were organized to take the kids for rides alongside the highway. Our own kids were part of all the festivities, which served to build their excitement for our own traditional family Christmas.

I am still haunted by the memory of one particular Christmas Eve when finally, after a long, hard day, we managed to close shop for the night. Joan told me that there was one more "small" errand I had to help her run. It had been an unusually harsh winter, which had blanketed the area with a thick layer of snow, adding to the already treacherous driving conditions. She and several of her friends had each prepared a Christmas dinner, complete with a stuffed turkey and all the trimmings, to be delivered to some of the families in greatest need. The family Joan had chosen was only accessible with an all-terrain vehicle.

Generally, when it comes to Christmas, I am of the "humbug" persuasion. It was customary in those days for businesses to show their appreciation by treating their customers to a drink or two, but, as always, toward the end of the day every lush in town insisted on claiming his part of the cheer and good will. It usually took considerable cunning to persuade the last of the thirsty raising their glasses to our health to save part of their charitable wishes for their other "best friends." Moreover, our contributions to these Christmas activities had to be crowded into what was the busiest time of the year for the service station, as people made travel plans to join their families in other parts of the province.

I was in no mood to play Santa Claus.

"Christ, woman, don't we have our own kids to worry about?" I hissed at poor Joan, who had not only pulled all of her weight during the day at the shop, but had also run back and forth to the house to supervise the cooking and baking. It was no use, of course. Off we went.

Following some footprints, and up to our knees in snow, we arrived at a scene that could have been from a horror movie. It was a little tarpaper shack, no bigger than the one that had served us during our first winter in Chetwynd. The inside walls were not sheeted or insulated in any way and were covered with soot and grime. A single low-wattage light bulb and the glow of a red-hot potbellied woodstove illuminated the place, giving it a cave-like appearance. There were six children, the oldest perhaps 10, the youngest 2 years old. Several of them were barefooted, running among puddles of spilled beer frozen to the plywood floor and stumbling over discarded bottles, the only sign that adults may have shared the space with them earlier in the day. I recognized none of the children as having been part of the festivities downtown earlier in the evening.

Joan moved quickly to clear the table—the only piece of furniture in the room, aside from the beds along the walls—shifting all kinds of rubble to make room for the meal. The children, anxious and frightened at first, quickly gathered around to explore what was being piled on the table, their dirty, groping little hands ripping the wrappings off the containers.

We remained only long enough to get them started on what might have been the only decent meal they had tasted in days. None of them even looked up as we made our way back through the snow to our truck. Both of us were too stunned to express our feelings. On our way past the hotel, we could see the lights of a Christmas tree (partially obscured by the smoke that enveloped the place) in the Ladies and Escorts section of the beer parlour, which appeared to be doing a roaring business. The parents of the children we had just left would be among the patrons. If they survived the hazards of the slippery highway they would have to cross in their drunken stupor and didn't freeze to death in a snow bank on their way home, they would be greeted by the dull, dirty faces of their frightened children, huddling together to protect one another from the abuse they could expect from their parents in their present state.

Back at our own comfortable place, we parked in the driveway and sat in silence for some time, Joan holding my hand in hers, both of us fighting back tears, until Ursula and Isabell ventured out into the cold, wondering why we would want to delay what we had planned together and dreamt about for so long. I tried not to look at Joan as we went through our ritual of the traditional prayers and songs of a southern German Christmas, knowing that her voice would fail her and that she would no longer be able to hide her tears. What deprived me of my own composure was the memory of my mother's tearful face at a Christmas so many years ago when, after those terrible years of unemployment and despair in Germany during the 1920s and '30s, our parents could, for the first time, afford some small presents for their children.

Incidents like this make it almost possible to justify the policies of an earlier federal government, which had called upon Christian churches to provide a solution to the Native problem. The intent had been, in just one generation, to familiarize Native children with, and assimilate them to, the values of western civilization and our Judeo-Christian principles by forcibly removing them from their homes and parents. But as well-intentioned as it may have been at the outset, the residential-school program was not only terribly misguided; it was the most egregious of the horrendous injustices perpetrated by the Canadian government on its own Aboriginal citizens.

It would be easy to condemn the parents of the children we had visited for being irresponsible, lazy, and lacking ambition to help themselves out of their desperate situation. But how are we to know what in their pasts made them what they were? Certainly it wouldn't be difficult to imagine that as children growing up in such desperate situations, they would never have had the chance to break this cycle of despair. Those who put their faith in the Father, the Son, and the Holy Ghost for a solution through the simple act of baptism must also be disappointed and frustrated. As the proponents and willing collaborators in this crude attempt at cultural assimilation, the hierarchy of the Christian churches must share much of the guilt for having contributed to compounding the problem.

This issue confounds the rules of social science and the best efforts of social engineering to this day. Nevertheless, it took hold in my conscience and in no small way sparked my own interest in searching for political solutions to the problem.

Toward the end of my first term as mayor in 1969, I was glancing over some mail at the village office and stumbled upon an opportunity I thought too good to be true. The federal government was making a direct appeal to small northern communities, inviting them to enter into partnerships designed to improve the living conditions of the off-reserve Native population. Eligible municipalities would be required to contribute the land and pay for the installation of services such as water, sewer, and roads. The federal government, under the Central Mortgage and Housing Corporation's Rural and Native Housing Program, would put up the money to build homes for families qualifying for social assistance, rental subsidies, and housing allowances. The town would be responsible for administering the arrangement, but would be guaranteed payment of monthly rents, including municipal taxes and services.

How could we lose in such an arrangement? Not only would it be the solution to the deplorable housing situation of a significant part of Chetwynd's population, but it would also make the Native residents productive citizens by adding them to the tax base—the people who pay for the amortization of municipal services and the improvement of roads, schools, and other infrastructure.

The idea was not without its flaws. The people targeted by the program would not find it easy to make the transition from their semi-nomadic lifestyle to living in and caring for a modern home. The maintenance costs for which the village would be responsible might far outweigh the benefits. But what if I could persuade the federal government to modify the program to allow the clients to participate and work on the development of the project, earning them some equity in the houses they would eventually own? What could the difference be between subsidizing the rent for a public housing unit and a subsidy that could be applied to a mortgage?

Some of the eligible Native people had never had any regular work experience. None had ever experienced the pride of building and owning their own home as a marketable asset. Wasn't this a one-time opportunity for some to break out of the cycle of hopelessness, deprivation, and poverty to which they were shackled?

My brain was in high gear. Joan was as excited as I was, but when I shared the idea with my council, the reception was less than enthusiastic.

"Nobody has ever built me a goddamned house," one of the aldermen declared.

"How long do you think it would be before they take the power saw to the place and cut it up for firewood?" another wanted to know.

It became a classic confrontation. Initially, only one or two of the aldermen bought in to the economic argument and offered support for exploring the idea further. Perhaps if I could convince the ministers in Ottawa and Victoria, where we would have to go for approval for the extension of our boundaries, the rest might come around at least to recognizing the financial benefits for the town.

I made my way to Ottawa. Our member of Parliament, Bob Borrie, had arranged a meeting with the federal Minister of Housing, the Honourable Ron Basford, a native British Columbian. Borrie himself, his secretary informed me, had discovered a conflict in his schedule and would not be able to join me in meeting with his colleague. Perhaps he was aware that I had stayed loyal to the Diefenbaker faction in the 1968 election, but as it turned out, I didn't need his help. The Liberals under Pierre Elliott Trudeau were now in power, and the proposition I was about to advance would not be too hard to digest for the disciples of his "just society."

Indeed, Ron Basford had no difficulty at all embracing my idea. He arranged for me to meet with Gene Rheaume, a consultant to the Native Housing Secretariat of Central Mortgage and Housing, to flesh out the proposal and write a report that he could take to Cabinet for approval.

"This sounds like a winner," he said as we shook hands on the deal. "You can count on my support."

Gene was one of those rare characters who, brilliant to the point of being bored with the world around them, teeter on the edge of insanity. A Métis with *voyageur* blood in his veins, he served for a term in Parliament, representing a riding in northern Manitoba, but, unable to deal with the ignorance and complacency of the people on whom he would have to rely to make a career in politics, he left to find more challenging vistas for his restless spirit to roam in.

There could not have been a better person to complement and augment Gene's exceptional talents than Louise Hayes, his executive assistant and perhaps the only person in the world able to keep him focussed and occasionally help him fight off his demons, which usually came in a bottle. A beautiful blonde with an encyclopedic memory for names, Louise was as well connected to people in high—particularly political—offices as anyone I have ever met. She also had a deep-rooted understanding of, and compassion for, the plight of Canada's Native people that bonded her to their cause for justice.

The two of them could not have been better matched, and the proposition I laid out for them was just the kind of thing to get their creative juices flowing. After a brief brainstorming session, Gene laid out a strategy.

"Don't worry," he said. "I'll see to it that our friend the minister keeps his word. I'll present him with a deal he can't refuse."

He also had some very positive ideas of his own and just the right connections in Victoria to get the provincial government involved in securing the land we would need for the project. I had estimated that about 30 to 40 families should be targeted, but had no idea what criteria would have to be met to determine eligibility.

Before I left, Gene gave me all the data we would need to conduct a survey and develop profiles of the families we wanted to include.

"It will take me a few days to write up the report the minister will need to get his ducks in line," he said, "and as soon as that's done, we'll meet in Victoria to dazzle that crowd with your harebrained scheme. In the meantime, you grease the skids at your end so that we can get this thing off the ground before anyone changes their mind."

I could hardly wait to get back to my hotel to call Joan with the good news. Compared to some of my other half-baked proposals, like opening a gas station in the middle of nowhere, this was one deal I had no trouble selling to her.

My friends and fellow town councillors were another matter. At the next regular meeting, during which I laid out the proposition, I failed to get their approval, even in principle, to proceed any further. They did, however, promise to think about it.

"Study all you want," I told them, "but in the end this thing is going to happen if it's the last thing I do."

Joan and I decided to sort out our friends and seek help from those willing to support us and invest their faith in what we were proposing. They would also have to live with the abuse from the community's bigots, who were already organizing to defeat the project.

Within just a few days, Gene Rheaume called to tell me that he had arranged a meeting in Victoria with Grace McCarthy, deputy premier in Bennett's government, and Dan Campbell, the provincial Municipal Affairs minister, to align their support.

"I've booked a room for you at the Hotel Vancouver for next Thursday, and I have a ticket for you to fly to Victoria the following morning," I was told.

If only my grandfather could see me now, I thought, as the bellhop at the famous hotel deposited my cardboard suitcase on the metal stand

and opened the curtains, letting the daylight in to illuminate the palatial surroundings of a suite that easily could have accommodated several of the families who would become involved in our enterprise. The bathroom alone was at least twice the size of any of the shacks in which they presently lived. Gene and Louise, who had already checked in, suggested we meet in Gene's room for a drink and a strategy session. When I presented myself there, it was clear to me that another drink was the last thing Gene needed. He kept us in stitches for two hours without once touching on the subject at hand, apart from telling me that he had been given full authority and a substantial budget to put together a demonstration project in Chetwynd along the lines I had suggested.

I was in no mood to spoil the moment by telling him that my compatriots on the Chetwynd village council were not at all enthused about the proposal. Word leaking out of the auxiliary council chamber— the laundry room at Maurice Hayward's Windrem Motel, where dissident members made it their practice to retire after formal council sessions at the village hall—was that a strategy was being developed to scrap the project before it saw the light of day.

I excused myself to make time for a haircut before the dinner Gene had booked in the upstairs dining room.

"There's a great barbershop in the basement," Gene said. "I'll give them a call and tell them you're coming."

"You must be Mr. Oberle," the maître d' greeted me at the door. He must have recognized me by my double-knit suit and white socks. "Come right this way and I'll introduce you to Julia, who will be looking after you."

Julia presided in a spacious private alcove, where she relieved me of my jacket and tie and led me to the chair. The discussion with the architect who had designed our house in Chetwynd was less complicated and involved than the one which determined the style of hair best suited to my personage.

"Carol," she concluded, "will do a manicure and a pedicure while I see what can be done with your hair." Julia, as her strong eastern European accent indicated, was an immigrant like myself. Her matter-of-fact demeanour did not invite even the slightest disagreement, particularly since that would expose my ignorance about the words "manicure and pedicure," which had not yet registered in my English vocabulary.

She had me in a horizontal position with the back of my head perched over a sink before Carol launched her assault. To my absolute horror, I could feel myself being stripped of my shoes and socks, which were surrendered to a young male attendant who quickly fled the scene. My feet were then treated to a warm sponge bath before the mutilation of my toenails, presumably the intended purpose of the exercise, commenced.

The entire ordeal lasted well over an hour, during which time I was making some quick calculations about how big a slice of my very limited budget this procedure would absorb. Since the trip was not officially sanctioned by my council, it had to be at my own expense, and with the use of credit cards not yet in vogue, I was contemplating the prospect of not being able to pay for the room, which no doubt would cost a small fortune as well. Carol was unwrapping a brand-new pair of black socks to cover up her deed when Gene entered the arena. He presented each of the women with a beautiful red rose and a most generous tip and thanked them for restoring his best friend, who had been marooned in the far north among a wild tribe of Indians, back to civilization.

"You bastard," I said to him. However, much to my relief, he also charged the bill to his own room—no doubt to be listed under "miscellaneous items" in his "generous" budget. It was, as Louise explained to me later, a crash course in "Gene-ology."

The following day was almost anticlimactic. Grace McCarthy promised to take a personal interest in the project, and Minister of Municipal Affairs Dan Campbell offered to sponsor an Order-in-Council for the extension of the village boundaries as soon as I could provide him with a proper survey of the area we had in mind. The province, Grace offered, would supply the land without cost to either the village or the project.

"The ball is now in your court," Gene lectured as we parted ways at the airport. "The sooner you can get me the list and profiles of the families whose lives you are about to change, the quicker we can get up and running."

"And don't mess up your hair for a while!" he shouted over the heads of my fellow passengers as I made my way to the departure gate.

Back home, Joan had not been idle. She had already recruited Father Jungbluth to help out with the selection of the potential clients. Before I reintroduced the subject at another council meeting, I solicited the help of a number of leading citizens whose influence, I felt, could be mobilized to tilt the council's decision in our favour.

The core group consisted of Father Jungbluth; Ed Hoffman, the accountant at our sawmill enterprise; Frank Bonnetti; Jim Matear, the current public-works superintendent; and Dr. John Lennox, who had just recently arrived with his wife—also a doctor—and their family to set up shop in anticipation of a hospital.

Dr. Lennox, who had spent most of his professional career in the mission field in Africa, was full of ideas on how to structure the project to optimize the social benefits to the individual families. After many hours and late-night meetings, the ground rules had been established.

Thirty-two families in all were identified as partners in the project. With the exception of two or three for whom special arrangements had to be made, all were required to contribute their labour, which, together with the serviced building lot, would count as the down payment for the house they would eventually own. Only one or two professional tradesmen and builders would be hired to train and supervise the workforce. A company was incorporated to serve as the legal entity, with Ed Hoffman to keep the books and act as the comptroller. The toughest job initially fell to one of the Natives, Harvey McFeeders, who was put in charge of keeping everyone on the job and keeping track of the hours every individual contributed to the project.

It was now time to introduce the village council members to the plan I had agreed to on their behalf. Backed up by the supporters I had invited to the meeting, I laid out the commitments the two senior governments were prepared to make and explained the financial benefits, which would far outweigh the initial costs the village would incur in developing the subdivision. To ease the pain even further, Frank Bonnetti offered to take on the contract to supply the water and sewer services at cost. Dr. Lennox contributed his expert opinion on the positive impact this project would have on the social development of the families involved.

It was no contest. Only one of the aldermen timidly suggested an in-camera meeting before a final vote was held. I reminded them that they had already had several weeks to think about it and that it was now time to fish or cut bait. The vote passed.

Yet it was not the end of the matter. An in-camera meeting, to which I was not invited, took place in the laundry room immediately following the public session. Not being privy to the agenda either, I can only assume that the mutineers discussed ways to rescind the decision they were too cowardly to oppose in front of the delegation and to find a way to scuttle the entire project for good. The village clerk, obviously sympathetic to their cause, advised them that since the Order-in-Council to extend the boundaries had already passed the provincial legislature, only a petition signed by a prescribed number of the electorate could overturn and stop the process.

They waited until I was away on an errand to Toronto, retrieving a car that had been stolen from our lot some time ago and had ended up in a police compound. Joan gave me the news when I called her from a phone booth somewhere on the Prairies on my way back.

"You better get back here fast," she said. "Word is out that the council has received a petition against the project, and it has been forwarded to Victoria together with a resolution to rescind the council's prior commitment to the Chetwynd housing project."

I had been feasting my eyes on the beauty of the rural prairie countryside, which looked so much more hospitable than it had on my first train trip almost 20 years earlier in midwinter. Now I riveted them on the road. Making my way back, I used all the experience I had gained driving Ed Williams's Chevy pickup to the Ashcroft hospital for my son's birth and ferrying the Chetwynd ambulance to Dawson Creek. I stopped only to inhale my diet of chocolate bars washed down with Coke to stay awake and keep myself nourished and focussed.

My mind was occupied with deciding which of the cowards I would strangle first.

I arrived late at night and allowed myself to be persuaded by Joan to get a good night's sleep before I did something we might regret later. The following morning, the clerk at the village office confirmed Joan's news. He had already transmitted all the documentation required to support the council's wishes to the appropriate authority in Victoria.

I advised the good man to make no less haste than he had employed in this dirty deed to contemplate a career change. Next I confronted Bill Hoover, a local businessman who had organized the petition and was now deep into a bottle of whisky, nursing the pain of the tongue-lashing his wife, Marion, had laid on him for allowing himself to be used by "these village idiots" to do their dirty work.

After that, I got on the phone to Dan Campbell, the Minister of Municipal Affairs, to explain what had happened.

"It all sounded a bit too good to be true," he confessed, but he offered to consult with his officials to find a way to remedy the situation.

"If you promise to stay on top of it this time," he said when he called me back several days later, "we will pretend that a mistake had been made in the initial survey which, if corrected by adding three feet to the southern boundary, will form the basis of a revised Order-in-Council.

"Look, Frank," he added, "I am sticking my political neck out a mile on this. I hope you know what you're doing." Thank you, Dan.

Some positive results flowed from the debacle. Everyone in the village was now aware of what we were doing. Some even offered to get involved with the project, and most of the others relented to the point of admitting that there was nothing else they could do to stop it.

It was now late in the fall, and the committee, hoping to be ready to begin construction early in the coming year, busied itself during the winter with interviewing the families and getting them to make their selection from one of several models of modest house designs we had selected for them. In the end, all opted for identical plans.

Even before spring freed the ground from the grip of snow and frost, the men were out clearing trees and brush from the site. Huge fires sent heavy smoke billowing to the sky, the flames of the burning brush and debris reflecting in the eyes of the children, who were wondering what it was that had gotten into their parents; they had never seen them so excited.

Soon Bonnetti's bulldozer and excavating machines were busy digging the trenches for the water and sewer lines, and shortly thereafter the first series of building sites were excavated. For most of the crew it was their first work experience. After the first few weeks, Harvey, whose job it was to get everybody reporting for work, was totally frustrated.

"It will take us 10 years to build this project unless we hire outside help," he insisted. We reminded him of the strict rules we had made requiring the Native people to do the work themselves. In my view, even if it took 20 years, this essential part of the enterprise would not be sacrificed.

However, this policy was challenged from a most unlikely source. The welfare office, which serviced its Chetwynd clients out of Dawson Creek, had served notice on everyone involved with the project that their benefits would cease and that any money received during the time they were employed on the project would have to be reimbursed. The whole crew quit en masse.

My call to the regional manager of the welfare office in Dawson Creek merely netted me an accusation of being a co-conspirator in fraud, since I had openly counselled his clients not to report their earnings from Chetwynd Housing Ltd. This bureaucrat was not in the least interested in the fact that the money was not actually paid out, but instead credited to a building account that would bolster his clients' down payments on their new homes. In fact, he questioned the ethics and legality of the arrangement and threatened legal action.

It was time to cash in on a promise made to me by Grace McCarthy to take a personal interest in our project.

McCarthy proved true to her word. The very next day, one of the agency's officers not only delivered the cheques to the families in person, but also arranged with Ed Hoffman to hand out the future monthly support payments, saving their clients the inconvenience and expense of their monthly trips to the city.

Thank you, Grace McCarthy.

With every stage of construction, the excitement grew. So did everyone's effort and commitment. Don Swanton, the overall superintendent, proved himself more than a highly skilled manager and tradesman. He felt as deeply as we did about the plight of the people for whom the project was designed. He was told by the steady stream of visitors to the site from Ottawa, Victoria, and elsewhere in Canada how important the project was, if only for the hope it would give other communities to replicate what we were doing and build on our success.

Don had infinite patience in dealing with his crew. Halfway through the summer he was confident that the project could be completed over a two-year period. But even before the first 16 homes were close to completion, one could see a dramatic change among the participants. How, after all, could a man find the nerve to pry himself away from the job to visit the bar when his children, with their friends in tow, might come bouncing home from school to show off what their daddy had done that day? For both him and the children, this was a new experience, one that evoked unfamiliar feelings of satisfaction, happiness, and contentment—a change one would find easy to get used to.

There was now a bounce in the step of the workmen putting the finishing touches on their work. Only reluctantly would they stop to chat and politely answer questions. "Got to go," they'd say. "Don wants me to finish the tiles in the Calliou house." There was now an urgency to work toward the final stage of completion in an effort, perhaps, to dispel any lingering doubt that it could actually be happening.

The workforce had expanded to include women, who were now busy painting, cleaning the work areas to get ready for the carpets and tiles, and choosing the colours and patterns. The budget allocated for the individual homes was sufficient to outfit them with a stove, oven, and fridge. The delivery of the last few appliances coincided with Halloween and the first snowfall, signalling an end to the building season.

"Let me show you your Christmas present before we go home to help the kids open theirs," I said to Joan after we finally closed down the garage on Christmas Eve. I suggested that we take a detour through "Moccasin Flats," as the project was nicknamed, past the row of spacious new homes, nicely painted and decked out with all the modern conveniences.

Some already had strings of colourful lights mounted to highlight the entrance and roof line. Through the windows we could see the brightly decorated Christmas trees, adding colour to the flowery patterns on the window panes that Jack Frost had added to the festive scene. Everyone seemed to be home—home, indeed—celebrating not only the miracle that gives the festival its meaning, but also the miracle that had given their lives some new purpose, some hope. I again recalled that special Christmas so long ago in my own childhood, when new hope and the happy glow in their children's eyes were my parents' most precious gifts.

How sweet were the tears Joan and I shed on this occasion. Sure, just as it had been a couple of years earlier, the door at the entrance to the beer parlour was open, inviting a glance as we drove by. As we had then, we could see through the clouds of tobacco smoke the outline of a decorated tree. But what I noticed most of all this time were some vacant seats, and that, more than anything, gave us the courage to face what the following year might bring.

Actually, our work was done. The project had developed its own momentum. Commissioned by the Native Council of Canada and supported by the money in Gene Rheaume's "substantial" budget, a documentary film was produced that highlighted some of the families and recorded the various stages of the project. Patrick Watson, arguably the most prominent TV personality at the time and later the chairman of the Canadian Broadcasting Corporation, produced and narrated the script and visited Chetwynd on several occasions. The B.C. Association of Non-Status Indians had approached us with a proposal to take over the management of the second phase, earning itself recognition and valuable experience to sponsor similar projects in other locations. Charles Cato and his "Frontier Apostles"—young people, mostly university students from all over the world, who donated their talents and time to worthy causes—supplied a crew of volunteers for part of the second building season.

No one in town dared to voice dissent any longer.

We insisted that Ed Hoffman carry on as the comptroller and that Don Swanton remain as the overall superintendent. Not only did they manage between them to complete an entire 32-home subdivision project, but they also produced a sizable surplus of money which, in the end, everyone agreed should be used to build a community hall.

The enthusiasm for the community hall project was boundless. The plumbing and electrical subcontractors, perhaps a bit anxious at the beginning of the project over whether they would get paid, offered to donate their time and supply the materials for the hall at cost. Other businesses donated fixtures and appliances. The result was nothing less than spectacular.

In no time, the place became a beehive of activity. Father Jungbluth helped organize a kindergarten; wedding receptions and socials were held. Modelled after some of the friendship centres in the cities, the hall included an activity room for teens to hang out in and a place for women to gather.

None benefitted more, however, than the people who had helped with the planning and had worked so hard to bring the project to fruition. We were all rewarded with the pride and satisfaction that come from contributing to a job well done. Moreover, in the years that followed, the Chetwynd housing model was used to help thousands of families throughout Canada broaden their horizons, offering their children a better start in life.

CHAPTER 4

Sorting Out Our Friends

Everyone is a prisoner of his own experiences. No one can eliminate prejudices—just recognize them.

—Edward R. Murrow

Advocating for a hospital for Chetwynd was another epic battle that not only compounded our problem of juggling time and energy between the demands of family, business, and service to the community, but also caused us to sacrifice some of the friends with whom we had shared a few of the happier moments in our social calendar.

Despite the noble efforts of Wink Wheeler and the gallant work of our ambulance drivers, the future growth of both town and industry in the area depended on the establishment of a hospital. Clearly, it was unreasonable to expect young families to settle in a place where basic health services other British Columbians took for granted were denied. And without a permanent health facility, it likewise proved impossible to recruit any health-care professionals to the area.

Unfortunately, my efforts to end this stalemate cost me at least one friendship. The volunteer chairman of the committee to promote the hospital was a prominent member of the community, a member of the Chamber of Commerce, and the zone commander of the Royal Canadian Legion (RCL). He was also a strident opponent of the Moccasin Flats development and seemed to have a general dislike of the local Native population, despite the fact that many of its members had served with distinction in the Second World War alongside his other comrades.

He also served as the local (lay) magistrate, an office that allowed him to display his many talents and impulses. At one point earlier, when we were finally able to recruit a doctor to move to town, we were faced with an urgent need to free up chronically scarce living quarters and space to accommodate a medical practice. Most likely out of desperation, my former friend allegedly collaborated with the owner of an apartment building to solve the problem by evicting a current tenant. The eviction notice was given to Nelson Ghostkeeper's family on the grounds that Nelson suffered from a chronic tardiness in meeting the monthly rent. Also, the landlord felt that the apartment had generated a higher-than-usual cost for maintenance and repair. To upgrade and redecorate the place to a standard appropriate for the new doctor and his wife, the ever civic-minded zone commander himself offered his services as a contractor for the work.

Nelson Ghostkeeper had a steady, respectable job with BC Hydro, managing a crew charged with clearing and maintaining the power line right-of-way. There was no reason for him to be short of money, except that he was away from home for prolonged periods of time, during which Marie, his wife, was expected to make ends meet.

Nelson came to me for help, not so much to complain about the eviction, which he had accepted as a legitimate penalty for being part-Native, but because he had been presented with a bill for the zone commander's repainting work and for the allegedly required replacement of the fridge and stove. Nelson was wondering if I could do something to help him get possession of the perfectly good discarded appliances and, even more importantly, to dissuade the magistrate from placing a garnishee order on his wages, which, he had been informed by his employer, would result in his dismissal.

He had been told that the old stove and fridge had been taken to the dump, where he was perfectly welcome to retrieve them. But a thorough search failed to reveal any sign of the items in question. In fact, Nelson had heard it rumoured that they had been sold.

I had my own reasons to get mad at Nelson from time to time. It was up to me to keep his family supplied with fuel for the stove and heater until he got around to paying me for the deliveries, which were usually called for in the middle of the coldest nights of the year. However, it appeared to me that my friend, on this occasion at least, might have gone a bit far in operating his "one-stop" service enterprise.

I decided to give him a call to get his side of the story. He didn't even try to deny that Nelson's version was basically true. I suggested that perhaps 48 hours would give him enough time to rescind the garnishee order on

Nelson's wages. I also dropped a broad enough hint that writing off the bill for redecorating the apartment might be seen as a gesture of good will and charity that would persuade me, and maybe even Mr. Ghostkeeper, not to take the matter any further. That one of the young police constables had helped him with the work in no way improved the ethics of what had transpired and would certainly not have dissuaded me from proceeding with the threat.

One thing must be said in favour of the enterprising magistrate: He knew when he was licked. Nelson did keep his job and continued to hire some of the local Native people to help him with his assignments. As for me, I was told by my former friend that he would personally see to it that I would never again set foot in any of the legion facilities under his command. It was not due to my cowardice alone that I never bothered to put this edict to the test. Joan and I had spent many happy hours at the local Legion mingling with the members, some of our best friends among them, who were usually among the first to offer the premises and their charity for functions to benefit families who had fallen on hard times. But I no longer had any interest in enjoying the hospitality of any place of which our former friend personally claimed to be the host.

Despite his impressive record of community service and these considerable entrepreneurial talents—he was an active member of the Masonic Lodge, the Elks Club, and, of course, the Legion, as well as participating in Little League baseball and the Scout movement—my former friend and his committee never achieved much progress in getting us closer to a hospital or some sort of a medical clinic. They met dutifully on a monthly basis to exchange and collect anecdotal evidence supporting the urgent need for the establishment of a health-care facility in our town, but aside from writing the occasional letter and filing a polite response, nothing ever happened to indicate that anyone in Victoria was taking note of our plight. So, in the fall of 1969, it was suggested that I give my good friend even more cause for the high esteem and kind affection in which he held me by challenging him for the chairmanship of his dormant committee and using the contacts I had cultivated in the capital to press our case.

It was with reluctance that I successfully assumed this mantle, a duty additional to acting as Chetwynd's mayor. There are only so many ends from which one can burn a candle and only so much that could be expected from Joan, who was filling in for me at our ever-expanding business. On my next trip to Victoria to meet with my friends in Bennett's government on municipal business, I also raised the hospital issue with Ralph Loffmark, the Minister of Health at the time. I argued that as long as the province's economy remained heavily dependent on the prime resource sectors and so long as the government stayed committed to their ambitious agenda of developing and exploiting the vast storehouse of these resources in the province's north, then it appeared essential—to me at least—that the government must also ensure that the orderly development of social amenities and necessities keep pace and stay in balance with the industrial growth being generated.

The minister promised to have his officials do a survey of the existing facilities in Dawson Creek and Fort St. John to determine the extent of the actual demand originating from the Chetwynd area—at this point estimated to have between 2,000 and 2,500 people. But, he pointed out, the Dawson Creek hospital was at an advanced state of planning for a major expansion, making it unlikely that another new facility in the area could be justified.

The minister nevertheless agreed to my request that any decision on the Dawson Creek plan would be delayed until the Chetwynd factor was added to the equation. To resolve this issue, I would be pitted against the charismatic chairman of the Dawson Creek hospital board, Ron Witherspoon, who was not only a good friend but also a valuable business associate. Ron and Don Phillips were the principal owners and partners of Aspol Motors, a prosperous Ford Motor Company franchise in Dawson Creek, and they had helped us get started in the automotive trade at our new automotive service facility. We had moved to this much-expanded business after we had outgrown our lease at the more moderate Chevron gas station we had opened in 1958. The new business operated as a sub-dealership of Aspol Motors, which was supplying us with automobiles and parts.

It was a classic struggle. Ron defended the perfectly reasonable notion of a central facility, sufficiently large and integrated to afford the latest in the costly diagnostic and treatment services necessary to attract specialists and other highly qualified health professionals to the area. I, on the other hand, insisted on a facility for Chetwynd that could cater to the more basic needs of our community, such as emergency treatment and obstetric and pediatric care and services. In the end, my argument won the day, but not without sacrifice to the personal friendship Ron and I had shared in the past. Chetwynd was allocated provincial funding for a hospital, causing Dawson Creek's expansion to be delayed.

Over the next two years I made a total of 15 trips, a number of them at my own expense, to consult with the architects and fight with the bureaucracy in Victoria over every hinge and doorknob in the new hospital. There were occasions when Joan and I had to ask ourselves whether the rewards and personal satisfaction that accrue from service to one's community could be reconciled with the personal sacrifices and the lost business opportunities we suffered as a result.

My health, too, was suffering. All too often, I had traded lunch for a chocolate bar and a Coke to make up for lost time as I attended to urgent situations requiring my personal attention at the business. A painful stomach ulcer was the reward for that habit.

I readily accept that I may well have only myself to blame for much of the organized resistance to the causes I led and helped to promote. Certainly, my own aggressive, uncompromising approach to issues about which I felt strongly did not endear me to anyone other than our best friends. Since my service, even in the mayor's chair, was largely voluntary and required Joan and me to sacrifice precious time we would have much preferred to spend with our children, I adopted the attitude that if people didn't like what I was doing, they always had the option of relieving me of my duties. Perhaps some regarded this as the same kind of attitude I later learned to detest myself, when I found it in people on whose judgement my future career depended—an attitude of bullishness and arrogance. But communities and nations are not build by timid people, and great things are not accomplished by leaders without conviction.

I had neither the time nor the patience to persuade those who, for reasons known only to themselves, or because of jealousy—and without regard to any consequences—opposed whatever was put on the agenda for discussion. Small-town politics, as I soon discovered, is not for the thin-skinned. Personality conflicts get in the way of reason and common sense.

Nothing brought home this painful reality more than the feedback we were getting from our children. Once, when we were discussing over lunch the upcoming municipal election in which I would compete for a second term as mayor, Frank suddenly broke out in tears for no apparent reason.

"I don't want you to be mayor any more," he said through his sobs, when finally he was able to speak. It was obvious that the vicious rumours spread in the community by my opponents about my "Nazi past" and my exploitation of my council and board positions for personal advantage had been overheard by their children. As cruel as children can be at that age, the bullies among them had targeted our kids for punishment for my alleged misdeeds.

I was devastated. For days I wrestled with my conscience. Perhaps our past was catching up with us after all and there was a line that immigrants, certainly the most recent ones, ought not to overstep. Perhaps it was expected of newcomers that they should show their gratitude by simply conforming to the way things are and keeping their own ideas to themselves. But there was still so much to do, so much unfinished business.

And what about the Moccasin Flats children? What was in *their* past that meant they should be deprived of the right to have their voices heard?

Finally, Joan and I decided to put ourselves through the ordeal. I won a second mandate as the mayor and for one whole day at least, in the fall of 1971, all seemed to be forgiven and forgotten. The occasion was the official opening of the Chetwynd and District Hospital.

There were no dissenting voices now. The schools declared a holiday to allow the children to meet the premier and some members of his Cabinet, who had come to help us celebrate the event. MLA Don Marshall and Premier Bennett left no doubt in anyone's mind about whom they shared the credit with for bringing the project to fruition. In fact, despite the bouquets thrown at me, much of the praise belonged to Marcel Lamar, the resident manager of BC Hydro who, acting as my vice-chairman on the hospital board, shouldered much of the burden with me. He was a great travelling companion and a tireless worker.

Like all the other building blocks that shaped the town and gave it its character and soul, the hospital immediately became a focal point, a beehive of activity. There were bake sales to raise funds for additional equipment. A ladies' auxiliary recruited volunteers to supplement services not covered by the health plan. They also organized a contingent of candystripers to assist the nurses, who would become their role models. Isabell's future nursing career was inspired by that experience.

But, even more importantly, we were able to attract two highly qualified and equally well-motivated doctors. Well in advance of the hospital's completion, Ruth and John Lennox had arrived to work at the new facility, enticed by the prospect of being able to contribute to the planning and design of the core components. Chetwynd had become a place to which businesses and their people were ready to make long-term commitments.

W.A.C Bennett, at the new hospital's opening, holds a replica of Chetwynd's *Little Giant of the Mighty Peace*.

Canadian Forest Products, having bought out Gordon's sawmill, committed to a major expansion. Another bank and a variety of smaller businesses generated at least some diversity in the local economy. The town could now afford to properly outfit the fire department and offer the chief and some of the volunteers a small stipend for their service. The provincial government established a regular ambulance service with proper equipment and trained personnel.

Sadly, with this new stability, a part of the spirit that motivated people to volunteer their time and money in support of local causes withered away. For example, it was now more difficult to recruit people to operate the ambulance equipment.

Likewise, the larger companies with their headquarters in the southern part of the province were not as attached to the community as those owners and operators who had grown up with the town. During one of my trips to Victoria, I stopped by to visit with the principals of the company that had bought the sawmill assets from the Moores to ask for some concessions on the price of the lumber we would need for the Native housing project; the request provoked a torrent of crocodile tears to back up their lament over the slim profit margins the company had generated from the Chetwynd location. So moved was I by the plight they described that I contemplated taking up a collection among the Natives in Chetwynd to help out. We ended up paying the same price Canfor was charging its customers in the U.S. and eastern Canada for lumber from the Chetwynd mill.

Another example of the changes was the water system. Gordon Moore's Fort St. John Lumber Company had constructed a small dam on Windrem Creek to supply the needs of the hotel, the sawmill, and some of their staff houses. This turned out to be an inadequate source when it came to serving a town of the size to which Chetwynd, at least in the minds of Chamber of Commerce members, was destined to grow.

"This puddle," opined an engineer sent by the provincial government to make an assessment, "won't make a living for a family of ducks."

When a proper system that drew water from the Pine River itself was eventually built, Gordon Moore and his enterprises agreed to pay a hefty premium to allow for the timely amortization of the project. But when Canfor came along, it was a different kettle of fish—or ducks.

First, we suddenly experienced a massive increase in consumption, prompting us to recall the engineer who had designed the system to investigate the cause. When it was discovered that the Canfor mill was using the new system to fill their log pond, pumping water at great expense from a source close to a kilometre away and to a much higher elevation, the town insisted on a metering device to measure the volume of water going to the mill. It should never be said that large integrated companies tend to stifle their employees' individual initiatives: one of them promptly bypassed the meter. Repeated efforts to persuade the company to install a more effective, less polluting waste disposal system were usually met with the threat that if we made things too difficult, they would have no choice but to move the mill to a more remote location, where they could escape municipal taxes altogether.

These experiences of dealing with the area's dominant industry undoubtedly helped lead me into one my wildest and most hair-raising ventures: getting involved in a partnership to build and operate a sawmill of our own, taking on the big boys (at least in the labour market), and competing for a share of the timber in the region.

CHAPTER 5

Exploring New Horizons

The chief obstacle to the progress of the human race is the human race.

—Don Marquis

The chief instigator of this sawmill scheme was Lorne Dalke, a volatile, independently minded hulk of a man who, like myself, had come through the school of hard knocks. He was not averse, given the slightest provocation, to make use of his fists to articulate his thoughts and press his point on someone contrarily inclined, otherwise disagreeable, or even likewise disposed—just for the pleasure of having a good fight for the sheer sport of it. My own physical assets paled in comparison to Lorne's; however, my comparative good looks and a healthy, full head of hair, which he lacked, made him green with envy.

When he first arrived in Chetwynd with his wife, Connie, late in 1963, he was a member of the trucking fraternity. He had come to work on the Peace River hydro project and had secured a contract to transfer freight between the railhead at Chetwynd and the construction site at Hudson's Hope. But it wasn't long before he branched out to cash in on other opportunities as well. Related to the Moores (Connie was Helen Moore's niece), Lorne began trucking logs for the lumber company and, after Gordon Moore sold the mill to Canfor, Lorne became one of several major logging contractors the mill used to supply the raw materials.

He was a disciple of the Ayn Rand approach to business, with an unbridled enthusiasm for free enterprise in its purest form. For example, when he discovered that he was paying out too much money to fuel his fleet of trucks, he bought the Pacific Petroleum bulk plant. I got involved with him when he came to the conclusion that the new mill owners were getting the best by far out of their contractual relationship. He started to explore the idea of complementing his trucks and fuel plant with a sawmill of his own.

As in most small towns that are bereft of lawyers' offices or other more formal settings for weighty business discussions, this enterprise was launched over a cup of coffee with Gordon Moore at his hotel.

"What you fellows should be doing is cranking up a little sawmill to cut up all that timber that came through the fire last year," Gordon suggested. "Canfor is certainly not interested, and it would be a crime to let it go to waste." He had maintained all his customer contacts in the U.S. who, he was sure, would put up some money to help us get started.

Naturally, it wasn't my expertise in the lumber business that sparked their interest in me as a partner in this new enterprise. Rather, it was the mistaken assumption that Joan and I were rolling in dough and that we were blessed with the "right stuff" when it came to matters of business. The local banker was discreet enough not to disclose the true nature of our financial situation and, since I was taught that people generally like dealing with successful businessmen, I never considered it in my interest to dispel this myth. The reality was that we now had four children to support and, still struggling to deal with a sizable debt related to our latest business ventures, we were struggling to "normalize" our relationship with the banks.

"Why don't you let me make a call to Ray Williston in Victoria?" Gordon offered. "I'll feel him out on the idea of allocating some of the timber in the area that might be surplus to Canfor's needs."

"No harm exploring the idea," said Lorne—and no need, I thought, to get Joan agitated over such a harebrained scheme until, of course, it looked like we might actually be able to pull it off. After the third cup of coffee, I suggested we had better break up the discussions before Lorne got the idea to buy the hotel as well.

Well, the seeds, planted in such fertile ground, germinated quickly. Gordon suggested that we invite the Demeulemeester brothers, Peter and Paul, also in the logging business, to join the partnership. Tom Wilson, considered by everyone to be a cutting-torch genius when it came to patching together gyppo sawmills, should be brought to the party as well.

The proposal was to set up a sawmill on a patch of land Gordon owned just a mile or so north of town on Jackfish Road. It would produce a precision-type, two-by-four lumber product for which Gordon Moore's former customers on the eastern seaboard of the United States seemed to have an insatiable appetite.

When I gingerly broached the subject, Joan seemed to think I had taken leave of my senses.

"Haven't you had enough of gambling on others?" she wanted to know. "How could you even consider risking everything we have worked so hard for, now that we are so close to reaching our goal?"

Valid questions all of them, but this was different. This was Big Time Stuff. Besides, I wouldn't have to commit much of my personal time or money, or so the argument went. Our contribution would mainly consist of some equipment, which had already been acquired for the ranch and could be shared between the two operations.

It wasn't an easy sell, but in the end, as always, Joan relented. And, as always, things turned out somewhat differently than as planned. The last thing we worried about at the time was trouble from either Canfor or the International Woodworkers of America (IWA), who dominated the labour scene in the province. At the time, the forest-products industry and its union were still by far the largest and most important sector in the economy. Neither Lorne nor I were great fans of unions, but we decided to cross that bridge when we came to it.

We started construction of our sawmill in 1969, about the same time that the hospital was built. With the backing of the three partners, the bank was initially quite generous in advancing the credit we needed to assemble the plant and get it into operation. Tom Wilson hauled equipment from as far away as Eugene, Oregon, and managed to fit it all together so that it looked like a sawmill. We even acquired a sizable generating plant to produce the necessary power, thus avoiding the costly expansion of the hydro grid to the site.

Only the weather failed to co-operate. When it came time to start up the plant late in the fall, unseasonably warm weather and poor road conditions prevented us from getting access to the burned timber the province had allocated to our plant. Our line of credit was predicated on the assumption that the enterprise would become operational soon after the first frost, sometime after the middle of November. In view of the unavoidable delay, the bank insisted that the crew still working on the finishing touches to the plant be laid off, to keep a check on the rising debt we were accumulating.

All of the construction workers, except three individuals who had expressed an interest in getting a permanent job at the plant, were laid off.

Difficult as this situation was for us, apparently it was an ideal time for the IWA to organize and get the plant certified in order to protect the future workforce from the capitalist tendencies of these new upstarts. With just three employees left on-site, it was an easy job for the shop stewards of the Canfor mill to get the required majority to apply for certification. With the plant substantially complete in early December, but without any change in the weather conditions, we were left with no option but to shut down completely. The union, with two of the remaining workers signed up, saw this as an opportunity to press charges against us under the provincial labour code, alleging that the shutdown was planned to avoid certification, thereby depriving the two employees of their right to freedom of association.

Lorne and I attended a court hearing in Vancouver, as did one of the aggrieved workers, who acted as the union's main witness. During the time afforded him by the layoff, he had wisely moved to Vernon, B.C., and had enrolled in a government-sponsored millwright-apprentice training course. Fate, however, intervened, forcing him to accept an invitation from another government-sponsored institution, one that catered to individuals found to be disagreeable to the police and the criminal justice system.

Although he served jail time in that instance, it would be ungrateful in the extreme if this champion of workers' rights, a recent immigrant from Europe like myself, were ever to complain about the justice system in his new homeland. In its infinite wisdom, the labour court, to diminish our defence, not only disallowed any testimony regarding the witness's character, but also simply chose to ignore a letter from our bank indicating that credit line limitations had caused the temporary shutdown. We were found guilty of unfair labour practices and were ordered to rehire the two people in question, and pay them full wages for all the time they were off work.

When finally, after several more weeks, we began hiring a crew to begin operations, Lorne had some useful advice for our recently released friend who, having served his short sentence, showed up to be hired as a millwright, even though he had not completed his course.

"Get yourself an extra-sturdy hard hat," he said. "You never know when one of these heavy steel beams you're supposed to know how to weld might come down to hit you."

"Loophole" Lewin with Frank and Joan.

The court confirmed certification of our plant and ordered us to bargain in good faith with the union toward our first contract. This was where I made my first acquaintance with the legendary Jack Munro, then president of the IWA.

Larry Lewin, or "Loophole Lewin" as he was affectionately known by his peers in Dawson Creek, was our lawyer and had agreed to act on our behalf at the bargaining sessions. It became a classic confrontation. Jack had to concede that our wage-and-benefit package would cause little acrimony in our relationship, since in most areas it exceeded what the union was demanding in other provincial contracts. However, there was the small matter of the so-called union security clause. This made it obligatory for an employer to ensure every employee was a union member in good standing by initially making membership a condition of hiring and also by automatically deducting union dues from workers' paycheques.

"Now, hold on a minute here, Jack," I responded. "Have you never heard of freedom of association, one of the cardinal principles of our democracy? And do you mean to say that I, the employer, must impose membership in your union as a condition of employment?"

"That's exactly what I mean," he boomed. "And there is no goddamned way we will ever sign an agreement without it."

"Well, Jack," I told him, "there's no goddamned way I will ever sign a contract that denies anyone who chooses to work at our mill the basic rights the whole world spent six years fighting a war over. Not even Hitler," I pointed out to him, "made it compulsory for working people to join his so-called Labour Party."

It would have been utterly useless to debate the subject any further. Loophole Lewin, pointing to the fact that his meter was running, suggested that it would perhaps be advisable for everybody to think about the issue until, as required by law, we met again the following year.

It wasn't the last we heard from Jack and his local representatives. Just a short time later the union called a strike at the Canfor plant during which the boys decided to establish picket lines at our mill as well. When I arrived at the scene, Lorne was making plans to fire up one of his big Caterpillar loaders to clear the way. I suggested a more conciliatory approach.

It was a typical cold, blustery, late-fall day, making the picketing job most uncomfortable for the boys.

"Look," I told them, "let's be reasonable about this. If you let us get on with our business here, we will extend the lunch hour for as long as it takes for a delegation from your group to convince our crew, in the comfort of their lunch room, of the virtues of your union. The only condition we will attach to the deal is that I get equal time to present our side of the argument." There was a brief, somewhat acrimonious, discussion among those assembled, but finally, everybody agreed.

We were treated to the classic "solidarity forever; the union makes us strong" sermon. I had heard it all before from Pat Miller, at the gold mine in Pioneer.

"Would you consider it fair," our boys were asked, "to enjoy the benefits that the union has fought for over the years without contributing your dues to make sure we're allowed to keep what has been won? Do you believe for one minute that Lorne and Frank here would pay you the wages and benefits you are getting without the union breathing down their necks?"

Good point, perhaps, but most people in the room had a hard time comparing Tom, Lorne, or me with the big copper bosses or some greedy capitalist driving a Cadillac while smoking big cigars. Much to the contrary, in fact; Tom Wilson usually ended up doing the dirty jobs nobody else wanted, and the most capitalist thing people ever saw me doing in the mill was sweeping the floor around the machines on the platform.

In my rebuttal, I pointed out that we had no objection whatsoever to any of our employees joining a union or forming one of their own. We would welcome it, in fact, providing we could all agree that our first concern must be the health of the business. I even offered to gladly collect dues for the IWA and accept the union as their bargaining agent, providing we had written authorization from everyone who wished to join to deduct the dues from their paycheque.

The union had no chance. We didn't exactly have a pro-union bunch, anyway. Several of our employees actually commuted to work all the way from Taylor and Fort St. John, 150 kilometres away, to avoid having to join a union. At the end of the session, when nothing else remained to be said, the union delegation was politely told by our crew to leave them alone.

Neither Jack Munro nor Lorne and I ever moved from the positions we had taken at our first meeting, so from a legal standpoint the issue was never resolved. That did not spare our mill from being harassed and targeted for special treatment by some of the hotheads in the movement. At one point, when I drew attention to our situation through the media and compared one particular incident, in which a truck of Lorne's was vandalized, to gangsterism, the union sued three newspapers and me for defamation of character.

The newspapers opted for printing an apology, leaving me to decide whether to fight the issue on my own. At the time I was naive enough to think that some of the giants in the forest industry might be inclined to support an action challenging the unions on the issue of compulsory membership. But the so-called captains of industry, while giving me lots of advice and encouragement, declined to become involved. Better to live with an archaic, adversarial labour model than to rock the boat—in their case, the yacht—that depended for buoyancy on the balance sheet's bottom line. I chose the coward's way out, which was also the only sensible solution.

And so I learned quickly that, just like municipal politics, the lumber business is not for the faint of heart. No industry is more cyclical, nor, as a price-taker, more vulnerable to the vagaries of the market, which is mainly foreign. To compete, one has to be more efficient, utilize as much of the raw material as possible, and become less labour-dependent. During good times (usually leading up to an election in the U.S.), the government demands a higher royalty, making it difficult to build reserves to help bridge the downward cycle.

As a result of this, by the time we arrived, the industry—encouraged by the province—had undergone a period of consolidation and only a few small independent companies were left on the scene. Despite that, with the help of Gordon Moore's contacts and our own proclivity for hard work and swimming against the stream, we managed to cobble together an impressive enterprise that employed up to 150 people which, together with the private contractors we had hired, added significantly to the local economy.

Canfor, as might have been expected, resisted every effort we made to gain access to a stable supply of timber, leaving us with very little collateral to offer the banks as security when we wanted to extend our credit limits. The supply of timber damaged by fire was soon exhausted, leaving us at the mercy of the government to grant us temporary access to some remote location that had not yet been allocated to the other companies in the area.

Further compounding our problem, the province brought in a long-overdue policy to reduce waste. In 1970 it became mandatory for the solid-wood sector to remove more of the tree from the bush and to convert as much of the waste fibre as possible to wood chips for the pulp mills. We estimated that the required modifications to our plant would cost upwards of a million dollars, which of course we could not expect to raise unless we secured a permanent supply of timber.

This was easier said than done. With the enormous political power the forestry industry was able to assert because of its dominant position in the provincial economy, our prospects for survival became rather bleak. Peter Bentley of Canfor actually told me that his company, no doubt for good reasons, would jealously guard the quota allocated to it and would resist every effort by an interloper to intrude into its area. He suggested to me "as a friend" that I find a graceful way to extricate myself from the business. What saved us in the end was a change in government or, more precisely, the industry's reaction to it.

In 1972 the unthinkable happened. The socialist hordes, as W.A.C. Bennett liked to refer to the New Democrats, penetrated the ramparts, bringing his 20-year coalition to its knees. Dave Barrett and the NDP swept the province. Although Bennett's Social Credit Party was more of a coalition of different political viewpoints than a party, it leaned strongly to the right of the political spectrum—so far, in fact, that the NDP by comparison was regarded by some as the lunatic fringe. Overnight, all of the industry's major plans for expansion were cancelled or postponed. Wherever possible, production was reduced or relocated out of province in order to starve the invaders out of existence as quickly as possible.

Premier Dave Barrett's response was just as swift. He was no ordinary shop steward, but a shrewd, populist politician who had no trouble interpreting the signals he was receiving. Publicly, he lamented the fact that the main engine of the provincial economy was grinding to a halt because most of the large, by-now totally integrated, companies had suddenly lost faith in their industry's future prospects. Meanwhile, Barrett assumed some timber quotas would be abandoned and could be reassigned to anyone with a more positive outlook on the future of the trade, so he extended an open invitation for applications from anyone fitting that description.

Lorne and I did, and were successful in stabilizing our situation with an adequate supply of timber that Canfor, legitimately perhaps, considered essential to their own operation's longer-term stability. Naturally, we would have preferred to reach for a lifeline thrown by a government more in line with our own political orientation, but for someone drowning, it's never prudent to question the motives of the party that throws you the rope.

We now had ample collateral for a loan substantial enough to enter the big leagues, but we underestimated the power and influence the big boys wielded in financial circles as well.

The manager at the local bank breathed a sigh of relief when told the good news about our timber allocation. Perhaps he was as naive as we were, but he anticipated no trouble at all in getting head office's approval for the new loan. Instead, he was told that not only was additional credit out of the question, but that he was to reduce the bank's existing exposure at our plant.

Much to our dismay, the reception we received at several other banks was equally cool. None were in the least interested in sharing the great fortune we were planning to build. Anyone with just a little less faith than my own in the integrity of the banking system and the individuals serving on the boards of directors might have been forgiven for suspecting conspiratorial motives.

Now we were desperate.

Fortunately, our broker, Dan Broderick, had by now developed a strong dependency on the products we were shipping to his clients along the eastern seaboard of the United States. He offered to introduce us to his own banker, who also counted several of Dan's main customers among his clients. Lorne and I were soon off to Pittsburgh to be introduced to the Yankee way of doing business.

The bank manager met us at a client's office. In less than half an hour, which we spent mainly discussing such weighty issues as hockey and some of the peculiarities of the Canadian political system, we walked away with a million-dollar credit line, supported only by our good looks (mine more than Lorne's) and the banker's trust in his other clients' positive recommendations.

There really was no reason to pay a visit to our own bank's regional head office in Vancouver, but we wanted to tell our tormentors what we thought of their tactics and to give them a lesson in venture-capital financing, American-style. We intended to deposit the money itself in their local Chetwynd branch. It turned out to be a not-very-friendly encounter.

I was still looking for the position that would offer optimum comfort to my posterior in the plush armchair that was part of the decor in the upper-floor executive suite of the bank building when an aide entered to summon Lorne to the telephone. It was a call from our plant. Much to my relief, one of the stone-faced creatures opposite me at the boardroom table leaned over to whisper into the ear of a man whose appearance indicated a somewhat higher degree of importance than the other assembled executives. To this point, no other sign of life had been discernible among them. However, I did sense that they might be preparing to deliver an unpleasant message. Presently, Lorne re-entered the room, his face drained of every last drop of blood, his nostrils vibrating like the wings of a hummingbird.

Fight time! His jaw set, he strained to push the words past his rage.

"Which one of you connoisseurs of male genitalia"—an approximate translation of his words in Canada's third, unofficial language—"called our note and gave instructions to bounce our employees' paycheques?"

"Now, now, Mr. Dalke, there is no need … " That was all the important-looking one was able to get out of his mouth before Lorne pulled him across the table with a firm grip around his throat. Having decided to let his fists carry the rest of his contribution to the dialogue, Lorne set out to deliver a very brief message indeed.

By the time I was able to react, he had the poor man—terror-struck, with eyes as big as the dial on the bank's vault—propped against the window, one hand around his throat and the other cocked to deliver a punch that would no doubt have landed the recipient among the pedestrians on the street 18 storeys below. I had to reach very deep to muster my last morsel of diplomatic talent to bring the situation under control.

"I had him lined up for a clean hook," Lorne assured me on the way down in the elevator. "He would never have felt the impact."

Eventually, we managed to persuade another bank to accept the million-dollar deposit on the condition that they take us as a client and help out with a smaller operating loan so we could carry on with our business.

Our relationship with Jack Munro also improved in that we acquired respect—not for one another's positions, of course, but at least for the uncompromising commitment we felt in defending them. We carried on with the obligatory annual meetings in Loophole Lewin's office, which, after a time, turned into almost friendly encounters. Actually, Jack became a good friend and a powerful ally in some of the crusades I organized later in my career.

Our armistices with the bank and the union were not the end of all our troubles, and Lorne's dream of expanding the mill to the point where some day it would exceed Canfor's production never came to fruition. But the enterprise flourished until eventually, like others before us, we found that it was altogether too irresistible to sell the assets we had worked so hard to acquire to a larger, more integrated forest company.

CHAPTER 6

Man's Best Friend

If you pick up a starving dog and make him prosperous, he will not bite you; that is the principal difference between a dog and a man.

—Mark Twain

Chetwynd was no different from most smaller northern communities where the canine population competes for prominence in the affairs of public life. Everyone can recite a litany of remarkable dog stories. If you couldn't always count on your friends, you certainly knew where you stood with your dog.

We shared our lives, certainly as long as the children were still at home with us, with several dogs over the years: some big and ferocious-looking, some small and cuddly, and each with its own mixture of breed and peculiar character. But judging by their behaviours, King was by far the smartest.

King, a white Alsatian, came to us on the back of a tow truck. Lorne Proctor, one of the garage mechanics, had been out on a mission and had found him scavenging along a logging road miles from anywhere, lost and hungry. King was fully grown and once he was fed back to health he started to compete for the position of alpha male among the staff and patrons of our Esso garage. Since I was the only challenger, he eventually accepted my dominance.

King had the traits one looks for when hiring new staff. He was a self-starter, rapidly becoming one of the managing directors at the office. I don't recall ever engaging him in any training exercises. He just knew what needed to be done. He decided that Joan was not only in more need of his protection, but was also the most deserving of his efforts and affection. In my absence, he would stretch his body across the full width of the door leading to the office, blocking the entrance to anyone who had not been invited to enter. When I was there, he considered protecting Joan to be my job.

King accompanied Joan everywhere she went and made sure she was protected when she got there. When she treated herself to a cup of coffee at the hotel, King would position himself between the double doors, closing off all traffic until she, or I, relieved him of his duty. He even insisted on acting as the lead dog on any of Joan's outings by car or truck.

One of the assets I had brought with me from the old country was a driver's licence, which had been required for my job as a journeyman baker at Kästel Fritz's bakery and noodle-works back in the Black Forest. But for Joan, driving, like everything else, was self-taught. Learning it was a matter of sheer necessity, and apparently simple enough—everybody else seemed to do it. Only King appeared to sense the dangers associated with her early attempts at venturing out in a car—at first, on the wide open ranges of the ranch in an old, dilapidated pickup truck we kept around the place, but soon thereafter on the village streets. She quickly graduated to driving not only the family car on our biweekly outings to our lakeside cabin, but also our one-ton tow truck and the service vehicles at the dealership.

Barred from riding with her in the car to assist her in the performance of her new skills, King did the next best thing by running no more than three feet ahead of the right front wheel everywhere she went, giving everyone ample notice of her whereabouts and the associated risk. On the tow truck, he was content to coordinate local traffic from its back deck.

Everyone in town, including RCMP constable Morley Kitchen, assumed that Joan had a driver's licence and King, slavishly loyal as he was to his mistress, never caused anyone to think otherwise. It was out of the question for her to take a course at the driving school in Dawson Creek since it would have taken another slice out of her already hopelessly overcrowded work schedule. Somewhere, however, she did acquire a driver's manual, which she studied religiously while doing the laundry or waiting for the bread dough to rise. Given the advantage she had over others by being in the business of servicing cars, she considered it a waste of time to attend school.

But she did get her licence eventually. During one of our infrequent outings to the bright lights of Dawson Creek, where we had taken the kids to visit the dentist, she just happened by the government agent's office and decided to drop in to try her luck. On our way home, Joan boldly announced that she would do the driving so that she could try out her newly acquired certificate. Luck must have been with her on the day she got it, because if someone had taken her out for a road test (apparently not mandatory in Dawson Creek in those days), they would at least have insisted that she avoid the habit of using her right foot to operate only the gas pedal. Her logic told her that with the advent of the automatic transmission, the left foot was left with nothing to do and was therefore free to assume the chore of manipulating the brakes. The potential hazard of operating both at the same time never seemed to bother her. Indeed, 45 years later, backed by the evidence of a perfect driving record, she still insists that it's the proper way to operate a vehicle.

King's protectiveness extended itself to relatives. When Emil and Berta were visiting, Emil liked to stroll down to the garage and sit with the boys during their morning coffee break. King immediately sensed a certain danger in Emil having to cross the highway on foot, so he made it his routine to leave the garage at precisely five minutes to ten, giving himself just enough time to meet his new friend as he was leaving the house and guide him down the main street. When they got to the highway, King dashed ahead to position himself in the middle of the road, stopping all traffic to facilitate Emil's safe passage.

At noon he would remind Joan with a friendly nudge that it was time for her to attend to her kitchen chores at home and for him to get a respite from his duties. However, he was never quite happy around the house, where he had to compete for our affection with the cat.

Ah yes, that cat. She made her debut as a kitten that had been born to a stray under the altar in Father Jungbluth's church. (There was no room at the inn.) Frank had brought her home after Sunday Mass as payment in lieu of 25 cents, his usual stipend for service as a senior altar boy. King and I thought it was a rotten deal, but by the time we got home for lunch, the small beast had already wormed herself into the hearts of the rest of the family.

King, noticing my displeasure, observed the new arrival with disdain and looked at me as if to say: "You insisted on being the alpha male, so do something about it before it's too late." But it was no use. My outright declaration that there was no place for a cat in this house was greeted with a flood of tears, forcing me to opt for an honourable retreat.

"Maybe we'll try it for a while, but don't get too attached to this flea-bitten varmint," I said firmly.

In no time at all she had taken charge of our once-peaceful home. The kids accepted her as a competitor in games of marbles, for which she trained at all hours of the day and night. In the middle of the night she took great delight in chasing her favourite toys down the carpeted stairs onto the linoleum-covered hallway, where she would lose her footing and crash into our bedroom door.

The upstairs was staked out as my alpha-male domain while I was at home. King was allowed access only to the lower environs or to a certain point at the top of the stairs that permitted him to be part of the scene. In my absence, though, Joan accommodated him with certain other liberties, which included sleeping on the couch upstairs. The cat recognized this immediately as a flagrant abuse of the rules and took it upon herself to enforce them. As soon as King entered the house, she took up position at the top of the stairs, from whence she repelled any of his attempts to invade with a quick swipe across his nose.

Needless to say, King was much happier around the garage, where he was the sole beneficiary of the affection due to him. During the summer months he extended his territory to include the Dairy Dream ice-cream parlour next to the service station. Several times during the day he would visit the establishment to collect pay "in kind" for his guard duties during the previous night. Everyone was aware of his weakness for a certain flavour of ice cream, which he preferred to have served in a cone. To the delight of patrons, he could hold it between his paws to be devoured only after the last drop of its delectable content had been licked away.

Funny thing about dogs and cars. King's predecessor at the Chevron garage, a German shepherd called Rex, liked to spend the entire day defending one of the pickups parked on the lot. Unlike King, he would delight in tearing the seat out of the pants or sleeves off the jackets of anyone making even a friendly gesture toward his domain. Harmless enough when allowed to roam free, he turned into a vicious monster inside a car, as Henry Hryciw, Morley Kitchen's successor at the cop shop, discovered on one occasion.

Henry, as was his practice, had stopped off on his rounds to catch up on the latest gossip over a cup of coffee, and the police cruiser was parked in front of Norm Stirling's hardware store when a neighbour, familiar with

Rex's antics, politely opened the door of the cruiser to invite Chevron's chief of security inside. Henry was not amused, to say the least, at having to call me to the scene to liberate and restore Her Majesty's property to his control. It doesn't need to be pointed out that this particular dog's term of employment was brief, since his demeanour was incompatible with our customer-service policy.

Others among the canine population of Chetwynd were blessed with a level of intelligence at least equal to that of some of their contemporaries among *Homo sapiens*. Father Hanna, the Anglican priest who was later elevated to bishop, had as a companion an ugly brown bulldog named Judas, who had a passion for travel—even without his master's company.

Judas's preferred mode of transportation was the Greyhound bus that stopped at the hotel on its way up and down the Hart Highway between Prince George and Dawson Creek. Judas had managed to familiarize himself not only with the schedule, but also with the routine followed by the bus driver during his Chetwynd stopover. Once the passengers had disembarked to stretch their legs after the long, torturous haul up the unpaved road from Prince George, and the driver was inside the depot exchanging insults with Jean Ray, the agent, Judas swung into action.

Jean, the reader should know, chain-smoked a particular blend of long-grained Russian tobacco—and, some suggested, horse manure—rolled into cigarettes that she manufactured herself. Any visit to her domain had to be brief. Even the heartiest of Chetwynd's mosquito or blackfly population quickly succumbed to the pesticide Jean emitted from every pore of her body.

Judas therefore had to be quick, his timing planned to the split second. He would spend the first part of his journey to the city hiding under a seat as far removed from the driver as the size of the bus allowed. After a certain passage of time, known among airline captains on transoceanic routes as the point of no return, Judas would nonchalantly ease himself into a more comfortable position on a vacant seat, from whence he could observe the wonders of the passing landscape. As one of the more frequent patrons of the bus line, he was usually treated to a free meal and a hospitable stay at the Dawson Creek terminal until it was time for his return trip.

One of Judas's outings was written up in the *Chetwynd Chinook* with what I considered a particularly unkind remark: "Judas," the story said, "was not nearly as smart as one might think, or he would have known that none of the Dawson Creek stores were open for business on Wednesdays, obviously not a good day to visit the city."

Some people would have us believe that dogs have a soul and are thus entitled to share space with us in heaven. Don Titus would certainly be among these believers, and the canine that one might meet upon arrival in the other world, in closest proximity to the "Great One," would undoubtedly be Don's best buddy, Butch.

Don was one of the business partners—Fred, Sandy, and Gordon Moore being the others—who founded modern Chetwynd. After building the hotel for the partnership, Don traded his equity in the hotel and its liquor dispensaries for the remainder of the real estate they had acquired, which he set out to develop. It was not the wisest decision he ever made, inasmuch as he was by far the best customer and most lucrative patron of the hotel's beer-and-liquor dispensaries.

Wherever Don went, his trusty friend Butch was sure to go. He was sort of a mid-sized mongrel, black and white in colour, and must have had inherited all the best aptitudes and traits of the several breeds of which he was comprised. His master was lost without him. They were inseparable except when, as so often happened, Don surrendered himself to the control of his demon. Butch was able to gauge the exact degree of his master's inebriated state, at which point he would set out on his own to summon his mistress to the rescue.

But when Don was away on business, where he had to rely on strangers to get him to his appointments or to the airport for the trip back, it was not at all unusual for him to literally get lost. Indeed, he was once missing for a whole week when he boarded the wrong flight in Vancouver and ended up in a Hawaiian hospital, where he had been taken in a comatose state after being found on a beach suffering from severe sunburn.

Don and Margaret (Effie), his wife, whom everyone respectfully referred to only as Mrs. Titus, were avid gardeners, taking great pride and satisfaction in contributing their bountiful fall harvest of potatoes, carrots, and other assorted fruits of their labour to all the local churches for dispensation to the poor. It kept them busy.

No greater tragedy could have befallen Don and his good wife than the untimely demise of their loyal companion. Everyone in town knew and liked Butch. According to the doctor, he must have ingested poison, but it was not thought to have originated from any malicious source.

It was natural, of course, for the grieving couple to seek solace in their faith and to insist on a prayer service to assure Butch's transition to the other dimension. However, they weren't quite certain which of the many denominations offered the best guarantee for his heavenly salvation.

Situated as we were at the end of the world, it was not surprising to see every conceivable variation of Christian and other religious fellowship represented, all engaged in fierce competition for our souls. The most dominant was Father Jungbluth's Catholic Church, but there was also an Evangelical Free Church, Pastor Roy Hubbeard's Chetwynd Gospel Tabernacle, the Seventh Day Adventist Church, the Peace Fellowship Baptist Church, and the Zion Presbyterian-United Church. The Lutherans held their services at the Rex Theatre, until Don Titus donated a piece of property and established a more dignified place for them to worship and confess their sins.

Only two of the resident ministers found it difficult to accept Don's invitation to officiate at the funeral service; Father Jungbluth was not one of them. Everyone was asked to attend a brief service at the home of the deceased, after which they were to join in a procession from the house to the garden, about half a kilometre away, where Butch would be laid to rest.

It was a strange sight. Here was Don Titus, in a dark suit no one had ever seen him wear before, carrying the box he had fashioned to contain his companion's remains, and with him, his wife and five clergymen who would rather have been struck dead than be seen in one another's company at any time, let alone on this particular mission. All were deep in prayer, their eyes downcast, as they walked in solemn procession, calling on their respective deities to comfort Don in his deep sorrow and to prepare an appropriate place for his friend in heaven.

None of them, at least as long as Don lived, would suffer any shortage of spuds, carrots, or whatever else his garden, with God's help, would yield.

Rather than supplementing the comfort dispensed by the clergy with enhanced dosages of liquid spirits, as one would have expected, Don instead derived the inner strength from the tragedy to defeat his demon. He swore off the booze.

Even with the help of Father Jungbluth and the others, no one has ever quite been able to interpret the message God sent in answer to his earthly representatives' prayers. On his very next trip to Vancouver, Don, for the first time ever, did not miss his return flight. Moreover, he was at the airport in plenty of time to call his wife and then catch the Canadian Pacific Airline DC-6B flight that crashed near 100 Mile House on July 8, 1965, killing all 52 aboard. My own theory is that God, in his infinite wisdom, decided that even with all the amenities Heaven had to offer, Butch was just too lonely without his friend Don.

This time all the ministers were in attendance at the funeral, with their entire congregations in tow. In fact, almost the whole town turned out to offer their condolences to Mrs. Titus and to show their respect for two exceptionally generous and kind fellow human beings.

CHAPTER 7

A New Canadian

Natural ability without education has more often raised a man to glory and virtue than education without ability.

—Marcus Tullius Cicero

As the landlords and neighbours of the police establishment, Joan and I enjoyed a special friendship with all of its initial tenants—Morley and Carol Kitchen, and their successors, Henry and Etta Hryciw.

Morley had a passion for practical jokes and spared no effort in this pursuit, whether it was enrolling some poor unsuspecting fellow's name in the Lonely Hearts Club or disguising his voice to call *Chinook* editor George Peck to report a flying saucer landing at Mount Lemoray, 50 miles south on the Hart Highway. Actually, the latter was done as a favour to our circle of women friends. Several of them had threatened to boycott that year's New Year's Eve festivities rather than be subjected to bachelor George's exuberant kisses and tactile ways of conveying his best wishes. George, diligent investigative reporter that he was, never made it to the party.

It was Morley who gave Joan one of the worst frights of her life when she applied for her Canadian citizenship in 1960. On this occasion, he came to the service station and gave Joan a list of about a dozen suspects purporting to be on the RCMP "wanted" list, each with an extensive dossier typed out on official stationery. Since all of them were either of German descent or German tourists, he suggested that by some odd chance she might recognize one of the names. I sensed that he was up to something when he paid me a visit at the back of the shop, making idle conversation as he waited for Joan's reaction.

The 1962 Chetwynd RCMP detachment.

It wasn't long in coming. Joan, white as a bedsheet, came rushing out, pointing to one of the papers. "They're looking for me," she stammered.

"What are you talking about? What could you have ever done to attract our attention?" he asked.

"Well, just look at it. There can't be any mistake," she blurted out. Sure enough, there it was in black and white. They were hunting for a woman fitting Joan's precise description, with her date and place of birth, and even her maiden name. It was alleged that she had walked away from a legal marriage in Germany that had not been declared on her application for landed-immigrant status. She had then entered into another marital relationship with a man whose last whereabouts was in Pioneer, a gold mine in the interior of B.C. The charge was bigamy.

"Look," Morley said, "there is obviously some mistake here. No need to get upset. I'll have this straightened out in no time." But as it turned out, the matter became just a bit more complicated than that. Not so much for Joan, but for Morley himself.

As it happened, this incident took place when Joan was studying for her citizenship exam. It seemed only natural to her to assume that she would be confronted and perhaps even arrested right on the spot and forced to answer to this ridiculous charge. She was devastated; I smelled a rat.

After a day's reflection, we decided to put the good constable's feet to the fire. We told him that we'd decided to inform the judge of the impending charges and to apply for a postponement of her application until the matter was resolved. This time it was Morley gasping for breath.

"That's the worst thing you could do," he declared. "Just let me handle the matter. I don't want you to lose any sleep over it."

But we left him dangling on his own hook, keeping him guessing about what we would do. I know how relieved he was to learn, early on the morning of the appointed day, that Joan had gone to Dawson Creek in the company of Ray Rebagliati, to whom he had confessed his dirty deed so as to make sure Joan would not say anything silly in front of the judge.

The same approach Joan had used to acquire her driving skills guided her through her studies for the citizenship exam. She knew from my experience that she would have to appear before a judge, flanked by an officer of the RCMP, and be tested on her knowledge of Canadian history, the meaning of our symbols, and a little about contemporary politics. She went without sleep for a week. Our good friend Ray, the provincial-railway superintendent who had resisted Emil Breitkreitz's advice to change his name, and Peter Eales, another Aspol Motors' partner, were recruited to appear as witnesses and to lend whatever support she would need to get herself through the ordeal.

Nothing, from the Vikings' occupation of Newfoundland, to the battle on the Plains of Abraham, the War of 1812, and the assassination of Darcy McGee, had escaped her scrutiny. She could name the 10 provinces and the two territories; she knew the names of the prime minister and all the premiers, as well as those of our region's members of Parliament and the provincial legislature. But it was all for nothing. The good judge wasn't interested in any of it. He wanted to know who owned the BCR—British Columbia Railway. She was stumped.

Terror-stricken, she turned to look in the direction of Ray, who was seated at the back of the room. Her hand hidden from His Honour's view, she inquisitorially pointed her finger at him, reasoning that he certainly *behaved* as if he owned the trains. Sensing her thoughts, he urgently shook his head in denial. In desperation she ventured to suggest that it might be one of the three deities: God, in the person of Premier Bennett, Ben Ginter, the proprietor of the province's major construction company and a brewery, and Phil Gaglardi, the Minister of Highways. It was good enough for His Honour, who lectured the assembly before him that the government did indeed own the railway, but only on behalf of all of us citizens of this great province. So, on November 22, 1960, the same year John F. Kennedy was elected president of the United States, Joan came away from her citizenship ceremony not only a proud new Canadian, but also part-owner of the railway.

Is this a great country or what?

The experience also left her far better informed about the history, symbols, and institutions of power and jurisdiction in our great country than many young people graduating from high school in Canada at the time. Very few would have heard about the War of 1812, unless it was in connection with the history of the United States, where all the textbooks were published. The fact that Americans came away the losers would no doubt have been sufficient reason for them to ignore the event.

Despite the happy outcome, our lust for revenge against Morley for causing Joan such anxiety burned deep in our hearts, and it didn't take too long before we got the chance to even the score.

In order to earn the respect and support of the local people, who provided much-needed help in critical situations, every one of the first RCMP officers stationed in Chetwynd worked hard to be accepted in the community. Morley Kitchen regularly attended the meetings of the volunteer firemen, whom he recruited as his eyes and ears, so as to keep tabs on anyone inclined to overstep the limits of propriety. At one point, he pleaded for help with a particularly nasty problem involving a suspected two-legged chicken thief who, on a regular basis, appropriated for himself some of the inventory of one of the outlying farms.

After just a few days, Cliff, the grader operator at the Highways department, reported sighting several chicken heads, covered in copious amounts of blood, along the road toward Jackfish Lake. Sure enough, Morley, upon attending the scene, discovered the first real clue toward solving the mystery. His next logical move was to recruit anyone engaged in the automotive-service sector to be on the lookout for evidence of blood mixed with chicken feathers, similar to the mess he had saved in the trunk of the police cruiser.

"The tire marks," he explained to all our staff, "would indicate the use of a pickup in connection with the crime."

But he suggested that we also inspect the trunk of any passenger vehicle, particularly from the Jackfish Lake area, to look for evidence that might help him connect the owner to the crime. "Perhaps," he suggested, "you might offer to check the air pressure of your customer's spare tire to gain access to the trunks of any passenger vehicle as well."

This incident happened around the same time we secured the contract to decommission the old police cruiser and install its siren—and all the other gadgets that distinguish a cop car from a normal vehicle—on the detachment's long-overdue replacement for the old jalopy. In the process of preparing what was left of it for resale to an unsuspecting buyer, it had to undergo a thorough cleaning and detailing to highlight some of its few remaining assets and disguise those that were in an advanced state of decline. Joan, involved in the operation, was the one who discovered the remnants of the chicken-caper evidence.

Our time to unburden our souls of their dark intent had arrived.

On Morley's return from Dawson Creek, where he had gone to exchange the old car for the new version, I reported to him that on that very morning we had serviced a car in whose trunk we had noticed some chicken feathers covered with blood.

"Look, Morley," I told him, "I have to make a living in this town and I don't need any more trouble than we already have. We are dealing here with one of our steady customers, whom we can't afford to lose. I'll give you the licence number of the car, but the rest is up to you. We haven't told any of our staff, and you've got to promise that whatever you do will not be traced back to us."

"You can take my word for it," he promised.

The Chetwynd detachment had not yet been outfitted with a teletype, so his inquiry into the ownership of the licence number had to be routed through the Dawson Creek office. His colleagues on highway patrol decided to deliver the response in person. It was very brief: "Licence No.——, being the subject of your inquiry, has been issued to the detachment of the RCMP in Chetwynd, British Columbia."

It wasn't too often that anyone got the last laugh on Morley Kitchen.

To the best of my knowledge, the chicken crime was never solved; however, the extent of the dragnet guaranteed that no other chicken in the area fell victim to any other than its rightful owner's dinner table for some time.

Both Morley and Carol, his wife, were among our most trusted friends and supporters. Not having any children of their own, they showered ours with their affection. Life was hard for both of them. Morley was frequently called out to deal with sensitive situations that in normal circumstances would require backup. Carol spent many sleepless nights anxious and worried about his safety.

It was not unusual for him to be called out in the middle of the night to attend a complaint. Such was the case on the particular night when Mrs. Gary, who owned one of the grocery stores with her husband, called to report her suspicion that someone had broken into Norm Stirling's hardware store next door. She had called Norm's house, but both he and Beverly were out of town.

At the time, we were still living above Lee Phillips's store, across the back alley from the hardware store. I woke up thinking that someone was calling me and sure enough, there it was again.

"Frank, cover the back door. I'm going in through the front."

I was sure it was Morley's voice, so I jumped into my clothes to investigate. I was not yet out the door when a shot rang out and all hell broke loose.

When Morley, dressed only in a shirt and pants, had pulled up in front of the store, he had discovered a broken window. The thief was still inside the store and Morley ordered him to surrender. It was when the intruder moved toward the back door that Morley had shouted, using my name to give the impression that it was covered as well. However, the thief decided to fight it out and attacked Morley as he tried to leave the same way he had entered.

In the scuffle Morley, pistol in hand, tried to hit the culprit over the head and the weapon discharged. When I got to the scene, Mrs. Gary had already gone to fetch the doctor. Someone was stretched out in the middle of the road, his brain leaking out through the back of his head, the dust on the dirt road absorbing his blood.

Morley, both hands held to his head, was walking around in a daze.

"I'm all right," he kept saying. "Where is that doctor? Will someone please call Carol and tell her I'm okay?"

Carol was certainly within earshot of the scene, so I ran back up to tell Joan what had happened and ask her to take care of Carol until we got things straightened out.

The robber was later identified as a railway-construction worker stationed out of Williams Lake. A visit to his home yielded a cache of stolen merchandise that was traced to several major break-ins all over the north. But he was also a member in good standing of the Legion at Williams Lake, and had plenty of friends who came rushing to his defence. "Trigger-Happy Cops," was the headline in one of the local papers. Surprisingly, few people were inclined to have any sympathy for Morley.

The force—much too quickly in my opinion, at least—arranged a transfer for Morley, moving him to general duties in Prince George until his fate could be decided. As it turned out, it was the wrong place and Morley was there at the wrong time as well. Just a short while after the Chetwynd incident, a drunk stumbled out in front of his cruiser on a dark, wintry Prince George night. His death was as sudden as the end of Morley's career with the force.

No finer, more dedicated, more able person will ever grace the uniform of the Royal Canadian Mounted Police.

Henry Hryciw and his wife, Etta, succeeded Morley and Carol at the post in Chetwynd in 1961. They, too, were ideally suited to serve in a community our size. In no time at all, everybody had claimed Henry as their best friend. He made it his practice to be on the road when school was out, just to show the kids he was looking out for them and to enjoy as his reward the friendly smiles and waves that they returned.

Joan and I will never have better friends, even though Henry never let me forget that had it not been for him, I would not have survived the arrival of our youngest son, Peter.

Joan, like Eleanor Krass, had to make two trips to the hospital in Dawson Creek to give birth. The second trip was not quite as hectic as the ordeal Joan endured between 100 Mile House and Ashcroft for Frank's birth in 1957, but it was close. Joan Eales, the wife of our friend Peter Eales, was the attending nurse when we arrived at the emergency entrance of the hospital late on the evening of March 23, 1962.

"Look," I told her, "this baby was supposed to be born on my birthday, which is not until tomorrow. Whatever you have to do, I want the delivery postponed until after midnight." Whatever it was they did to oblige, Joan, ever so anxious to please, co-operated with them. Peter and I share the same birthday, 30 years apart.

I didn't get the chance to meet my new son as soon as I might have, because on my way home from the frantic hospital trip, I decided—as was customary in those days—to stop in at the hotel to treat the patrons in the bar to a round in celebration of my good fortune. Obviously sensitive to my emotions, Marvin Phillips, who was Lee's son and the bartender at Gordon Moore's hotel, allowed himself to be carried away by his own enthusiasm and spiked each of several glasses of beer I managed to imbibe with a couple of ounces of vodka.

Henry and Etta had long since retired for the night when they discovered me in a comatose state at the front door of their office. My desire to share the good news with our best friends may well have saved my life. Thankfully, Henry was no stranger to such emergencies. He knew just what to do to my stomach to expel the evil contents that had poisoned my blood. Etta kept the operation supplied with copious amounts of coffee, while Henry spent the rest of the night forcing me to stay on my feet, marching me all over the neighbourhood. Given the circumstances, it wasn't until very late the following afternoon that Joan was given the chance to introduce me to our new son.

At that time, fathers weren't allowed to be present in the delivery room to share in the miracle of the birth. Only the pain-distorted features of her face and the happiness and joy radiating from her eyes helped me to comprehend the nature of the drama that must have unfolded behind closed doors.

"Happy birthday, darling," she whispered as our lips touched, and I tasted the salt from the tears that welled from her eyes. It was another of those so very precious moments that have kept the bonds between us so strong and spiced the love we feel for one another. It took me much longer to recover from the ordeal than it did her. So much so, in fact, that we decided not to expose my life to further risks by adding to the size of our now-perfect family.

Henry, over the years, gave me plenty of opportunity to discharge the debt due to him for saving my life. He enjoyed the outdoors more than anyone else I knew. Many times I was deputized to accompany him on a mission up the Sukunka Valley to deal with the kind of job-related stress that we both suffered in abundance and that only the peace and tranquility of nature's undisturbed domain could dispel. Joan had to take up the slack in the business while I was away, but considering the major improvement in my disposition after such therapy and the knowledge that Henry's official police patrol kept the area safe from any criminal elements, she gladly stepped into the breach.

Off we went, equipped with fishing gear and hunting equipment to explore every creek and crevice that nature had carved into the rugged, mountainous terrain. There are no words to describe the beauty and splendour of the area, particularly in fall when Mother Nature drapes herself in her most colourful dress, as if to celebrate the life that has fulfilled its purpose and must now lie dormant to be reawakened in spring, when she will spring forth anew, enticing us through our senses to share in her exuberance.

It was not uncommon for us to get carried away in our quest to find out what undiscovered wonder might lie over the next hill or around the next bend of an uncharted trail. On one occasion, while fording a creek, we managed to submerge the police cruiser in three feet of water and we spent the rest of the day working ourselves out of our predicament. When finally we had managed to clear the carburetor and siphon out the water that had invaded the gas tank, we headed home. Henry, with the lights of Chetwynd already in sight, decided to stop for tea, just to make the day complete. His theory was that the most memorable trips were the ones where we got stuck and where, in the end, we triumphed over the elements. One should always take a moment to reflect on such an experience to be sure it remains committed to memory. In the meantime, of course, back on the ranch, Joan had to juggle even more balls to stave off the crises, the avoidance of which had made the trip necessary in the first place.

There were times as well when Henry, faced with real emergencies, had to call for assistance. Not long after Constable Ray Keelan had arrived to serve as the second member of the Chetwynd detachment, Henry jolted me out of bed at about five in the morning. He needed a ride up the highway to where Ray was having a picnic with five sports fans who were making their way north from Vancouver, where they had allegedly withdrawn large amounts of money from several banks without obtaining consent.

Henry and Ray had been manning a single-car roadblock all night, spelling each other off, when finally the thieves arrived on the scene and simply ignored Ray's effort to stop them. Without regard to what would happen if he caught them, Ray gave chase. He just barely managed to get out a garbled radio signal calling for help before he was confronted by all five of the suspected bank robbers.

Their car had, in police terminology, failed to negotiate a rather sharp curve near Sundance Lake, on the road to Dawson Creek, sending it rolling along the ditch. When it came to rest, everyone managed to climb out to count their limbs, giving Ray just enough time to skid the cruiser to a halt and to take hold of his trusty '38.

Visitors from the Lower Mainland area of the province always tended to be somewhat underdressed. It was a very cold, late November night with plenty of frost on the ground, making it miserable for the burglars to participate in the Mexican standoff that followed. After Ray had everyone convinced that he would not hesitate in the least to use his weapon for what it was intended, he invited the whole crew to put both their hands on top of the cruiser and leave them there until he decided what to do next. Not knowing whether his message to his boss had got through, Ray himself soon felt the effects of the cold and the dicey situation that was developing.

"Can you fire up that hot rod of yours"—referring to my pride and joy, a fire-engine red Ford Mustang—"and meet me out front right now?" Henry asked when he called me.

From the tone of his voice I knew not to ask too many questions. When we arrived at the scene Ray, shivering from the cold, was still holding on to his gun, which by that time must have weighed a ton. Between him and Henry, they managed to bundle all five of the culprits into the back seat of the cruiser and tie them up into a neat bundle, with the help of two sets of handcuffs and a few swift kicks administered by Ray's frozen footwear.

By the time I embarked on my second term as mayor in 1970 (with the seven-vote margin), Henry and Etta had been transferred to Vanderhoof to take charge of the somewhat larger RCMP detachment there. Henry's successors in command of the now three-man Chetwynd detachment could afford to discharge their duties more in line with "the book." Unlike Vern Williams (Chetwynd's first RCMP constable, who had served the community out of a trailer stationed outside town), Morley Kitchen, and Henry Hryciw, who had all operated one-man shows, the new complement were less dependent on the support of the community to help them with their thankless job.

I was at war with them right from the beginning. The first major battle was fought over who had jurisdiction to issue permits for dances and other social events at the community hall. Certainly the police had a formal role in issuing permits for the consumption of liquor, but that was not a factor with the group of teenagers who wanted to use the hall for a New Year's Eve dance. I had already given out the key to the hall on the condition that there was to be no alcohol to fuel the festivities. Joan and I and some of our friends offered to chaperone the crowd to make certain that the kids kept to their promise.

It wasn't good enough for the new officer in charge of the Chetwynd detachment, who had obviously received his training in the same kind of police academy as had Ernst Meier, the policeman back in the Old Country who had arrested me at 13 on a rather flimsy charge, right after the war, and threatened me with internment in an institution for incorrigible Nazi boys.

The intrepid sergeant was forced to back down in front of all the teenagers, which did little to establish him as an authority in whom they could place their trust and respect. Neither did it make my job any easier, because it thwarted any effort to prevent our respective authorities from clashing or to allow the exercise of any discretion to enable sensible solutions to even minor problems. That his authority as an officer in charge of a police department reporting to the provincial attorney general far exceeded that of a small-town mayor—and that he availed himself of every opportunity to exercise it—kept both of us at loggerheads for the rest of the time we had to spend as neighbours in a small town.

As I got more and more involved in the affairs of the community, our various business enterprises started to blossom as well, challenging our ingenuity and demanding an ever-greater commitment of our time and resources. Often, only our raw ambition and the fear of failing to reach the goals on which we had set our sights kept us going. These were turbulent times for us. Only the war years had been more tumultuous than the 1960s were turning out to be.

Like most people, I often find that one's memory is refreshed by linking important events in the affairs of mankind to particular places and times in our personal lives.

It was in 1961, for example, that the Berlin Wall was built and, in 1963 that President Kennedy was assassinated. I remember that in 1966 Germany once again came away the loser of a war against England. Thankfully, this time it was the final match for the World Cup and it was fought out on a soccer pitch. In 1967 Christiaan Barnard of South Africa performed the world's first heart transplant. That was also the year Canada played host to the world during Expo '67 in Montreal. Finally, on July 20, 1969, who could forget U.S. astronaut Neil Armstrong setting foot on the moon, thus accomplishing mankind's single greatest technological feat of all time?

As well, my memories of important events—particularly of happy or difficult periods in our lives—are often sparked by music that was popular at the time. Joan and I are particularly fond of Simon and Garfunkel's "Bridge Over Troubled Water," which was released in 1970, the same year The Beatles came out with "Let It Be," another of our favourites.

Along with the changing times, we began to realize that our family was growing up too. After completing her schooling, which had begun in Chetwynd's one-room facility, Ursula became the first among her peers to graduate, and went on to university in Vancouver to start working toward a teacher's certificate. Peter was beginning his academic career in a brand-new modern facility in Chetwynd. Isabell and Frank Jr., in Grades 9 and 7 respectively, became the beneficiaries of the extracurricular learning experience offered by being gas jockeys at our Esso service station.

Joan and I also improved our education, somehow managing to find time to feed our ravenous appetite for books, articles, newspapers, and all manner of educational programming and docudramas delivered on TV. They had replaced the funnies and the Eaton's catalogue as our means of nourishing our curious minds and satisfying our thirst for knowledge.

"Ma" Murray had once told me of the time she published an entire weekly edition of the *Alaska Highway News* without using the letter "R," which had become detached from the mechanism of the typesetter. In the same vein, in my business correspondence I became quite adept at finding substitutes for words I wasn't quite sure how to spell and that I could not find in the dictionary. No doubt there were many times when important business decisions would have benefitted from the higher education or advanced training that Joan and I both lacked, but then we couldn't afford the time, in the words of Mark Twain, "to allow additional schooling to interfere with our education."

We made mistakes, some no doubt costly, but fortunately neither of us dwelt on them, and we never allowed them to shake our confidence and faith in one another. There was never any recrimination; rather, we looked upon them as valuable lessons that even advanced business or university courses may have failed to teach.

However, missing the opportunity and privilege of achieving a higher education remains one my life's great disappointments. It became an obsession for Joan and me to make certain that our children would not have to live with the same regrets. We wanted to make sure they were educated, both in higher learning and by staying in touch with their German heritage. Our desire to send our kids to live with their relatives in Germany for a while after they had graduated from high school arose from the same motive that led me to write these pages. It was intended to help them discover their roots and perhaps, since we are who we are because of our past, also help them discover what may have shaped their parents' characters, their strong attachment to certain principles, and their uncompromising commitment to a certain path in pursuit of their goals.

When Ursula returned from Germany after her high-school graduation in 1970, she immediately left again to attend university in Vancouver. It was not an easy transition for her. Mature as she was for her age, it nevertheless proved a difficult challenge to absorb the culture shock associated with the move and managing by herself. No doubt her desire to please her parents was as much a factor in helping her cope as was her own commitment toward a professional teaching career. Indeed, after suffering through the ordeal for two years, she eventually found it preferable to finish her teacher's training at a university in Saskatchewan.

Ursula's visit to Germany in the summer of 1970 had been quite an adventure. Everyone was looking forward to meeting their cousin, niece, or grandchild and finding out what kind of young lady she had grown up to be, but the people in Joan's sister's house—Aunt Cilli's—were the most excited. Aside from Berta and Emil, who had gotten to know Ursula during their visit with us in Chetwynd, the only memory anyone else had of her was as a one-year-old baby, leaving home in her mother's arms on her way to meet her father in Canada for the first time, or as a 10-year-old flower girl at her uncle Rudi's ordination back in 1962.

However, in all the excitement they got their dates mixed up, so when Ursula arrived at the train station in Karlsruhe, no one was there to greet her. Luckily she had retained enough of her German to find a bus that would take her to Forchheim. Once there, she could only hope that she remembered enough from her previous visit to find her way to Aunt Cilli's. What a commotion there must have been when she knocked at their door to inquire whether she had come to the right place.

For all our kids, the experience was well worth the effort. They had the maturity to understand and admire everyone's compliance with the rigid rules and order that history has imposed on Germany and that have shaped its people's attitudes. Our kids found the young people with whom they came in contact better disciplined, less inclined to test the limits of tolerance established for them, and more in control of their inner conflicts. Young people, even in their early teens, already seemed deeply committed to a certain career path that had been chosen for them. But while much of it, compared to our Canadian way of life, might have been appealing to them, it was all too rigid and confining. It required too many concessions and compromises of the kind of personal freedom they and their friends enjoyed at home. The experience helped all of our kids to better understand what might have compelled us to seek our fortune elsewhere.

Sadly, there was one joy Ursula was denied during her visit. Her paternal grandmother, Rösel, in whose heart Ursula had occupied such a special place as a child, had passed away a year earlier.

We were given the sad news early one spring morning in 1969. Given the nine hours' difference between the Pacific coast and western Europe, early-morning phone calls always created some anxiety for us. Any news from our families overseas timed to reach us before we went off to work was usually bad. As always, it was my brother Erich who called to convey the news that, at best, our mother would have six months before her cancer, which had now spread throughout her body, claimed her life. He told me the news came as no surprise to Rösel, but when she talked about it in the presence of the rest of the family, she lamented the thought that she would never see me again.

"We talked about it," Erich said, "and I suggest that, if at all possible, you might pay her one last visit, even if it means you won't be here for the funeral." It seemed that for every one of the 6,600 miles that separated us, the painful reality of such news intensified by degrees. If there were times when I wished that somehow we could have managed to be closer to our families, it was on occasions like this.

I tried to be as cheerful as my emotions would allow when I called her on the telephone.

"Look," I said, "Erich called to say that you are really sick. I have some business in eastern Canada and Joan suggested that, if it is all right with you, I might extend the trip to pay you a visit." Her weak voice, choked by tears, did not allow her to contribute much to the conversation.

"Don't worry," I managed to say, "we'll have all the time in the world to talk when I get there, but I want you to try to get better so that you can show me around town and introduce me to all my old girlfriends, whose names I might have forgotten."

I remember how surprised I was by everyone's casual reaction to the crisis we had to face. In all the time I had been away, aside from some memorial services at the mine, I could only recall attending the funeral of my good friend Ed Williams, the building contractor in 100 Mile House who was killed in a car crash, and Don Titus's funeral in 1965. The dearth of deaths was due to a peculiar deficit in the demographics of the places where we had chosen to live in Canada. There were few, if any, seniors or retired people—certainly not in the logging camps where I worked or at the gold mine in Pioneer. Even in the relatively more established places, like 100 Mile House and Chetwynd, most of the grandparents only came to visit for short periods of time. Funerals therefore were events one would attend in faraway places.

The face of death in the established communities of the Old Country was now much friendlier than I remembered it from the war. It appeared to be part of everyday life. Supported by their faith, people found comfort in the certain knowledge that while death was painful for those left behind, the spirit of the departed experienced only the joy of being reunited with all who had preceded them in their journey. It seemed that for the women who had lost sons, husbands, or sweethearts, and whose bodies and souls were racked by memories of them and the war's horrors, death was almost welcomed as a relief.

Joan had insisted on sewing a dress for Mom. It wasn't that we thought Mom would ever be able to wear it, but Joan wanted to express her gratitude for the love and kindness Mom had shown her during the most difficult time she'd ever had to live through—during her pregnancy with Ursula, when she'd been ostracized by some of her own relatives for having offended the laws of the church and shunned the piety demanded of her as a child of a family blessed with a son destined to enter the priesthood.

When I arrived for my visit in late summer of 1969, I discovered that Mom had taken my challenge seriously. She had managed to mobilize every last ounce of her fading energy to look her best and make my visit as painless as possible. For weeks she had not been out of bed, but to everyone's absolute surprise, she found the strength to let us help her put on her new dress and to cling to my arm like a childhood sweetheart for a short stroll through the *Hauptstrasse* and up the steps of the restaurant next door, which Mom and Dad had frequented most of their lives.

As if it were the fulfillment of a dream she had harboured for a long time, the pride of having it come true reflected in her eyes and her rosy cheeks as friends and neighbours surrounded us on the street, curious about the visitor and genuinely kind in offering Mom their best wishes. Dad declared it a miracle. For the few days I was with her, she never once allowed herself to show her pain and made every effort to fight off the effects of the heavy doses of morphine one of the nuns came to administer on a regular basis. Even during the evening before my departure, when we last met as a whole family, she delighted us with her own special brand of humour.

Only after the car pulled up the following morning to take me to the airport in Frankfurt for my trip back home, when the rest of the family insisted I should have a private moment with her, did she acknowledge her awareness of the purpose of my visit. I sat beside her bed, holding her hand, groping for words. She put her soft hands over my mouth and wiped away my tears.

"Don't cry," she said, "God has made up for the pain and suffering we had to endure during the early part of our lives by giving Dad and me many happy years, and by giving us so many reasons to be so very proud of all our children. I am tired now and ready to die. I'll tell everyone that I have made you promise not to come to the funeral. I want you to remember me the way I am now. Please say goodbye to Hanna and the children. I love them so much." She struggled to speak through her tears. Then, after one last embrace, when nothing else needed to be said, she gently pushed me away.

Joan has much more experience than I do with the supernatural. My mind refuses to accept anything for which there is no logical explanation; no cause without an effect that is commensurate with natural law. In her youth my mother, as was more customary than might be now, once consulted a female psychic who predicted that she would bear four children; that her husband would take her away from her village; and that one of her sons would cross the big ocean to live in another country. Unfortunately, she was also told that this son would die at an early age. I always took Dad's side in the argument, insisting on sheer coincidence when some of these predictions actually came to pass.

However, on the night of October 23, when my mother passed away, I awoke to her calling my name. Not urgently, but with a soft, soothing voice, "Franz ... Franz." I had no sooner told Joan over breakfast the next morning that we should expect some bad news from home when the phone rang to confirm my suspicion. I have always been too preoccupied, too busy dealing with the realities of the world, to burden my mind with the mysteries of the other dimension. So I must accept it as fact that my mother's spirit, on its way to the other world, attempted to bridge the divide.

My mother, who had reached the age of 70, was laid to rest close to her parents and grandparents two days before her grandson Frank's 12th birthday.

Dad, of course, took it very hard. It was decided that he should give up the apartment in which they had spent their last years and move in with my sister, Lina, and her husband, Reini. For the longest time he visited Mom's grave every day, grieving his loss. Erich hinted that given the happy times Dad and Mom had experienced in Canada during their 1962 visit, perhaps he would find some solace and distraction in paying another visit to us. Adolf eagerly accepted our invitation in 1972, enriching our lives by spending the better part of another year with us.

CHAPTER 8

Addicted to Politics

The credit belongs to the man who is actually in the arena, whose face is marred by dust and sweat and blood ... who at the best knows in the end the triumph of high achievement, and who at the worst, if he fails, at least fails while daring greatly, so that his place shall never be with those cold and timid souls who know neither victory nor defeat.

—Theodore Roosevelt

So it was that Dad was there to see the start of my first foray into national politics—the very last thing, given his and his contemporaries' experience, that he would have wanted to become involved in.

By 1972 the Liberal Party, headed first by Lester B. Pearson and then Pierre Elliott Trudeau, had been in power for almost 10 years after beating Diefenbaker's Progressive Conservatives in 1963. The PC party was still the Official Opposition, now led by Robert Stanfield, with David Lewis at the helm of the New Democratic Party. Finally, to round out the political forces at play, the separatist Parti Québécois under René Lévesque had just emerged and was on its way to becoming Quebec's provincial government.

The current member of Parliament for our area was Bob Borrie, a Liberal who had been swept in by Trudeaumania in 1968 and was rarely seen in the more remote areas of his constituency. The riding of Prince George–Peace River, one of the largest in Canada, covered an area of over 230,000 square kilometres in northeastern British Columbia including Prince George, the area west of Highway 16 as far as the border with Alberta, and along the Rocky Mountain Trench to the Yukon border. In the 1968 election the Conservatives of British Columbia had been shut out completely, compounding the feeling of alienation that had manifested itself in the west generally and particularly in B.C., where the Rockies have historically been seen as a natural barrier to trade and the mainstream cultural activities of the rest of the country.

For B.C. voters east of the Rockies, this problem was compounded by our isolation from the provincial seat of power. Residents had a long list of historic grievances and concerns that they felt were not being heard by either level of government.

My route to becoming a candidate in 1972 was anything other than conventional. It started several years earlier with an adventure in provincial politics.

Larry "Loophole" Lewin's expertise extended beyond law, business, and finance; he was also a Godfather-like operative in the backrooms of provincial and federal politics.

"Okay," he would say, after the business that had prompted the visit to his office had been dispensed of, "let's turn off the meter and talk about things that really matter."

What really mattered to him, just before the provincial election in 1969, was that the government in Ottawa, on account of its overdeveloped left wing, was flying in circles, while the government in Victoria, whose flight orientation was in the right direction, was failing to attain the necessary altitude to clear the mountains that separated them from the hinterland. Perhaps it was time to dispatch a more aggressive representative to the provincial legislature to draw some attention to the needs of our area. Stan Carnell, the sitting MLA at the time, had served under the W.A.C. Bennett's administration and had, in Larry's view at least, represented us there long enough to fall out of touch with the real world.

"We have decided that the time has come for a change," Larry told me on one such occasion, "and your old buddy Don Phillips has agreed to take up the challenge. We need you to organize a contingent from Chetwynd to attend the nominating meeting, just in case Stan has any friends left to help him mount a defence."

With Don's high profile in the business community in Dawson Creek and the respect he had earned himself among the members of the various community service clubs to which he belonged, it was no contest. Neither, of course, was the election itself. The area of British Columbia across the Rocky Mountains to the northeast was hardly a hotbed of socialism, which would have been the only opposition Bennett and his Social Credit coalition ever needed to worry about.

Don took to the job like a duck takes to water. In no time at all, heavy-duty construction equipment and paving machines were invading our roads and highways, reminding me of the activities leading up to the building of the Siegfried Line at the beginning of the Second World War.

However, even before "Dynamic Don," as he was fond of being referred to, got his second wind, he was recalled by Ron Witherspoon, his senior partner at Aspol Motors, who was preparing to retire and needed Don to carry on with the business on which his retirement income would depend.

When Phillips announced that he would not compete in the 1972 election, Larry may have questioned his priorities, but when faced with the inevitable, he had no difficulty recruiting Don Marshall, a prominent local farmer and businessman, as a worthy successor. At first Marshall filled Phillips's shoes well, but after a time he found it increasingly difficult as a backbench MLA to rationalize and defend some of the policies and programs of the Bennett autocracy. Marshall began to show some sympathy toward an underground movement led by Darryl Warren, a charismatic young lawyer with a more moderate, more "progressive" conservative bent. He began recruiting support to reorganize the long-dormant Progressive Conservative Party of British Columbia, with the idea of luring its sympathizers out of Bennett's Socred coalition. The movement was intended to provide the kind of transition to which Alberta's Premier Ernest C. Manning had committed his Social Credit Party, when it became obvious that his "funny money" theory was running out of steam and that Albertans' desire for change had become irresistible.

Larry was among the first to be persuaded to join the conspiracy, which planned to challenge the government in the upcoming election. Needless to say, the "Godfather" called on me and the rest of the gang to be part of the revolution.

To position the new party for the next election, it was deemed necessary to allow the revolt to manifest itself in the legislature. As the first act of defiance, Don Marshall would cross the floor to the Opposition benches where he would sit as a Progressive Conservative to give the new movement a voice. Our task was to promote the idea locally and to recruit Don Phillips as one of the principal proponents. I knew Phillips had harboured such treasonous tendencies himself in the past and would therefore see it as his prerogative to march in the front row of the movement. The timing, of course, was most critical, but in the end it could not have been worse for us.

"Where is Don Phillips?" was the first question I asked Larry when I met him at the Fort St. John airport en route to Victoria to participate in this historic event. Unfortunately, Don was away on a well-deserved skiing holiday near Jasper and could not be reached in time to help write the headlines staring him in the face when he picked up his morning newspaper.

W.A.C. Bennett was no amateur when it came to reading political trends. By the time we were able to contact and meet with Don, Bennett had already called upon his loyalty to the Socreds, insisting that he take on the traitor in the upcoming election. The party, Bennett assured him, would find ways to assist with whatever it took to compensate Don's thriving enterprise for the time he would have to spend away in Victoria. No doubt he was also promised a voice in Bennett's next cabinet as a reward for his loyalty and that of the good burghers in the Peace River constituency.

Phillips, having acquired a taste for the political poison in his blood, had no choice. Two of the Godfather's capos would face off against one another in a fight to the death. By the time it was over Phillips had won the battle and regained the seat by a margin of six votes, but Bennett had lost the war. The newly revived Progressive Conservative Party managed to accomplish what Bennett had predicted throughout his tenure. They split enough of the free-enterprise vote to allow the socialist hordes led by Dave Barrett to take over the government in British Columbia.

The change in government left northeastern B.C. even more bereft of political influence. Given the complete lack of support from our area during the election, Barrett's New Democrats were even less likely than their predecessors to build any bridges to the hinterland. Loophole Lewin, now denied any sway in the affairs of provincial politics, decided to set his sights on the lunatics in charge of the asylum in Ottawa. This was where I came in.

Since 1968, the federal Progressive Conservative Party had not elected a single representative from British Columbia to Parliament, and the fact that two-thirds of our constituency's population lived west of the mountains, where I would be unknown, did not deter him at all. True, few people could recall having ever met or heard from our member of Parliament, but that shouldn't have been reason enough for me to justify flirting with the idea of offering myself for the job.

Lewin thought otherwise.

"Now," he argued, "as far as the people in the Peace River area are concerned, no one has better credentials. The good burghers of Prince George will know everything about you we want them to know, and unlike anyone from their own ranks, you have no baggage to carry around to slow you down." Larry had convinced himself that my past and my ethnic background could actually be turned into an asset.

Joan didn't need to tell me that this bordered on lunacy. We had two businesses to worry about, four children in school, and half the people of Chetwynd who actually bothered to vote in municipal elections were ready to ride me out of town on a rail. But the poison was already spreading through my system. Like any other addiction, it gets into your blood. It torments you, deprives you of your ability to be rational, and costs you sleep. There is an inner voice that keeps asking, "What if it could actually happen?" It promises to remind you for the rest of your life of the opportunity you were offered and were too much of a coward to pursue.

"Look what you accomplished as the mayor of Chetwynd," the voice would say. "Just imagine what you could do as a member of Parliament—just imagine how many places like Moccasin Flats there are in Canada and how many children there are waiting for their chance for a better life. What if someone got the government in Ottawa to focus some attention on the plight of the north: the discrepancy in the standard of services and social benefits between the urban centres and the rural areas?"

I had fought and won most of the battles with my inner voices before. I prided myself on having tamed my demons on many occasions, but this was not some minor skirmish, like fighting off the urge to smoke or denying my body some other potentially addictive pleasure, this was outright war.

Perhaps the mistake I made was to tell Larry and the boys that, "while I might be interested," I just couldn't see any way to extricate myself from my other responsibilities—Joan would never go along with the idea, and it would hardly be prudent to start a new career and find a new wife all at the same time.

It was no use. I finally settled on the coward's way out. I cleared my conscience by telling the inner voice that I would leave the decision up to Joan. I would make an effort to convince her, but the likelihood of that was even more remote than getting the party's nomination and actually winning the election.

It wasn't divorce Joan threatened me with when I finally found the courage to casually raise the subject, but her first reaction was just as categorical.

"Over my dead body," she said.

In response to one of Lorne Dalke's frequent tirades at the lumber mill about the antics of our federal government, I cautiously said to him one day: "You know, I have half a mind to run for office myself."

"Well," was his immediate response, "you might be lucky there; most likely that's all it would take."

I had already explored the idea with Gene Rheaume, who was still fresh in my mind from the Moccasin Flats project and the surprise manicure. Both he and his executive assistant, Louise Hayes, had close ties to the Progressive Conservative Party in Ottawa. Louise had served on Diefenbaker's personal staff, and Gene, apart from having served a term in Parliament himself, filled in as a personal aide for Mr. Stanfield, the new Conservative leader.

"Nobody coming to Ottawa as a rookie MP would have better manicured fingernails and cleaner socks," was Gene's immediate reaction. "I couldn't think of anyone better qualified for the job." The plot thickened.

Joan, thinking perhaps that the chances of my being elected to Parliament were as remote as King's learning to answer the telephone, finally adopted a more conciliatory stance. Her concern was as much about how I would deal with the humiliation I would surely have to suffer as it was about reconciling my new ambitions with our personal and business affairs. She certainly wanted no part in a decision that would leave me spending the rest of my life wondering what could have been, but she did make me promise to expel these crazy notions from my mind after I'd had my fling—and to shelter her and the kids from involvement.

The die was cast. Larry was ecstatic.

"The first order of business," he declared, "is a trip to Prince George to consult with the few faithful left there, after the drought that's dried up most of the support the party had in B.C. before the Trudeau revolution."

The reception in Prince George was less than friendly. Sitting around the boardroom table in one of the downtown law offices, it quickly became apparent that a local candidate was preferred. In fact, several people in the room appeared hopeful and anxious to have their own name suggested as a potential candidate. Some others, mostly the lawyers, expressed their willingness to commit their energy to the service of our great country, but only in an advisory capacity. Presumably their services would be rewarded in a manner assuring a commensurate measure of lucrative federal government business, should our party ever come to power.

Larry was not one to beat around the bush. He informed everyone that as a candidate, I would have the support of the northern part of the constituency. Then he delivered a testimonial to my character and accomplishments that only my mother would have believed without reservation. The group's reaction—to be charitable—was much less than enthusiastic.

"We have to move fast," Larry lectured on the way back in the car. "I'll need some pictures that tie you to your various business interests; and some of the family for a four-page tabloid we'll distribute to every household in Prince George. I want you to mobilize your contacts in Ottawa to produce an endorsement from the leader."

"Forget the picture of the family," I told him, conscious of my promise, but he insisted on having a little talk with Joan about that himself.

The following week Larry called to tell me that the Prince George crowd had settled on the former president of the riding association, who was also dean of the local college, as their choice. However, burdened with some contractual obligations relating to his current employment, he would not be able to announce his candidacy until later in the year.

"Here's the deal," Larry said. "I want you to arrange a phone call from Mr. Stanfield, telling the good man of his interest in your candidacy and asking him for his support. On the same day, coincidentally, we'll flood the city with our flyer."

"No problem," Gene said when I questioned him on the prospects of the leader agreeing to such a devious scheme. "Just give me the date and time and I'll make the arrangements."

And so it was. The man chosen by the Prince George elite, who was obviously much better qualified for the job than I would ever be, was not among the other fine people with whom I had to compete for the nomination. There were four of them. A series of meetings would be held throughout the constituency, allowing everyone the opportunity to assess the candidates' qualifications.

I was astounded at the wide range of political philosophies offered up during the debates. At some of the first encounters, I began to doubt whether I had chosen the right party. Karl Marx would have been proud of one of the aspirants' ideas. Another could have served as an outrider in Genghis Khan's cavalry. The latter was a prominent Peace River farmer who took his instructions directly from God, who in turn reserved it as his given right to allow anyone too lazy to work to starve to death. This man would, if elected, make it his personal mission to dismantle as quickly as possible any and all "socialist" ideas, such as universal health care and the Canada Pension Plan, that had found acceptance in Ottawa during 1960s.

He would have young vandals—who had recently terrorized the town by breaking store windows in the place where one of the meetings was held—serve a prison term in the high Arctic, where they would be housed in shelters without windows. There they would share space with those who had violated parole or attempted to escape from established penal institutions. Their stay would be only temporary in that they would be pardoned during blackfly season and required to fend for themselves in finding their way back to civilization.

My own contributions to these debates must have sounded positively boring by comparison. I tried to explain the values that in my view best define the anchors of conservatism: the accumulated wisdom gained through experience and history; the established institutions of a free society; and the essential relationship between personal freedom and responsibility. I explained that I committed myself to being guided by the wisdom of Mahatma Gandhi, who listed the seven sins of the world as wealth without work, pleasure without conscience, knowledge without character, commerce without morality, science without humanity, worship without sacrifice, and politics without principle. I told them of my belief that a society's worth is best measured by the way it treats those in the dawn of life, on the margins of life, and in the twilight of life.

Judging from the applause the other speakers received during the final meeting, I was more surprised than anyone by the margin of victory I had earned when the ballots were counted.

I had officially joined the Progressive Conservative Party of Canada in May of 1972 and was now the candidate to carry the banner in the election called for October 30 of the same year. I was up against Bob Borrie for the Liberals, Bill Close for the NDP, and Al Kruger for the Social Credit Party. The gravity of the situation began to sink in as I was bringing home a pickup full of paper Lewin had sent out to be folded and made ready for distribution. Sitting around the kitchen table one night, working on the second edition of Larry's tabloid, Peter made the observation that "a family that folds together holds together."

Poor Dad didn't know what to make of all this. He had a hard time understanding how it could be possible for someone with my past and limited education to aspire to such high office. He very politely asked whether I had taken enough time to think through what I was getting myself into. As much to convince myself as him, I tried to explain that in the New World, the concept of democracy and the idea of a free society have different meanings and embrace different values than those in the Old Country. More importantly, the best way to prevent such catastrophic events as those the German people fell victim to from ever happening in our new country is for good people to become involved in the democratic process.

None of us who were working on my campaign allowed ourselves to hope for success and certainly Joan and I made every effort to keep intact the bridges connecting us to the real world. But, having come this far, I was determined to have my say. In the period leading up to the election, Larry and the committee arranged for me to speak at the various service clubs and chambers of commerce on our side of the mountains. Given the disappointment our friends in Prince George had suffered over the nomination, it was most difficult to get anyone there interested in mounting similar efforts, much less contributing financially to the cause.

Larry and I made several trips to Prince George to drum up support, but the effort was mostly fruitless. We would be on our own, fighting an incumbent Liberal who made his home in the city and was well connected to the business establishment. He had served as the executive secretary to the construction association in Prince George prior to being elected to Parliament. Larry, as usual, saw that as an advantage in that the Liberals, well aware of the lack of support on our side, would see no need to mount an expensive campaign themselves.

Little did they know of the secret weapon we acquired halfway through the campaign. Lee Acott, a total stranger to us at the time, had driven by our Prince George headquarters late one night with one of her partners in a local real-estate firm and had observed us nailing together some lawn signs supplied to us by the party.

"Who the hell is in charge of your affairs here in Prince George?" she asked when she called me after she got home. "And why hasn't he found something better for you to do than nail signs together in the middle of the night?"

"I want you to go home right now and get some sleep," she ordered, after I had explained the state of affairs to her. "I'll be there in the morning to help you get the show on the road."

True to her word, she showed up the following morning with a truckload of essentials, including a giant coffee machine, paper cups, and even some fresh doughnuts. By the end of the day, the wake she created cutting through the confusion had washed in a small army of volunteers ready to go to work.

Soon the only major flaw remaining in a text-book election campaign was the presence of the candidate himself. My reluctance was due to the same impediment that had made me abandon my career as an insurance salesman at 100 Mile House. I just could not bear to be mistaken for one of Jehovah's personal witnesses or a Fuller Brush salesman invading the privacy of people's homes, interrupting people's suppers or a particularly crucial sequence in a hockey game or soap opera.

Lee insisted that I give it a try, but it was no use. If it is true, as most seasoned campaigners for political office would have us believe, that the margin of votes a candidate receives is determined by how many doors he or she has bruised knuckles on, mine would have been very small indeed. I would be willing to drive half a day to meet someone who was interested in what I had to offer, but could never bring myself to impose without being invited. Fortunately, the medium of television offered us a way around this difficulty.

At the time, Prince George had only one television channel. The local station was an affiliate of the CBC, but was required to broadcast local programming for much of the day and evening. Advertising revenues in markets such as Prince George were marginal and the cost of producing local programs prohibitive. Consequently, the more time one booked with the station, the less the cost. We decided to commit the major part of our budget to producing a series of half–hour programs, each with a special theme and similar to the fare offered by community channels today.

The advantage was obvious. We were playing to a captive audience, virtually knocking on the doors of 90 percent of the homes in the city and outlying areas all at the same time. The only option the viewer had was to shut off the TV. From among her legions of friends, Lee selected those with the strongest opinions to appear with me in those segments that were scripted to address their concerns. Here I was in the Prince George studios, debating complex tax policy with half a dozen local accountants. On one show, a group of teenagers talked about the lack of amenities in the schools, and on another, housewives complained about the postal service and the lack of daycare facilities in the city. A group of union members debated the concept of freedom of association, which was the only controversial subject. I played the part of the sincere, innocent bystander who was keenly interested in and concerned about the problems being raised.

Unlike my Liberal opponent, I wasn't blessed with any distinguishing assets—such as his dashing moustache—but by the end of the campaign, my recognition factor nevertheless exceeded his by quite a margin. Soon people were engaging me on the street to offer their opinions on the various topics that sparked their interest but, more importantly, one after another of the old-guard Conservatives started drifting into the committee room, sensing that we might actually have a chance to beat the odds.

Most of my campaign time was spent in Prince George. Larry already felt confident of a positive result in the north. Obviously, he thought, Tomslake and Tupper, the two Sudetan–German settlements, would cast all their votes in my favour. Little did I know that these people, too, were haunted by their past. To them, politics was a religion, the values and principles of which could not be sacrificed or betrayed. Their commitment to these principles was so strong that, when challenged by Hitler's New Order, they chose to abandon their homeland and most of their worldly possessions to defend them. At the beginning of the war, for fear of persecution, they escaped to England rather than see themselves reintegrated and embraced by the dictator's vision of a greater Germany. The British helped them negotiate an agreement to settle in Canada, where they arrived in the fall of 1939 to suffer further hardships in an epic story of perseverance and survival.

Much to my disappointment, just as the campaign got underway in earnest, Dad decided that his time had come to return home. The excitement was getting too much for him, and he was homesick for his friends and the rest of the family. Since I needed some time to reflect anyway, I decided to take a couple of days to swing through the southeastern part of the constituency on the way to taking him to the airport in Edmonton. Because of the path my life had taken, there had been very few occasions in the past for Dad and me to get to know each other and share one another's thoughts and feelings.

The trip took us through the Pine Pass to Prince George, then via Highway 16 to Jasper and on to Edmonton, and it coincided with the final game of the Canada–Russia hockey series, which was being broadcast on the car radio. Dad had become quite a fan, and as the excitement mounted during the last few minutes of the game, I stopped the car at the summit of the Pine Pass, where the reception was good. When it was all over and Paul Henderson had stickhandled his way into the annals of Canadian sports history with his tie-breaking goal, we just sat and talked for the longest time, catching up on things we both felt needed to be said before we parted, perhaps for the last time.

He spoke of all he had sacrificed in his youth to earn the respect of his father-in-law and Mom's siblings. He reiterated again the opportunities he might have missed by not having had the courage to move away, abandoning whatever little comfort their families offered, and escaping the penalties that the victors of the First World War had imposed on Germany.

"The aftermath of the second war was not nearly as traumatic. Things are different in Germany today than you would remember," he said, "but not in your wildest dreams could you have accomplished what you have here or aspired to what you are aiming for now. You must not be too disappointed if things in the election don't turn out as you wish.

"Keep in mind that we always learn more from the things in which we fail than from any successes," he told me. It was a lesson I never forgot.

But I wasn't allowing any negative thoughts to sap the energy that my adrenaline kept pumping through my body. I would need it all to carry me through the rest of the campaign. On October 30, having spent the last few nights with very little sleep and, perhaps too tired to care, I was perfectly satisfied with our effort. We had even gone to Father Jungbluth's little church in Chetwynd the day before, just to make certain that if any divine intervention was forthcoming, it would come our way. Father Jungbluth allocated much of the sermon to praying for the enlightenment of our political leaders and reminding his congregation of their good fortune in having me as their future representative. Once he had lectured everyone on the absolute importance of voting, he pointed out how easy they would have it in this particular election.

"All you have to do," he said, "is put your "X" beside the name 'Frank Oberle.'"

I could think of little else we could have done. I was ready to accept whatever verdict the people would render.

Joan and Frank with his ardent supporter, Father Jungbluth, in Fort St. John.

A typical end-of-October day greeted us when Joan and I set out to spend the morning of election day visiting the polling stations in Fort St. John and Dawson Creek. The plan was to cast our own ballots back in Chetwynd, pick up the kids, and leave for Prince George in the early afternoon to arrive there in time for the polls to close. The kindly reception we received from the people manning the polling stations in the various locations along the way gave us every reason to be in high spirits as we set out on the last leg of the trip, our rendezvous with destiny—and straight into the first major snowstorm of the season.

At the top of the 933-metre summit of the Pine Pass we got caught in a blizzard, with winds gusting to a hundred kilometres a hour, at times threatening to carry the car off the road. We ploughed through snowdrifts that overwhelmed the capacity of the wipers to clear the windshield. Complete white-out conditions periodically forced us to a full stop and put us in danger of becoming completely buried in snow. The kids, crowded into the back seat, were terrified, begging me to stop or turn around, which up to a certain point would have been the sensible thing to do. However, once committed to the descent of the western slope of the summit, that was no longer an option. Nor would it have been fair to Lee Acott and the multitudes of people she had invited to the ballroom of the Simon Fraser Hotel to celebrate either an upset election victory or a wake.

It was nearly time for the polls to close when miraculously, and much to everyone's relief, we saw the faint lights of the commercial establishments at McLeod Lake penetrate the darkness and the storm. However, still out of range of the Prince George radio stations, we decided to suffer through the rest of the way rather than stop for a respite and some much-needed nourishment.

Finally, about 50 kilometres outside Prince George, the car radio crackled to life with early reports from eastern Canada pointing to a tight race between the Liberals and us. It wasn't long before we got news of the first results in our own riding; they were not encouraging. In the early going, there were one or two polls that showed us with a slight margin, but the majority soon indicated a steady trend in the other direction.

The noise coming from the ballroom as we finally made our way through the hotel lobby indicated a full house. We managed to sneak up the stairs to the room that had been reserved for us and back down to the coffee shop to feed our starving kids before we were discovered by one of the reporters, who demanded to know what on earth we were doing eating a casual meal at a time like this. Joan provided him with a lecture about a mother's priorities in looking after her children no matter what the circumstances.

My own preference would have been to find a quiet place to collect my thoughts and prepare myself for what would be expected of me, no matter what the outcome of the election might be. Nothing I could say or do, I knew, could possibly do justice to all these incredibly generous, loyal, and wonderful people who had invested so much faith in me and so much time and energy in our cause.

The last days had been particularly frantic. Because we had waited until the last two weeks to put up most of the election signs, that job had to be done with military precision. Armies of young people canvassed the streets and shopping centres, handing out brochures and reminding everyone to vote. The campaign headquarters had been a beehive of activity. One committee's job was to contact every name on the voters list to solicit their support. Another prepared a list of all those who had responded positively to their solicitation and targeted them for a "get out and vote campaign" on the day of the election.

What Joan and I felt now was mainly a sense of relief that it was finally over. We knew that the odds were not in our favour, but no one throughout the entire campaign had ever allowed us to even consider the prospect of losing. It would be the toughest speech I would ever have to make, and I had not prepared for it at all.

Word of our arrival had now filtered into the ballroom. Back in our room, I did not even have time to switch on the television set before Lee announced herself at the door. The emotions reflected in her face deprived me of the last hope for a miracle.

"Lee," I said as we hugged each other, "you must know that no one could have done a better job or done more than you have. We have nothing at all to be ashamed of or to apologize for. Joan and I have no regrets; perhaps it just wasn't meant to be."

I suppose I just hadn't gotten to know Lee as well as I did later, during the many years of our lifelong friendship, or I would have known that in situations such as this, she was more likely to swear than to cry.

"What the hell are you talking about?" she exclaimed, as she pushed me away and ran over to turn on the television set. "We've won! The results have just come in from the north; we've taken it with a landslide!"

To this day, I worry that I'll wake up to discover that it was all just an impossible dream. At the time, we simply allowed ourselves to be carried along in the wave of emotion and jubilation that greeted us as we entered the ballroom.

Peter and Frank in the ballroom at Prince George after the victory.

It had been decided that the bar service would be suspended to allow for some formalities, including an inspirational message from the new member of Parliament—a ceremony not unlike, I suppose, the virgin blessing my brother-in-law, Rudi, was expected to dispense on the occasion of celebrating his first Mass. However, I could sense that the content and length of my acceptance speech was not nearly as important as the brevity of the drought. Still, it took numerous attempts for me to find the right words of praise and thanks for the support we had received and the selfless effort made by most of the people in the room.

I also judged it the ideal time to alert my future constituents to my humble beginnings and to point to the greatness of our country that made it possible for someone like myself to be counted, not only among the world's most blessed people, but also as a member of the most exclusive club in Canada. I remember as well spending perhaps a little too long praising Bob Borrie, our Liberal opponent, who had conducted himself as the fine gentleman that he is. Not once throughout the whole campaign did he make any reference to my background or try to exploit the shortcomings in my education, both of which he must have undoubtedly been aware.

In fact, I was still in the midst of heaping him with praise when he entered the hall with a few of his own team to concede the election and to offer me his very best wishes. This brief interruption provided Lee with the opportunity to announce the reopening of the bar and the commencement of the festivities.

Fortunately, during some of my weaker moments spent speculating on the possibility of a victory, I had actually given some thought to a few catchy phrases suitable for the television fans we had acquired during the campaign, and for the hungry media representatives who demanded most of my time for the rest of the evening. I was only allowed some reprieve from the glare of the lights when it was announced that Bob Stanfield, potentially our new prime minister (the national results were still too close to call), was holding the line, waiting to speak with me. The steady flood of phone calls that followed finally gave Joan and I the excuse to retire to our room.

The rest of the night would almost pass before we managed to get some much-needed rest. Gene Rheaume and Louise Hayes were among the first to offer their congratulations and, more importantly, their commitment to help me launch my new career in Ottawa. Lots of other calls came, too, from a legion of friends—most of whom we'd never met—but who nevertheless were claiming singular credit for our splendid success.

The last call I placed myself. It was the one I had rehearsed the most and the one that would give me the greatest joy and satisfaction. It went overseas to Germany. Dad was too overcome by his emotions to add much to the conversation, but he did recall the promise I had made to him so long ago that one day he would have reason to be very proud of me.

"If only your Mom could have lived long enough," his shaky voice stammered, and I only managed to say, "she knows," before we both embarrassed ourselves in front of those listening in and trying to make sense of what was being said.

The following morning the results showed that the people of Chetwynd had invested more of their faith and trust in me as their member of Parliament than as their mayor. A convincing majority had taken the advice of Father Jungbluth. In fact, we had won by a comfortable margin in all but two of the polls east of the mountains. Bill Close, the NDP candidate, had been favoured by the Sudetan–Germans in Tomslake and Tupper.

The Liberals were completely shut out in Chetwynd. The Prince George results were not nearly as one-sided, but we had registered enough support there to take us over the top.

All in all, we had won eight of the 24 seats in British Columbia. Nationwide, the Liberals eventually managed to cling to power with a margin of just two seats over the Conservative Party. They had 109 seats in the House of Commons; we ended up with 107. The NDP held the balance of power, with 31 seats.

The next day, after a series of interviews with the local media and meetings with the campaign team, Joan and I finally found ourselves alone in our room with some time to reflect. We realized to our horror that neither of us had given much thought as to how our lives would be affected by the pervious day's events. Once again we had thrown all caution to the wind. Instead of pursuing the plans we had been making for a career change into ranching and perhaps a more active role in our lumber business, we now would have to abandon the comfort of community and friends. Once again we would have to strike out on our own, on an adventure that would lead our lives into an entirely new direction along an uncertain path.

MEMBER OF PARLIAMENT FOR
PRINCE GEORGE–PEACE RIVER

1972–1985

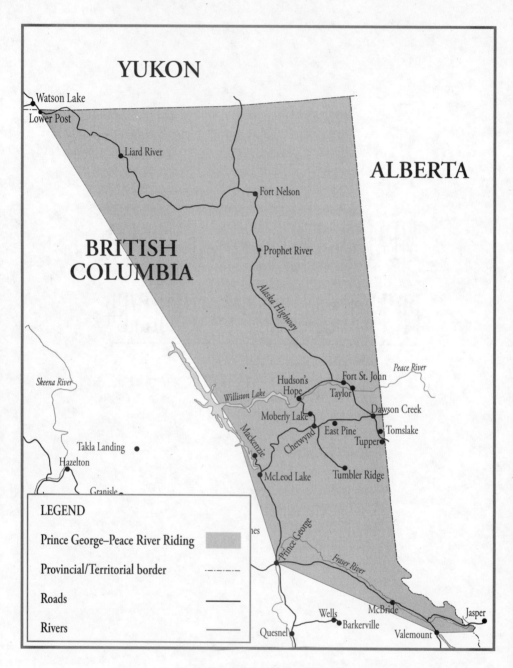

Prince George–Peace River Riding

134

CHAPTER 9

An Innocent in Ottawa

A king may make a nobleman, but he cannot make a gentleman.
—Edmund Burke

The next few days were filled with both excitement and trepidation as the reality of the situation finally sank in. With no idea of what might be expected of me or how I might be compensated for travel and other inevitable expenses, it was impossible for Joan and I to make plans.

Nor did we know how long to plan for. Given the delicate balance of power between the parties, it seemed obvious that the 29th Parliament would have a short life span indeed. Altogether too many loose ends needed to be tied up. The first priority would be to plan for an orderly transition of our various business interests to new management. With all this in mind, we finally decided that, for the time being, we would spare our family from being uprooted and would postpone a full move to Ottawa until we became better acquainted with our new situation.

It had taken us until late in the afternoon of the following day to make our way back through the mountains to deposit the children and to visit with a few of our Chetwynd friends whose encouragement and support had helped to sustain us through the election campaign. When we left, it was with their best wishes and the comfort of knowing that if things did not work out for us the way we all hoped, we would have a home to come back to and reliable friends that we could count on to help us get re-established in the real world.

It almost came as a relief for us when, shortly after leaving Chetwynd to attend the victory celebrations, as promised to our Dawson Creek and Fort St. John supporters, I lost control of the car and ended up hopelessly stuck in a snow-bank. There was no escape without the help of a winch-truck and nothing to do but wait for someone to relay a message about our predicament to Ted Hauck or one of the boys in the garage back at the service station. Once I had cleared the tailpipe of snow and settled back in the car, we took advantage of the first opportunity we had had for some time for a precious moment of intimacy.

"Tell them not to hurry," Joan told the Good Samaritan going in the other direction. "We are perfectly okay."

Other than congratulatory messages from my future colleagues, there had been no official communication from the party. Acknowledgment from Parliament of my new status would have to await the return of the writ, which could take up to a month. Louise Hayes suggested that I should nevertheless present myself to the whip's office in Ottawa and arrange to hire a secretary to look after my interests there as soon as possible. True to her word, she offered not only some valuable advice on what to look for in the selection, but arranged a number of interviews in advance of my arrival.

It was mid-November before I managed to get away for an exploratory mission to Ottawa. One of the first things that struck me, as one of the whip's aides guided me on a tour around the parliamentary precincts, was the predominant use of French among the security and clerical staff in the offices we visited. No doubt members of the House of Commons would have to rely heavily on these people for their support, pointing to the need for a French-speaking secretary.

Her name was Denise McCullough and she was the very first candidate Louise had scheduled for an interview. In her strong but pleasant French-Canadian accent, she referred to me as "Mr. H'Oberle." Joan would later comment that it was certainly more than just her good looks that guided my decision to hire her. Her agreeable demeanour and infectious enthusiasm made it a pleasure to be in her company.

The selection of an office was my first introduction to the pecking order in which I'd have to compete. No matter how spectacular the architecture or masterful the engineering, when a grand edifice has been designed to reflect the important purpose for which it was created, there are bound to be certain spaces inside where practical utility has been sacrificed to enhance the aesthetics and splendour of the outside. In the Canadian Parliament, such spaces are used to accommodate new members and to keep them in touch with their humility. Of course, exceptions are made for those who have a prior privileged connection to either the party or the administrative hierarchy of the place. I was not one of those people, so I was destined to start my new career as a member of Parliament from a position not at all unfamiliar to me: nowhere to go but up.

The first "office space" we were shown was slightly larger than a broom closet, with a 10-foot ceiling and a tiny window offering a view of the weather-beaten masonry on another part of the edifice. The other two choices did little more to relieve my sense of claustrophobia.

"Denise," I said, "I am sorry to put you to the test so soon, but I am afraid that our relationship will be short-lived unless you can charm someone into giving us some better accommodation. I just can't see myself spending the better part of my life in one of these cubbyholes."

I had no sooner arrived back home when she called with the good news that she had found us a much more spacious office in the West Block of the Parliament Buildings, with big windows overlooking the "Gatineau mountains." With all the other things on my mind during my last two visits to Ottawa, the presence there of any mountains must have escaped my attention, but I told her I was willing to give it another try. Later, I was told by people in the whip's office that Denise was totally convinced that Mr. "H'Oberle" would not come to Ottawa unless a more suitable office space could be found. My new secretary had already proven her worth.

The office proved to be quite a catch, as it turned out. It was not only spacious enough to accommodate two sizable desks (I preferred to have Denise share in the bounty of what she had conquered), but also an adjacent smaller room. There was a large window that framed the gothic-style masonry of the three principal edifices on Parliament Hill, and a view in the direction of the Gatineau Hills and the banks of the Ottawa River. The only serious drawback was that these windows also framed the spectacle of an array of Canadian Armed Forces artillery which, on the occasion of official visits by royals, the Governor General, and other assorted dignitaries, thundered their salutes, shattering the serenity of the place and rattling my windows. No doubt affronted by being singled out for such hostile treatment, some of my colleagues from Quebec maintained that the guns are always symbolically aimed across the Ottawa River toward their province. However, there is no record of injury to anyone in the target area. In my case, these noisy spectacles always triggered a battle with my instincts, honed during my childhood, to dive under my desk every time they happened.

My initials would determine the location of my seat in the Chamber itself. The Os occupied the very last row of the Opposition benches, but fortunately for the O'Reillys, the O'Sullivans, and the Oberles, there were enough Pattersons, Paproskis, and Reynoldses to assure a position close to the centre of the activities, right behind Bob Stanfield and John Diefenbaker, and facing Pierre Trudeau straight across the aisle.

Although Joan and I had decided it would be wise for us to carry on with the business as best we could until we got a better fix on our situation, I used the occasion of my next trip to Ottawa to stop over in Toronto to meet with my good friend Mr. Thomson, with whom I had consummated the deal to establish our second service station, and whose position with Imperial Oil had been elevated to that of vice-president. Emboldened by the fact that the company had every reason to be satisfied with the volume of business and quality of service at their Chetwynd location, I requested that Mr. Thomson consider one of two options to help me to extricate myself from my personal commitment to the enterprise. My preference was for Imperial Oil to buy the property from us and lease the business back to our capable staff; failing that, I asked them to release me from the product agreement and allow me to offer the facility to one of their competitors.

I was pleasantly surprised to receive an immediate response and a most generous offer to purchase the property. Marshall Peters, who had been managing the place in our absence, was offered an infinitely more generous lease agreement than the one we had with Standard Oil, our first landlord, at the Chevron station across the street. Given our circumstances, we were now as ready as we could be for me to finally be sworn in as a member of Parliament, earning me the distinction of being the first German-born citizen of any British Commonwealth country ever to qualify for such an honour.

Parliament opened on January 4, 1973. Ahead was a sitting scheduled to last until the end of June, 1973, followed by a two-month summer break and then the fall session.

Given the tenuous balance of seats in the House, the government had to tread lightly, introducing only minor changes such as the imposition of some restrictions on foreign investment in the resource sector—a precursor to the National Energy Program, perhaps—and the odd resolution on abortion and capital punishment designed to embarrass and exploit the weaknesses among the members of the Progressive Conservative Party. In the main, however, it was events abroad that were attracting media attention. In the United States, the people had re-elected Richard Nixon as their president. He dominated the world stage with his visits to China and the Soviet Union, and assured his place in his country's history by planting the seeds of the Watergate crisis that resulted in his downfall. It was also the year of the Summer Olympics in Munich, Germany, where a group of Arab terrorists assassinated 11 Israeli athletes, and in the United Kingdom, the British moved to impose direct rule over Northern Ireland.

I left Chetwynd between Christmas and New Year's to get settled in a small bachelor apartment within walking distance of the "Hill." During the first caucus meeting, some attempt was made to help new members become acquainted with the job, but nothing could have prepared me for the humbling experience of walking into the Chamber for the first time and finding myself in the presence of the most powerful people in the country. Others sitting near me in the back row of the Opposition chairs were equally traumatized by the experience and the prospect of—someday soon—having to stand up in their place, establish their presence, and account for the reasons that brought them here, but no one could have been more intimidated and terrified than me. The place has the ambience of a cathedral during High Mass on a Sunday morning, except that everyone in the congregation is expected to be familiar with the rituals honouring hundreds of years of British parliamentary tradition and, at certain times, to take his or her place in the pulpit.

Mercifully, the first day's session was intentionally brief to allow for the customary receptions and parties celebrating the beginning of a new Parliament. When it was all over and I was ploughing my way through a mountain of fresh snow back to the apartment, I felt as much confidence and enthusiasm for what the next day might bring as I had done after my first shift as a pipefitter's helper, 800 metres underground in the gold mine at Pioneer.

I couldn't recall ever feeling more intimidated or unsure of myself. Unlike during my introduction to the harsh and dangerous environment of hard-rock mining, this time I was all alone. No one like Nick Labuschka showed up with a case of beer under his arm to help me build my confidence or reinforce my courage. How could I ever bring myself to stand in the presence of all these eminent people and make a speech? How could I ever measure up to all the expectations I had brazenly created back home during the election?

A photo shoot in the House to show off the new MP with Bill Kempling, MP for Burlington, Marcel Lambert, MP for Edmonton West, and Bill Clarke, MP for Vancouver Quadra.

Fortunately for me, the day's activities had exhausted all my energy, forcing my system to shut down for a few hours of sleep. But getting into the elevator the next morning did little to boost my morale. My pad was located on the eighth floor of a 12-storey building and, thanks to the building's proximity to Parliament, it was occupied almost entirely by civil servants. All I got in response to my greeting in the elevator from the people who had boarded above was a blank stare. Perhaps, like most of the people I had encountered outside the Chamber on Parliament Hill, they were all French and didn't speak English, I reasoned, thinking that I at least should make the effort to learn a few phrases in the other official language. That theory was destroyed as additional passengers came aboard at the lower floors; still not a word, not the slightest sign of recognition passed among any of them. I concluded that perhaps government employees were assigned the appropriate floor levels commensurate to their rank and that it was against the rules of conduct to fraternize and associate with persons of lower echelons.

Welcome to Ottawa.

Thankfully, it appeared that my trusty secretary, Denise, preferred to operate contrary to any such rules. She was bubbling over with excitement when I got to the office. She had seen me on television the previous night, coming out of the Chamber, cutting an impressive figure.

"Will Mrs. H'Oberle come to Ottawa for the Governor General's ball?" she needed to know. She had organized a schedule for the day that left little time for introspection or negative thoughts. A list of phone calls and dozens of letters required my personal input and attention. Thought had to be given to the committees on which I would serve, so she suggested that I meet with Mr. Stanfield, now leader of the Official Opposition as well as party leader, to ask for guidance about what might best suit my interests.

During the election campaign, Gene Rheaume had managed to arrange a visit by Bob Stanfield to our riding even though, given previous results, we had not been given much of a chance of winning and were therefore not on any priority list for campaign visits by the leader. I had introduced him to a packed school auditorium in Dawson Creek as the next prime minister of Canada and someone with whom I had a lot in common. Both of us had gotten our starts in Halifax, Nova Scotia: he as the heir to the Stanfield underwear fortune, me as a dishwasher at the Green Lantern restaurant.

Little did I know at the time how close he would actually come to being prime minister or how wide the rift between us would be, not only in terms of our vastly different backgrounds, but also in the way those backgrounds had shaped our outlook on life and our respective philosophical orientations. I should not have been surprised, since he was after all the choice of those in the party who, in 1966 and '67, had plotted the political assassination of my idol, John Diefenbaker, who had personified my own dreams and inspired my interest in politics and love for my new homeland.

As Opposition leader, Stanfield led by surrounding himself with people like Flora MacDonald, David MacDonald, and Joe Clark—all highly competent, respectable, and decent people, but the NDP would have been a much more comfortable home for them. This group, known as the "Red Tories," were at odds with the more traditional Conservative faction, including such notables as Jack Horner, Don Mazankowski, and George Hees. When I spoke with Stanfield, I found little to boost my confidence and little understanding for the causes I wished to champion.

Despite all of that, I got to know and appreciate the man as a thoroughly decent individual who treated people with the utmost courtesy and respect. I have no doubt that, had he allowed his partisan instincts, rather than his laudable principles, to guide his judgement and his conduct in either the 1972 and 1974 elections, he could have taken the party to power.

In fairness, Stanfield understood and showed concern for the critical role of Canada's forests, not only for their importance in securing a healthy economy, but also for a myriad of social and environmental considerations. He accused the current administration of outright neglect, and asked me later on to act as the party critic on forestry matters and to explore what useful role a future Progressive Conservative government might play in this area. He was instrumental in convincing the party to adopt most of the policy recommendations proposed by the caucus committee that I chaired.

When we met in his office, Mr. Stanfield did offer words of encouragement and sincere interest. He was most generous in his praise for what I had accomplished as the mayor of Chetwynd, and suggested I work with Joe Clark, the shadow-Cabinet critic for Indian affairs and Northern Development, who would be heading the appropriate caucus committee. Robert Stanfield was a very private person, more shy than aloof, and I would have only one other personal encounter with him, but not until Joe Clark had succeeded him as party leader.

All members of Parliament find themselves jostling for a position on the more powerful and prominent parliamentary committees such as Finance, External Affairs and Defence, and Justice, although the leader is the one who directs these appointments. I was still very much preoccupied with finding my way around the place, so I was not at all unhappy to be assigned a minor role on the team.

I was told by one of the senior clerks whom I had befriended and who was sensitive to my despondency that it was not unusual for new members to feel out of place, unsure of themselves, and wondering what justified their presence here. For most, however, it takes no time at all to ask that same question of everybody else. Indeed, after just a few sittings in the House of Commons, it appeared that the only contribution required by a private member of any party was to shout insults at whoever on the other side was speaking at any time. Or, conversely, to pound on one's desk, not unlike what you'd expect from a bunch of monkeys in a zoo, and shout, "Shame! Shame!" or "Hear! Hear!" to signal one's response to what was being said. (Mercifully, this primeval practice fell into disuse when TV cameras began recording proceedings live in October 1977.)

The House of Commons itself, one soon discovers, is not what most people perceive it to be. It is in the main a theatre that plays to the audience back home or to the various people and groups interested in the subject under debate. The most important drama acted out on a daily basis is Question Period. Most members make it a practice to attend. Ministers, when in town, are expected to be there and to be accountable for their departments. During regular sittings, unless the prime minister or one of the party leaders was participating in the debate, only a corporal's guard of a few members would be grouped around whoever had the floor, to fill the TV screen. At various times, the place could be the scene of high drama or the equivalent of a "gong show."

The press plays a major role in determining the agenda of Question Period in the House of Commons. No one expects to change the minds of any of the members opposite, no matter how impassioned the plea or histrionic the delivery of the speech. Lasting 45 minutes, Question Period adds some spark to the otherwise mundane routine. Members are allowed to question ministers on matters pertaining to their realm of responsibility, with the questions carefully crafted to expose the respective minister's vulnerability. Only rarely would anyone be thoughtful enough to give notice of the question to the minister, who is expected to respond spontaneously. The general rule is never to ask a question for which the answer is not already well known. The Speaker, who presides over the proceedings, receives a list from the respective house leaders of the parties, giving him the names and the order in which the members are to be recognized. The exchanges are laced with venom, sarcasm, and sometimes humour. The rules, however, are very strict and crafted to safeguard the myth that everyone in the place merits the title "honourable."

The House of Commons is therefore an ideal place for anyone incapable of making the distinction between truth and fiction. To catch someone out telling an outright and obviously deliberate lie and accuse him of it can result in expulsion from the Chamber. Most participants in this charade, however, quickly learn to disguise their insults and expose the truth without offending the rules.

Mr. Diefenbaker was a master of this art. On one occasion, in response to a particularly abrasive young upstart who had gotten under his skin, he expressed his esteem and affection for him in the following manner. (Note: I have paraphrased this and all other Hansard excerpts used in this volume.)

Rt. Hon. John Diefenbaker: Mr. Speaker, you know how much I pride myself on being able to quickly and accurately assess the special talents honourable members bring to this august Chamber when first they arrive. In the case of the Honourable Member to whom you had just given the floor, however, I must confess that my talent has failed me. Instead of being some kind of a wit, which was my first assessment, I now find that I was only half right.

Some Hon. Members: Hear, hear!

"The only thing that prevents me from calling the Honourable member a barefaced liar is his beard" was another way some members used to get their point across.

Tommy Douglas treated one of his adversaries to this comment: "My honourable friend said that being challenged, 'he could eat me for breakfast.' Had he actually managed such a deed, he would undoubtedly have found himself with infinitely more brains in his stomach than his head."

To participate in this kind of dialogue and match wit with some of these experts was a major preoccupation for many of the members.

In 1974 I earned the distinction of being named the contributor of the funniest statement of the year by *The Parliamentarian*, a journal published by the Parliaments of the Commonwealth. It came about through another of those many ill-fated attempts at humour and political satire by the Canadian Broadcasting Corporation. *One Honourable Member*, which was broadcast as part of the *Up Canada* series, was to be the Canadian equivalent of the immensely popular BBC series *Some Honourable Members*. Unfortunately, one of the main characters in the first episode, George Fraser, was not only portrayed as coming from the west coast, but he also lived on the same Ottawa street on which MP John Fraser made his home. (John Fraser, later Speaker of the House, Environment minister, and Minister of Fisheries and Oceans, was the member from Vancouver South.) As usual, the program was promoted for weeks in advance as another of those gems that only the CBC can produce from time to time.

Here is the question of privilege I raised in response:

Mr. F. Oberle: Mr. Speaker, on January 8, the night before last, our government-funded national television network aired the first episode of a new series called *One Honourable Member*. I, and I am sure most Hon. members appreciate the media's recognition of our presence here in Ottawa, but we must object to the use of the network in creating false impressions about our activities here.

The scene to which the audience was treated during this first episode showed one Hon. member from the West Coast, whose name and address were almost identical to that of one of my colleagues from Vancouver, in bed with another Hon. member's secretary. The male actor, presumably for Canadian content, was clad in a Hudson's Bay blanket that covered only his vitals. The lady, suitably dressed for the sport in which the couple was engaged, was devoid of any attire apart from a set of false eyelashes and fingernails.

Soon an argument ensued over the impending arrival in Ottawa of the Hon. member's wife. The lady decided to "split the sheets" and made her way to the telephone to summon a taxi, which arrived in an instant to take her from the scene.

Now Mr. Speaker, I would expect that the minister responsible for the financial health of the corporation would make every effort on our behalf to stop any future broadcast of this exhilarating cultural experience so that we do not create the impression in the country that any Hon. member, or his secretary for that matter, can call a taxi here in Ottawa and expect it to arrive in any time less than half an hour."

Some Hon. Members: Hear, hear!

To stave off any potential libel action that John Fraser would have had every justification to launch, the CBC informed us the following day that there would be no airing of any further episodes.

The excerpt of my statement was reprinted on the front page of the *Ottawa Citizen*, but the best compliment came from the Right Honourable John Diefenbaker who, on his way out of the Chamber, congratulated me and said that he would be hard-pressed to think of anything funnier he'd heard in the House for a long time.

He may have harboured a bit of a bias perhaps because, for obvious reasons, he had taken a liking to me right from the beginning. Throughout his political life he much preferred to relate to the ancestry of his first wife, Edna, who was of Scottish descent. I was among the very few people to whom he would confess and show pride in his Germanic origins. Although he was born in Canada, his roots were planted in the region of Baden Baden, not more than 30 kilometres away from my ancestral home.

For my part, it was John George Diefenbaker (a common name in the Black Forest), who, ever since I first heard his name mentioned during the elections in the late '50s and early '60s, had sparked my interest in Canadian politics. I liked his message and sympathized with his beliefs.

I can still hear him: "I am a Canadian free to speak without fear— free to worship in my own way—free to stand for what I think is right—free to oppose what I think wrong—free to choose those who shall govern my country. This heritage and freedom I pledge to uphold for myself and all mankind."

No one could have offered a better interpretation of the dreams I had for my new homeland. It was because of him and my desire to vote for his party in the election of 1957 that I obtained my citizenship that same year. Diefenbaker was a statesman and a consummate politician. He served as our prime minister only for six years, from 1957 to 1963, but he loved and respected Parliament and thought it a privilege to serve as a member of it—in his case, right up until his death on August 16, 1979.

Most of all I shared Diefenbaker's idealism, something I found little evidence of by the time I arrived in Parliament. It was astounding to me that neither my own party nor the Liberal Party could point any longer to a set of principles or philosophical moorings by which they could be identified or which could be seen as a guide to their approach to governing. Surely, as the word implies, Conservatives should be counted upon to demonstrate a stronger attachment to traditional values and be cautious about change that has not been tested by history and time-honoured conventions, customs, and traditions. Unlike Liberals, who believe it's due to the failure of society as a whole that individuals defy its rule of law, Conservatives traditionally attach more guilt to the individual for failing to live up to the responsibilities every citizen must assume as a member of a free and open society.

On one occasion, Stanfield ordered a weekend retreat of our Progressive Conservative caucus to debate the issue of the party's philosophical base, but the results, at least to me, were most unsatisfactory. I knew few colleagues in Parliament, even among our opponents, who were not committed to promoting prosperity, health, and happiness among our fellow travellers within the brotherhood of man. No matter what the label, neither the right nor the left, the red nor the blue, could claim a monopoly on concern and compassion for the underprivileged or for those with special needs. The labels, it appeared to me, only identified the approach each would favour in working to remove obstacles in the way to attaining such lofty goals. People whose political orientation is left-leaning tend, for instance, to opt for higher minimum wages or for rent controls to improve the lives of the working poor. Those on the right ask themselves how many new homes or apartments or how many new jobs for young people making the transition from school to work such policies might produce. They would prefer to opt for ways to encourage individual initiative, sensitize the private sector to citizens' needs, offer incentives, and stimulate a free-market response.

After all, this was the approach that had led to the unqualified success of the Chetwynd Native Housing project. Rather than offering rent subsidies for substandard housing designed by some agency of government, we provided the targeted families with the opportunity to help design and build their homes—homes they would eventually own and so would have a vested interest in. Sadly, however, once the idea had been accepted and adopted throughout the country, most of the benefits were lost when the bureaucrats in Ottawa called in outside contractors to do the work. One of the First Nations leaders reasoned, when challenged on the new approach: "I don't see too many white men having to build their own houses."

There did seem to be one difference of note between the Conservative and Liberal parties: The Conservative Party's tendency was to stab itself in the back. The constant bickering between the right- and left-wing factions seemed our main preoccupation. Our friends in the Liberal Party don't seem as burdened by such internal philosophical conflicts. My honourable friend Pierre Gimaiel, the Liberal member preceding Lucien Bouchard in Parliament from the riding of Lac Saint-Jean, gave us perhaps the best insight into what constitutes Liberal philosophy when he spoke in the House of Commons in January 1982. Here is what he said:

> To be a Liberal in the pursuit of opportunities for development and progress anything can be justified. If the development of individual Canadians can best be achieved through socialization, the Liberal Party can turn socialist. If in order to promote our development the Liberal Party thinks we have to be communistic, we shall be communistic.
>
> This is what it is all about to be a Liberal.

Is it really any wonder that politicians in our country are held in such low esteem by the people they represent?

As I got to know my colleagues better and learned more about their motivations, backgrounds, and qualifications, I began to group them into categories.

The first and most prominent were the lawyers, whom I called "Judiciariens." They viewed politics as a branch of their profession—a specialty, perhaps. The Chamber was their courtroom, their constituents and the party, their clients. Few allowed themselves to be constrained by principles while pursuing their clients' objective, which was to either replace the party in power or to stay in power. The end justified the means. They were masters of focussing their argument only on those aspects of the truth that put their opponents in the worst possible light. In Opposition, they played the game of politics with the sole motive of stopping progress; then, having done so, decried the lack of it. When in power, their main preoccupation seemed to be to ensure that all government and Crown corporation legal-service contracts were allocated to those firms with the proper political credentials.

The "Juvenilians" were the next group of members, those whose mothers knew the minute they were born that they were destined to become prime minister.

Over time, some actually did. At an early age, the poor unsuspecting critters were dragged to every political meeting and introduced to every visiting dignitary in search of mentorship and inspiration. Most made an honest attempt to get an education but all too often, usually around the time of a critical exam, someone always decided to call an election to interfere with their commitment and distract their attention.

By the time they are sworn into office, they have usually served as assistants to their mentors or functionaries in the party's central office, qualifying them to enter the system in an elevated position in the pecking order. They are familiar with the rules of the game and conversant with the jargon of the profession. They are masters in the delivery of snappy, smart-assed comments meant to portray the person at whom they are directed as a complete moron, even if that person, for example, were the proprietor of a successful business, head of a corporation, or had practised medicine for 20 years of his life before offering to serve in Parliament.

Politics was their whole life. Like their lawyer friends, they divested themselves of any capacity to consider ideas or proposals generated by the Opposition as anything but a conspiracy against their right to life and the pursuit of happiness.

Another group, the "Zealotians," was made up of people who arrived in Parliament committed to a single-issue crusade, such as abortion, the right to life, capital punishment, or the metric system. The most principled among these were members of the New Democratic Party, who, to borrow Winston Churchill's words, believed that "the inherent vice of capitalism is the unequal sharing of blessings; the inherent virtue of socialism is the equal sharing of miseries."

Most of the Zealotians are highly skilled intellectual gymnasts, allowing them to effortlessly refocus the debate on their area of special interest, no matter what the original subject. The disciples of Major C.H. Douglas and his Canadian counterpart, William Aberhart, whose "funny money" theory had helped spawn the Social Credit movement in the 1950s, were among that group as well. They were singularly obsessed with the gap between

Canadians' capacity, on the one hand, to produce and on the other, to consume, and the combined banking and monetary system that stands in the way of closing that gap.

A small, but nevertheless important, group was the "Bureaucratians." They came to Parliament via the public service, where they had been joined by university professors and their former students trained in the discipline of political science. Like the Zealotians, this group was obsessed and singularly preoccupied with the rules and orders that govern conduct in the House of Commons. It was like a religion to them. The books of parliamentary procedure are their bibles; the authors, their prophets.

For most of the rest of the honourable members, their passion for politics is an extension of their dreams. They find comfort in the companionship of like-minded people who share the belief that there are better ways to achieve social justice and promote the brotherhood of man. Whereas most of the others tend to put their faith in bureaucratic authority, this group is of the view that society's needs are best served through the independent efforts of its citizens, through volunteerism and charitable public attitudes. Through their personal accomplishments, and respect for civic duty, they have earned the support of their peers and the people in the communities that have elected them to serve as their representatives in Parliament.

To them there is no higher calling, no greater honour; but they find being in the House frustrating and boring, preferring committees as more effective arenas to have their views heard. (In fact, several honourable members, including one of my predecessors representing our constituency, never uttered a single word in the House of Commons in all the time they spent there, yet they were usually re-elected several times and were recognized for their outstanding service to their constituents. For certain others, who felt the urge to pontificate on every issue that reached the floor of the House of Commons, it might have been wiser to remain silent and be thought of as a fool than to seek every possible opportunity to remove any doubt.)

Naturally, one couldn't help but be impressed by the exceptionally gifted orators—men and women—who inspired others to follow in their footsteps: People like Tommy Douglas, John Diefenbaker, Pierre Trudeau, and Brian Mulroney made Parliament come alive. What an honour it was to walk among them, for they were born leaders and truly deserving of the respect they commanded from their peers. Many others among these gifted politicians also deserve praise for their success in their professions or their business enterprises. Had they been motivated by money alone, they certainly would have been in the wrong place. Instead they sought their reward in the satisfaction that comes from serving their community, helping others, and the belief that through their service the world could become a better place.

Some, a small minority to be sure, were particularly undeserving of the title "honourable." I soon discovered that, just as wealth does not guarantee happiness, so is knowledge by itself no substitute for wisdom. A professor in one of Canada's more prestigious law schools liked to introduce his new students to the profession by telling them that the courses they would be required to attend were designed to sharpen their minds by narrowing them. Indeed, I found among the most learned of my new friends some of the most narrow-minded and ignorant people I have ever met.

I was also appalled by how many of my "honourable" friends lacked not only the wisdom and the prudence to judge their saturation point in the consumption of alcohol, but also any social grace or control over their inner demons. How could they be trusted to uphold their oath to the office and fight for justice in the world while being slaves to their own weaknesses?

CHAPTER 10

First Session 1972–1974

The strongest bulwark of authority is uniformity; the least divergence from it is the greatest crime.

—Emma Goldman

Having taken Mr. Stanfield's advice to work with Joe Clark on the Indian Affairs Committee, I soon realized that at least one of us had to be in the wrong place. Joe's approach, no doubt conforming with the rules of political gamesmanship, was simple and straightforward. On the issue of Native affairs, everything the government was doing or attempting to do had to be exposed as an act of genocide, without any exploration of its merits, including my experience with the Chetwynd housing experiment, for which Ron Basford, the Liberal Minister of Housing and Urban Affairs, deserved a good share of the credit. And, in an effort to promote ours as the party of choice for every clear-thinking Native person in the country, everything suggested to us by some of the more vocal First Nations chiefs across the land—no matter how outlandish the idea—was to be embraced as our policy.

According to the Royal Proclamation of 1763, Natives were to be treated as sovereign nations and were to be compensated for any land surrendered for settlement by European immigrants. However, with the passage of time, during which the Aboriginal peoples had every reason to become increasingly distrustful and suspicious, it became necessary for commissioners negotiating surrender treaties to make ever-more generous promises, some of which they no doubt knew could never be delivered. As more and more Native land became alienated for other uses, one such promise would lead to conflict over time: the Aboriginal right to hunt and fish, and the guarantee of a land- and resource-based livelihood so long as the sun shone, the grass grew, and the rivers flowed.

Fortunately, others on the Indian Affairs committee and many enlightened Native leaders throughout Canada would have much preferred to depoliticize the process of alleviating the horrifying conditions in Native communities throughout the country and to work toward more sensible and practical solutions.

Needless to say, Clark and I got off on the wrong foot. I did share much of his passion, which was genuine, for the plight of the Native people, and his social conscience. But I judged his approach to some of the problems altogether ill-considered, naive, and superficial. It was partly my first impression of the man that made it impossible for me, later on, to consider him the right candidate for the leadership of our party. I felt he was motivated more by his own ambition than by any clear vision of where he wanted to take the country. His lust for power and control was spawned by his mistrust of anyone with the audacity to disagree with his view of the world. This mistrust was not restricted to the Opposition parties; it was also directed toward colleagues in our own party.

It wasn't long before I had overcome my fascination with the pomp, ceremony, and theatre of the place. To the casual observer these trappings may project an image of power, integrity, and stability but, once I began looking behind the scenes, I quickly discovered just how shallow the process really was for dealing with the complex issues that had to be faced every day—let alone the process for addressing issues affecting the nation's well-being in the longer term.

It can be argued, of course, that the British parliamentary system provides for an impartial, highly professional public service, to offer the government the advice and guidance it needs. However, that same advice is not available to any of the Opposition parties, who are expected not only to effectively critique the government's policies, but also to be prepared to assume the mantle of power themselves at any time. The public has the right to expect their representatives to form opinions on the entire range of issues with which the government must deal, but given the scarce resources available to members of the Opposition parties, it would be unreasonable to expect them to become more than 30-second experts on most of them.

I decided to examine how political parties in other jurisdictions defined themselves and what approach they could be expected to use if they were called upon to govern. In Great Britain, for example, the Conservative Party had the advantage, while in power or serving in Opposition, of balancing the advice it received from the public service with the findings of three different research organizations and several study groups, perhaps the most prominent of which was the Centre for Policy Studies (CPS), which operated at arm's-length from the party itself. The CPS regularly sponsors weekend public seminars to define and promote conservative values, principles, and ideology, on the basis of which future policy options are developed and chosen.

In the United States, the American Enterprise Institute (AEI) started out as a voice for business and free enterprise but developed into a sophisticated and comprehensive research organization widely recognized as the standard bearer of neo-conservative thought in the U.S. The Bookings Institute and the Research Division of the Republican National Committee were two additional sources of research and advice.

Naturally, I was particularly interested in and had studied the system adopted by the Federal Republic of Germany, arguably the most modern arrangement among western industrialized nations. It is of the most recent origin and benefitted in its design not only from Germany's own troubled history, but also from the experience of other countries. I led several delegations of fellow MPs and journalists to study the role of the various institutes attached to the main political parties.

The idea of periodic change of government is as fundamental to German democracy as it is to all multi-party systems. Flowing from this idea is the belief that the major political parties should, at all times, be able to contribute meaningfully to the national agenda and debate and be ready to assume the mantle of power. Prior to elections, each party is expected to publish its own detailed and reliable fiscal, monetary, and social policies, which, in Germany's case, no doubt, results in a public capable of making well-informed electoral choices.

The Konrad Adenauer Foundation and the Hans Seidel Stiftung are recognized throughout the world as important reservoirs of conservative ideology, but they too operate at arm's-length from the political parties—the CDU and its counterpart in Bavaria, the CSU—on whose supporters they partly rely for a major part of their funding. However, more than 50 percent of these institutes' finances are provided by the legislature, with the remainder coming from private individuals and corporations. The recognition of the important role they play in public education and the promotion of competing philosophical trends justify government support for these foundations.

In 1980 I produced a detailed report, titled *The Macdonald–Cartier Foundation: A proposal to establish a Canadian centre for conservative thought*, that I shared with my caucus colleagues and the leadership recommending the establishment of a foundation as the guardian of the fundamental principles on which the party should rest its fate. The name came from two illustrious conservatives: Sir John A. Macdonald, Canada's first prime minister, and another father of Canadian Confederation, George-Étienne Cartier.

Mr. Stanfield, to his credit, gave me an audience, the second in our relationship, to discuss the report. He expressed interest and afforded me the courtesy of a lengthy, handwritten reply, offering his opinion on the subject but disagreeing with my proposals. He considered it essential that the parties should "cast as wide a net, build as big a tent as possible" to attract and provide a home for supporters of the entire spectrum of philosophical currents.

For Pierre Trudeau, who in some of his musings could point to certain virtues of a single-party democracy, such an approach would make a lot of sense. After all, what is the purpose of a multi-party system, which is the essence of all western democracies, when all the parties compete for the same ground?

To their credit, Peter Blakie, the party president at the time, and Brian Mulroney, who was thinking of competing for the leadership of the Progressive Conservative Party, embraced the idea. Brian went as far as asking my permission to have the paper translated into French, and offered to pay for it. Both were positioned to leave the party with an important legacy, but sadly allowed other, perhaps more pressing, issues to dispel the opportunity.

As for the House, apart from the time and effort I invested in my role as the party's Forestry critic, I avoided it as much as possible, often trading my obligatory days of house duty with one of my friends, usually one of the "Bureaucratians," for some other favour. Unlike most of my colleagues who, in addition to their obligations to the constituency, spent most of their time and efforts preparing themselves for an occasional moment of glory during Question Period in the House or working in committees, I chose instead to concentrate on promoting my own causes and the agenda that had sparked my interest in politics and motivated me to aspire to parliamentary office.

During the election we had made several attempts to involve students in our campaign and to challenge my opponents to use schools as venues for some of our all-candidate meetings. Astonishingly, none of the high schools we approached showed any interest in having their students exposed to this sort of debate. This was, perhaps, understandable in that the standard curriculum offered little if any information about the institutions of Parliament, the courts, or the historic relationship to the British Crown. Politics was treated somewhat like sex and pornography, matters on which one must seek enlightenment from one's peers to satisfy one's curiosity.

Denise herself spearheaded our first extra-parliamentary effort, an attempt to remedy this problem. Entitled *A Look at Our Government*, it was a 50-page report on the structure and functions of the various levels of government. Designed to be distributed throughout the schools in the riding, the publication became popular with a lot of teachers, who made use of it in their classrooms as the only aid available to them on the subject.

Initially, the resources needed for individual members to pursue special projects and hire additional staff were only reluctantly granted by the Speaker. Matters got better after the 1974 election, when members saw a marked improvement. New funds were allocated for a modest office in the constituency, and a salary for an assistant to do research and help the member with their political duties.

Given the lively flow of correspondence into the office from people who found it more convenient to write in German, Denise and I decided that we should recruit someone with the necessary language skills. Gudrun Boyce, like myself an immigrant from Germany, answered the call and in no time at all had made herself indispensable to the operation. She was hired on a basis as permanent as a member of Parliament's circumstances would permit.

Projects became much more ambitious—the Macdonald–Cartier report for example—with each requiring the full-time attention of a research assistant, usually a graduate university student chosen for his or her special interest in the topic under study, as well as a general interest in parliamentary affairs.

Nothing about my new career was ever routine. The greatest challenge, given the vast distance between the office and the constituency, was staying in touch with the real world, but it also brought me the greatest satisfaction. The distance between Valemount at the southeastern extremity of my riding, near the border with Alberta, and Lower Post on the Alaska Highway at the border with Yukon, is approximately 1,800 kilometres. Given the remoteness and the special needs of the people along the highways and the small settlements in between, I felt obliged to be in personal contact as often as possible—at least once a year.

I had one advantage. Unlike large, northern constituencies in other parts of the country, mine was readily accessible by air, thanks to one of the most ambitious projects ever built to defend North America against foreign invasion. As much as a year before the declaration of war with Japan in December 1941, Japan was regarded as a potentially serious military threat to the United States, prompting President Franklin D. Roosevelt to join Canada in the building of a number of airstrips at 100-mile intervals between Edmonton and Fairbanks, Alaska. The move was intended to allow aircraft and supplies to be delivered to Alaska in the event of an invasion.

In addition, after Pearl Harbor, the U.S. Army Corps of Engineers was ordered to build a land bridge along the same route. Construction of the highway that was to link Dawson Creek with Fairbanks, a distance of about 1,550 miles, began early in 1942. The Canadian government had agreed to turn over whatever right of way was chosen along the route. The arrangement was that six months after the end of the war, the assets would be turned over to Canada, providing, however, that the new road be upgraded and maintained as a permanent link between Alaska and the lower 49 states.

It was not a good bargain. The road was built in less than nine months and, at the end of the war, it was not much more than a single-lane trail through some of the most rugged northern wilderness. It appears Prime Minister Mackenzie King was not at all in a hurry to accept the "generous" gift and the obligations that went with it. Even today, there are still people living in the area, suffering from the benign neglect of either the provincial or federal governments, who think it's a shame that he did.

In any event, King had no choice but to eventually allow our own military take possession of the "highway" and begin upgrading it for civilian use. It was not until 1964 that the project was transferred to the authority of the department of Public Works. Aside from the federal involvement with the Trans-Canada Highway and the ferry systems on the east coast, the Alaska Highway was the only major road system operated and maintained by Public Works Canada. It was also a major headache for the member of

During a parliamentary recess, the Oberles would hit the road in their motorhome or ride in local parades.

Parliament who cared for the residents and business establishments along the route.

Fort St. John, its history dating back to the establishment of a trading post in 1806, was nothing more than a small farm community dependent on a ferry service across the Peace River for its connection to the outside world. It can be argued that Fort Nelson, Watson Lake, and Whitehorse, as well as Fort St. John and today's modern commercial establishments along the route, owe their existence to the highway and the airports, some of which were retained and upgraded to accommodate modern commercial equipment.

Every year during Parliament's summer recess, Joan and I would crank up our motorhome and set out on a working holiday along the road that has since become one of North America's major tourist destinations. Telephone services along the route were chronically poor or non-existent. In order to alert our many friends, and to underline the importance of the persons involved in the mission, Gudrun and her staff in the Ottawa office made it standard practice to use the local radio stations' twice-daily information service.

"The next message is for our member of Parliament, who has left Fort St. John on his way to Fort Nelson and Watson Lake: Please call your Ottawa office for an urgent message as soon as possible," the announcer would say, giving everyone along the way the signal to load up their list of complaints. These would be about everything from poor postal service to the telephone system, with hazardous road conditions usually topping the list. In fact, the announcements were always welcomed, because they were also the signal for the works department headquartered in Fort Nelson to hurriedly dispatch maintenance equipment to spare themselves the wrath of the federal minister of Public Works, who would otherwise find himself strapped to the hot seat during Question Period in Parliament after my return to Ottawa.

Once or twice it was discovered that some enterprising locals, totally at their wit's end, had initiated the message themselves, hoping for the same results, even though I was nowhere near the vicinity.

We fondly remember these trips, particularly during the times when one (or more) of the children was able to accompany us. Of course, we had to put up with a torrent of complaints from constituents at every stop, but it was always tempered with a lot of good friendly advice and generous hospitality. At the end of every day we usually managed to park our humble abode on wheels beside a mountain stream, strategically positioned to reveal the optimum view through the picture window. Can there be anything more precious than that, and the smell of a freshly caught brook trout frying over an open campfire, in the best place on God's green earth?

I've mentioned the complaints, but in fairness to the government, and despite Trudeau's assertion that MPs are nobodies 50 feet away from the Hill, most of the ministers required their departments to give top priority to members' inquiries on behalf of their constituents. As well, I was surprised at how quickly people in the highest offices of the private sector invariably complied with requests coming from members of Parliament. For people in the rural and more remote areas of the country, their members of Parliament often provided the only recourse or protection against the bungling of either government or corporate bureaucracies. Given the desperate economic situation at times when jobs were scarce and unemployment had reached levels not registered since the Great Depression, the job could be extremely stressful. Coupled with periodic drought and other weather-related calamities, the impact on farmers in the Peace River area was particularly devastating.

On many occasions I found myself sitting across the kitchen table from a teary-eyed farm family in absolute despair, facing foreclosure on a property that had been carved out of the wilderness and in which they had invested not just their own lifetime of work, but all the hopes and dreams of their families' two previous generations. Not only would they be denied access to unemployment insurance, they would be forced from their homes because, in most cases, it was considered an integral part of the farm property, which was mortgaged to the bank or the government-sponsored Farm Credit Corporation. Only someone with direct experience of such situations could possibly comprehend the devastating impact on the lives of the people and the depth of their despair.

Many times I felt justified in appealing directly to the presidents of the largest banks for some period of grace until the government could be persuaded to deal with the crisis. I derived great pleasure and immense satisfaction from successfully intervening on behalf of some of my constituents who, due to no fault of their own, had got themselves caught in such desperate straits.

Other predicaments cropped up as well, where an intervention from a member of Parliament proved to be the last resort in dealing with often bizarre situations. In one case, I helped out a farmer whose barn had been demolished by a Greyhound bus veering off an icy road. The farmer had wrangled for two years with the insurance company and only had a lawyer's bill to show as the result. I called the CEO of the bus company who, to his credit, committed whatever it would take to restore the farmer's property.

Another time it required a direct call to our High Commissioner in Delhi, India, and my personal guarantee of the funds required to bail out the 19-year-old son of a local family after he had been jailed for suspected drug-related offences.

Then there was the case of the lost body. In desperation, one of my Prince George constituents, who had just lost her husband, called me in Ottawa (at 2 a.m. Ottawa time) to seek my intervention. She was frantically searching for her husband's remains, which had been shipped by air from Prince George to his hometown in Saskatchewan, where he had willed to be interred. The casket had not yet arrived at its destination, and any effort to trace the wayward remains residing in it was fruitless. The funeral service was scheduled for 10:30 the following morning.

André Gauthier, a good, old friend and a VP of Air Canada, who had been introduced to me by Louise Hayes and Gene Rheaume, was less than amused at having his sleep interrupted at such an ungodly hour, but he offered to make some inquiries. He called me several times during the rest of the night, perhaps more to get even than to keep me abreast of the progress he was making. His last call came in at 7:30 a.m.

"Look," he said, "it will take the contents of at least a bottle of the finest whisky, the brand with which you are familiar, and all the time the two of us will need to drink it, to fill you in on the details of what has happened. Let's just say that, even as we speak, the coffin containing your deceased friend is leaving Calgary on a special flight to its intended destination. My only worry now is that if you look after your living constituents as well as you do your dead ones, I'll have to put up with you here in Ottawa for a long time to come." Indeed, it would have been very difficult for anyone to lose an election with the reputation I was building up of being able to walk on water.

Incidentally, some time later, André did fill me in on the details of the lost coffin. However, the story did not lend itself to relaying to the bereaved family. The sensitive cargo, as it turned out, had to be transferred to another airline in Calgary. In the process, some of the boys among the freight handlers decided to engage in a little fun toward the end of a boring shift by opening the lid of the coffin and slightly rearranging the contents. Their unsuspecting colleagues later found the mysterious traveller in a dark corner of the freight shed, propped up in a sitting position with what looked like the kind of grin one would wear after cheating a Saskatchewan undertaker out of his job. For the bereaved back in Saskatchewan. there was little to smile about. Since the traveller had missed the first connection to his final resting place, the victims of the prank had decided to get even by delaying him and his coffin past the time of the next day's flight as well.

Not all such encounters and interventions had a happy ending. There were times when the only way I could deal with my own frustration and show my constituents how mightily I had laboured on their behalf was by competing for a spot during Question Period and attacking the minister responsible, shellacking him for the insensitivity and tardiness of his officials and burdening him with the blame.

CHAPTER 11

Rewards and Costs

I remember those happy days and often wish I could speak into the ears of the dead the gratitude which was due to them in life and so ill-returned.

—Gwyn Thomas

As we soon discovered, politics—at least the way I intended to practise it—is not a career for anyone who values being close to his or her family. Edmund Burke, the 18th-century British politician, told his electors in Bristol that "your representative owes you, not his industry only, but his judgement; and he betrays instead of serving you if he sacrifices it to your opinion." He lost his next election, but his truth nevertheless served as a guide for my own conduct as an elected representative.

The regular sittings in the House at the time were arranged to fit within a five-day week, from 10 in the morning to 11 at night. Only on the rarest occasion was there enough time to spend an hour at home for supper or to skip the odd weekend of travel back to the constituency. During the summer recess members were expected to be fully engaged in their constituency work. Considering the distance from Ottawa and the limited budget allocated for travel at the time, this imposed an additional hardship on those of us from the west coast. In my particular case, it meant flying either to Prince George or Fort St. John, where Joan would pick me up and act as chauffeur and personal assistant.

It should come as no surprise to anyone that all too many of our members of Parliament, once elected, soon find themselves having to choose between the obligations inherent in their oath to the office, and their marriage and family. All too often, it is the latter that is sacrificed.

Joan and I both treasure our privacy. She in particular found living in a glass bowl under constant public scrutiny most uncomfortable. Our ability to adjust and cope with the new reality was tested almost immediately.

Rumours spread that I had cunningly arranged for her to be on the public payroll as well. Challenged on that issue during a live interview by an overly aggressive reporter, I was able to dispel any concern my frugal constituents may have had in this regard by telling them that the pleasure she may have derived from sleeping with the boss, now only on rare occasions, was the only remuneration listed in her contract for employment.

Joan's first visit to Ottawa coincided with the Governor General's ball, which opens each parliamentary session. Had it not been for her past ex-

posure to some of the most horrific and tumultuous experiences life can offer, she might have found the whole affair altogether too overwhelming and too intimidating. But our self-confidence, reinforced by the success we had scored as a team, led us to believe that as long as we were together, there was not a mountain on earth too high for us to conquer.

In fact, Joan, who had learned sewing and fashion design from her mother, had enough faith in her ability and enough aversion to frivolous spending to decide she would design and sew the gown for the occasion herself.

Frank and Joan shine at one of Ottawa's many formal events.

We made good use of the precious hours leading up to the event. In no time at all, she had transformed my sparse little abode into a cozy little love nest, which, for the time being at least, became an insulated haven where we could be oblivious to the outside world. The ill-equipped kitchenette yielded the very finest of her special culinary delights, for which she would later become famous in Ottawa.

Several years earlier, our RCMP friend, Henry Hryciw, and I had fallen victim to the blandishments of a fast-talking fur salesman travelling the hinterland to sell his wares.

"Is there any reason," he had demanded, while giving us his sales pitch over a cup of coffee in the showroom of the new garage, "why ladies as refined and sophisticated as the two you have the good fortune to have as your wives, should not feel the urge on occasion to dress according to their status and in a manner that is both fashionable and suitable to the climate in this area?" One reason that came to my mind immediately, but that I lacked the courage to express, was the price. In the end, with the help of our friend from the bright lights, we concluded that our wives were indeed deserving, and after all was said and done, we managed to negotiate a deal neither of us could refuse.

Joan's and Etta's closets became the domiciles of two of the finest quality "centre-back muskrat" jackets money could buy. Needless to say, therefore, I felt somewhat miffed when Joan liberated from her luggage a mink stole to serve as the main feature of the attire she had assembled for the ball.

"I'm sorry," she told me, "Helen Moore and Beverly insisted that I wear it. They said it's the first impression that's important and they did not want us to leave behind any doubt about the good taste and refined culture of the people we came to represent."

No need for anyone to know that the mink, certainly in this specimen's state of health, was probably the only one to be found anywhere within a 200-mile radius of Chetwynd, nor that on a previous occasion—as we discovered much later—it had adorned the shoulders of another prominent Canadian at the same venue. Again at the urging of its owner, Helen Moore, it had graced the person of Margaret (Ma) Murray, when her husband, George, was elected to Parliament in 1949 and had summoned her to be presented to Governor General Field Marshal the Viscount Alexander of Tunis and Prime Minister St. Laurent, both of whom she had often demonized in the *Alaska Highway News*—the former for being British, and the latter for being French, and a "damned Liberal," like her husband.

In these circles it is considered an unpardonable sin for ladies to wear the same dress on more than one occasion or, even worse, to wear something either identical to someone else's, or handed down. Fortunately for Joan, neither Roland Michener, the Governor General at the time, nor his spouse, nor Prime Minister Pierre Elliot Trudeau recognized the offending mink that became the most prominent feature of Joan's attire as it made its way past the receiving line at the most prestigious event of that year's Ottawa social season.

How proud I was of her. Her dress elicited several inquiries as to its origin, given that no one had seen anything matching it in quality and masterful design outside the fashion capitals of New York or Paris.

The Germans have a saying that "*Kleider machen Leute*, [Clothes make the lady]," but Joan had no need for a pretentious wardrobe to be recognized for the lady she was. Nor did she waste much time figuring out who among the crowd were the pretenders and who were the ones deserving of the respect people generally show for the spouses of their elected representatives. Neither of us was ever overly impressed with the pomp and ceremonial theatre of the church in which we had grown up, nor did we therefore regard the ancient rituals surrounding the daily proceedings within the precincts of Parliament Hill in Ottawa as anything more than a reminder of the proud history of British parliamentary tradition and a powerful magnet for tourists from all over the world.

To anchor one's faith in the church or one's loyalty to the state in such rituals means to accept without question and have a slavish devotion to the principles and the myth they are intended to celebrate. It was not a given for either Joan or me to accept as absolute truth anything that has no basis in logic or is shrouded in mystery. To do so, a person must confine their thought processes and narrow their range of facts, the historic basis of which may well be in doubt, and should therefore be examined as to the relevance to today's world. It may be that the Catholic Church has managed to maintain its archaic ties to another age, but Edmund Burke's 18th-century Britain could well be in another galaxy when compared to our modern-day society that has adopted Pierre Trudeau's Charter of Rights. It is good and perhaps even essential to have faith, but it must be tempered with a healthy degree of skepticism and curiosity, without which the world would be starved for new knowledge, ideas, and progress.

Joan and I did not let ourselves be intimidated by the surroundings and the peculiar customs we now had to navigate. We found, in fact, that despite our humble beginnings, we were more conversant in the art of proper etiquette than many who, for example, had perhaps never learned the proper use of both hands in manipulating dinner table implements.

On one occasion, at a banquet in honour of her Majesty the Queen, I couldn't help but observe Joe Clark, our prime minister at the time, clumsily trying to tame a Cornish hen on his dinner plate that was making repeated attempts to escape his custody to the relative safety of the lap of Her Majesty, who was sitting next to him. If Her Majesty was fazed by the experience, she certainly didn't show it. No doubt both she and the Duke have been exposed on many occasions to similar or equally delicate situations and have learned to deal with them with grace and humour.

In fact, his Royal Highness, the Duke of Edinburgh, delights in confessing to an embarrassing etiquette lapse of his own when, during a visit to Whitehorse at a state dinner catered by the ladies' auxiliary of the local branch of the Royal Canadian Legion, he unwittingly offended local custom in the use of table implements.

In his defence, he might justifiably have assumed that the good ladies had undergone the customary pre-event training regarding the rules and etiquette of the royal household, which stipulate that at the end of each course one politely deposits any implements assigned to the various stages of the meal on the empty plate. However, in this instance, Madam President, who had taken on the critical role of serving the head-table guests herself, decided after the main course to gracefully remove the fork so deposited and place it back on the table, not to the left side of his place setting, but to the right. The Duke, trying to be helpful as always, once again picked up the fork to put it back on the plate. Not to be dissuaded, the good lady again picked up the offending object and planted it, this time more firmly, back on the table.

"Keep the fork, Duke," she offered with pride. "We got some pie coming."

Most of the encounters on the social scene took place at stand-up cocktail parties. I found them to be a sort of endurance test. For ladies wearing high heels as part of the "uniform," they were nothing less than torture. No great challenge to anyone's intellect here. According to the rules, the room must be filled to absolute capacity, presumably to prevent any of the guests not entirely familiar with their alcohol saturation limits from hitting the floor in a free fall. Everyone is required to speak at once, making it impossible to discern what is being said. One soon acquires the art of making just the right facial expression, occasionally either shaking or nodding one's head, to prevent the derailment of any train of thought being expressed by anyone trying to make a point.

The first session of the 29th Parliament, which lasted until the end of June 1974, went by in a flash. Given the delicate balance in the House, everyone was expected to stay close to the scene lest there be an opportunity to defeat the government on a surprise vote. For new members, it was equally important to be seen in the constituency as often as humanly possible so as to solidify their mandate, cultivate additional support, and assure readiness for another election, which everyone expected within a year.

For most of the time, any contact with the rest of my family was by telephone only. It soon became apparent that the practice followed by most of my colleagues of commuting between the office and home would not work in our situation for any length of time. By the end of the summer we started making plans to move the family to Ottawa so that we would have at least some time together. Neither option would ever be totally satisfactory, since I would still have to divide my time between the constituency and the office in Ottawa.

Ursula was still enrolled as a student at the University of British Columbia and living in residence, while Isabell was in her last year of high school in Chetwynd. Nevertheless, we decided on the move in the fall of 1973, in time to enrol Frank and Peter in an Ottawa school.

First, though, we had to tie up some loose ends. The sale of the business's real estate to Imperial Oil had been approved. Well aware of the risks and the uncertainty of the political situation, we attempted to maintain as many of our other ties with Chetwynd as we could.

Conscious of certain moral obligations we felt toward the people who had helped us and given us their loyalty in our businesses over the years, we arranged to turn most of the inventory and assets over to them, except those not directly tied to franchise. In return, we expected Ted Hauck and Ray Schreiber, our ranch manager, to look after whatever assets we retained for ourselves at the ranch. Both were also offered shares of the proceeds that the management of these assets would yield.

The arrangement was not entirely unselfish on our part in that it helped us to stay attached to the place that had become central to our dreams for the future. It would provide us with security for our declining years and, in the old tradition of our ancestors, afford our family a home base. Sure, it might only be just that, a dream. We could already sense that our children, and certainly our grandchildren, would not be nearly as encumbered by such ancestral hang-ups. The Industrial Revolution served to liberate western civilization from the yoke of subsistence farming, when a large family and ownership of sufficient land to sustain it was the only security measure for old age. Today's technological revolution will shift the paradigms even further, making it irrelevant to own property other than, perhaps, one's own home. But the ranch had given us the psychological freedom to invest our energies and vigour in yet another, entirely different, career.

We also hung onto our house in Chetwynd, renting it out to Andy Teslyk, the new village clerk, and his family. It was painful to part with our cabin at Moberly Lake and to say goodbye to King, who had proven himself such a loyal and trustworthy member of the family. The crew at the garage, which was after all his real home, promised to take good care of him. When it came to moving our children, we discovered, sadly, that they were not nearly as adventurous as their parents had been at their age. It took all our powers of persuasion to help them overcome their reservations about the move.

Louise Hayes helped us find an apartment in her own neighbourhood on Monterey Drive in Nepean, just outside Ottawa, for Joan and the male contingent of the family to settle in. Peter and Frank Jr. enrolled in Nepean's Sir Robert Borden High School, while Isabell embarked on her post-graduation trip to spend the summer with family in Germany. Only now did I realize how much I had missed them all and how sad it was to think that our children were growing up and the time when we could always be together had passed.

I should confess that, despite my early discovery of the drawbacks of my new profession, I did allow myself to take some pleasure in the adulation and notoriety I received, at least from some quarters.

Six months after my election, we acted on a promise Joan had made on our behalf to her sister, Cilli, that we would attend her son Gerhard's wedding in Forchheim, taking advantage of the concession afforded all members of Parliament to make use of any surplus space on military transport planes to visit our troops stationed abroad. Our keepers of the peace as far away as Cyprus could thus boast more regular contact with their representatives in Ottawa than the average citizen living two blocks away from Parliament Hill.

However, I was more inclined to visit our armed forces attached to NATO in Europe, whose contingent was stationed in the Black Forest in Lahr, near Baden Baden. Despite the time constraints, Denise managed to book us some surplus space on a military flight that would take us from Ottawa to Forchheim in much less time than it took to get to Chetwynd.

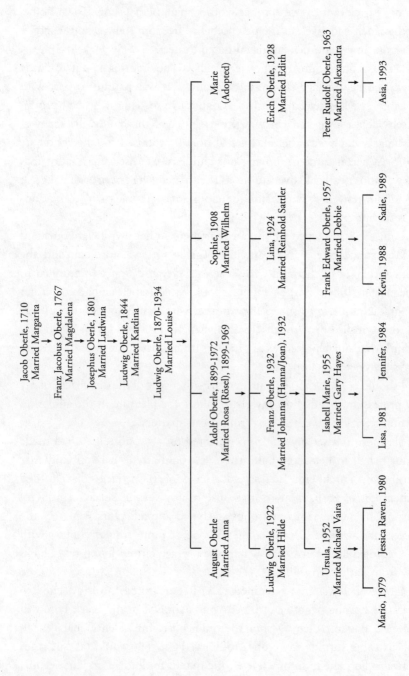

Jacob Oberle, 1710
Married Margarita

Franz Jacobus Oberle, 1767
Married Magdalena

Josephus Oberle, 1801
Married Ludwina

Ludwig Oberle, 1844
Married Kardina

Ludwig Oberle, 1870-1934
Married Louise

Marie
(Adopted)

Sophie, 1908
Married Wilhelm

Erich Oberle, 1928
Married Edith

Lina, 1924
Married Reinhold Sattler

Peter Rudolf Oberle, 1963
Married Alexandra

Frank Edward Oberle, 1957
Married Debbie

Asia, 1993

Kevin, 1988   Sadie, 1989

Adolf Oberle, 1899-1972
Married Rosa (Rösel), 1899-1969

Franz Oberle, 1932
Married Johanna (Hanna/Joan), 1932

Isabell Marie, 1955
Married Gary Hayes

Lisa, 1981   Jennifer, 1984

August Oberle
Married Anna

Ludwig Oberle, 1922
Married Hilde

Ursula, 1952
Married Michael Vaira

Mario, 1979   Jessica Raven, 1980

Brother Erich, now a senior executive with the *Badische Neueste Nachrichten*, the dominant regional tabloid, was bubbling over with excitement when he picked us up at the air base in Lahr. My election to Parliament had made front-page news, and the news of our first homecoming after the event had spread like wildfire throughout Forchheim. The mayor had contacted Erich to inform him that the town council had voted to hold a reception at city hall in my honour and to extend an invitation to the rest of Joan's family and my family. Our former classmates had also requested a date for a reunion, and dozens of people had put in requests for meetings with us.

What a homecoming it turned out to be. Dad, sister Lina, and the rest of the family were already there when Joan and I arrived at the *Rathaus* [City Hall], to be greeted by the mayor and his council. We were ushered into the *Bürgersaal* [Hall of Honour], a spacious reception hall just one floor above the jail I had visited briefly 27 years earlier—and right next door to the room where I had been interrogated about Uncle Otto's hidden motorcycle by the local police authority in the person of the intrepid Ernst Meier.

The mayor's greeting was delivered in the typically cultured High German but my response, framed in the colourful dialect of our region, showed that we were still firmly attached to our roots and won us the praise and the hearts of the good burghers in attendance.

Ernst Heil, Mayor of Forchheim, presents Frank with a pictorial memento of Forchheim on April 25, 1973.

Both of us were showered with flowers and gifts, but I found my greatest reward and satisfaction in sharing the occasion with my Dad, whose eyes reflected such pride. Tall and erect, with his chin held high, he followed the proceedings, vindicated at last. Not one among our relatives, who had treated us so shabbily at times in the past, had ever received such high honour and recognition; none had reason to be more proud of their children. There was no reference to my mother's maiden name, Leibold, by which we had always been known during my childhood because Dad was an immigrant from the neighbouring village of Mörsch. The invitation was simply addressed to Adolf Oberle, the honour of whose presence the mayor himself had requested.

It was hopeless for us to try and take a stroll through the familiar streets. When we attempted it, we were stopped along the way and surrounded by dozens of people wanting to shake our hands and wish us well. As his contribution to the festivities, my old friend Kneisel the butcher, by now a successful restaurateur, had laid in a mountain of my favourite sausage at Berta's, as usual.

It would have been nice to bask in the glory for some time longer but duty called. On the way back to the air base, as Erich's car took us by the bus station in front of the Leibold store, I couldn't help but be reminded of the scene just 22 years earlier when I said my goodbyes and set out on my adventure. In none of our wildest dreams could Joan and I have come anywhere close to predicting what destiny held in store for us.

Revolutionary advances in modern transportation technology had made the world a much smaller place and goodbyes no longer seemed as final. Sadly, in Dad's case, this one did turn out to be the last.

Erich and his friend and neighbour, Dr. Miller, had accepted my invitation for a fishing expedition to the west coast of Canada the following year, which turned out to be the first of many memorable visits and great adventures we shared together. Just before they left, Dad had been admitted to hospital to deal with a recurring stomach ailment. On his way back, Erich and his friend stopped over in Ottawa and they were with us when we received word of Dad's passing on August 1, 1974. A good, old friend at Air Canada managed to free up a seat for me on Erich's flight to attend the funeral, although he couldn't prevent them from losing my luggage on the way.

What a pitiful sight I must have been, standing by the grave, wearing an ill-fitting black suit borrowed from Erich, exhausted from jet lag, and unable to contain my emotions. The men's choir to which Dad had belonged all of his adult life was there to pay tribute to him, as were dozens of his former colleagues at work and hundreds of people who simply wanted to pay their last respects to an honourable true gentleman.

It was the first of several funerals Joan and I had to attend. Berta was mercifully called home a few years later, as was Emil shortly thereafter. Joan had been with me during a particularly gruelling trip when we received word that Reini, sister Lina's husband, who had been suffering for some time from throat cancer, had passed away. As usual, Gudrun managed to secure two seats for us on an overnight military transport plane to Lahr in the Black Forest, getting us there just in time for the funeral.

The immediate family, as is the custom in Mörsch, Forchheim's neighbouring town, occupies a place of honour near the coffin at the front of the cemetery's chapel, as people gather to pay their last respects. Reini had been a long-time active member of the soccer club, the voluntary fire brigade, and numerous other fraternities and so the procession must have lasted close to two hours. In such situations, where private thoughts and prayers are best experienced with closed eyes, it requires a special kind of skill to keep one's head erect and refrain from snoring. Here, too, Joan and I worked as a team. Each time one of us dozed off, the other used an elbow to restore consciousness. When the time finally came for the priest to commence his service, Joan tugged on my sleeve to point out to me that he was speaking German, as if the logic had escaped her that it is customary in Germany for priests to use that language.

When we reflected on the lives of those who had been so close to us and whose untimely death we were left to mourn, we managed to draw some comfort from the fact that all had come to visit us in Canada. They had shared with us some of the good times that we were given to enjoy together and to dispel some of the lingering bitter memories of another time.

Joan, however, never quite got over losing her sister, Cilli, who died at 56 years of age in 1983. It was during a routine—and in her family doctor's opinion, unnecessary—exploration of her heart by means of an angiogram at a prestigious specialty clinic and it resulted in a cerebral aneurysm from which she did not recover. The two had a bond that was forged by experiences and secrets they shared about events too horrific to recall, and by the sacrifices they were forced to make in helping get the family through the war and helping their mother attain God's grace by inspiring and preparing her son to His service.

Cilli was the only anchor Joan had to her past. When she died, a part of Joan died with her. When Leo, Cilli's husband, rushed into a new relationship perhaps a bit too soon, not even Rudi could prevent Joan from losing interest in anything that connected her to her youth and childhood.

Nor did her faith help her find comfort after losing the only intimate friend she ever had. The circumstances of Cilli's death only added to the lingering pain Joan had brought with her to the New World.

It was almost a year after her move to Ottawa before Joan accompanied me for the first time on a trip back to Chetwynd. There were just too many memories and too many good friends that she would find hard to say goodbye to again. As we drove up to the garage and service station we spotted King at his customary place next door at the Dairy Dream, not wasting too much energy moving his head, just rolling his eyes in a radius of 210 degrees to spot the next sucker that might spring for an ice cream cone.

Joan was certain that he would remember her, so she decided to stay in the car while I paid a short visit to Marshall and the staff at the garage. But our loyal old friend had a sixth sense as good as his nose. Even though we got away without a tearful reunion, he knew we were in town and decided to catch up to us. In no time at all he was scratching and throwing himself against the front door of the old house, making his presence known. When Ann Teslyk, our tenant, inquired about the cause of the commotion, he invaded his old domain and cleared out the little dog that had made its home there instead. Upstairs and downstairs he ran, exploring every nook and cranny until finally he decided to position himself at the foot of our bed, where he was sure we would find him. It was only with great difficulty that Marshall Peters, who had been summoned to help, was able to extricate him from the scene.

Had we abandoned one of the kids to an orphanage, we could not have felt worse. I can't help but think that when it comes to loyalty and love, most of us humans could learn a lot from our four-legged friends.

The next time I visited Chetwynd was at the request of Father Jungbluth. Our friends at the village office were threatening the people of Moccasin Flats with foreclosure of their community centre unless they cleared up the taxes that had been accumulating for several years. Dr. Lennox, Father

Jungbluth, and I attended a meeting of the council, making a reasonable argument in favour of a "tax-free" status for the facility. We pointed to the fact that, like all of the local churches and most of the other community infrastructure, the facility was built almost entirely with volunteer labour. Surely the council could agree that the community centre—which was used entirely for activities relating to social, cultural, and educational purposes, none of which produced any commercial benefits—should be classified for municipal tax purposes in the same way.

In retrospect, it might have been better had I not been part of the delegation. Even though none of the councillors presented a challenge to the proposition, I could sense that some of them at least could see it as a way to get even for the defeat they had suffered at my hands in opposing the Moccasin Flats project in the first place. We were discharged with the promise that the matter would be taken under advisement and that we would be informed of their decision in due course.

It took them another year before they found the courage to render their decision. The manner in which it was communicated allowed for no recourse or further appeal. Without informing anyone, they simply hired a contractor to raise the structure from its foundation and move it from its original location to the new airstrip, not more than 400 metres away, where it has served as the terminal of the Chetwynd Municipal Airport ever since.

The people of Chetwynd should consider themselves fortunate in at least two respects. First, I know of no other town that has benefitted as much from the charity of some of its poorest citizens. Second, I know of no group of people other than my friends at Moccasin Flats that would have reacted to such blatant discrimination, such insolence and injustice, by simply turning the other cheek.

In the end, fate prevented Joan and I from realizing the dreams we had build around Chetwynd and the ranch in the Pine Valley, with its spectacular natural surroundings, as the place to which to retreat in our declining years to enjoy the serenity, comfort, and security for which we had striven so hard. When the time came beyond which it would have been senseless to hang on any longer, the decision to sell the property was at least made less painful by the knowledge that, despite the many friends we would leave behind in Chetwynd, we could hardly be comfortable and secure living among people who had used their positions of power and privilege in such an utterly callous manner and whose most powerful instinct was to attack and punish the most vulnerable and defenceless among us.

Joan and I were not to be denied some personal satisfaction for having committed so much of our energy and sacrificing so many of our friends over our involvement with the Moccasin flats project. Years later, as it happened, we were in a line-up at a check-in counter at the Vancouver airport when Joan, obviously in distress, drew my attention to the fact that we had been followed by an RCMP officer, who now appeared to be making his way in our direction.

"Hi, Mrs. and Mr. Oberle," he said, as Joan manoeuvred herself into a position behind my back. "I don't suppose you would remember me. I'm Noel Stoney from Chetwynd, from Moccasin Flats. How have you been keeping?"

Well, considering the odds that we would have occasion to meet and compliment each other on what we had accomplished in life, given our pasts, we had been keeping very well indeed.

I can only speculate on the rush of emotion Joan must have had to wrestle with at the time. It wasn't until we were comfortably settled in our seats on our flight back to Ottawa that she took my hand and confessed through her tears that this incident alone was worth all the sacrifices we'd made in support of our Native friends and neighbours.

Noel's case was not an isolated one. Most of our Moccasin Flats children graduated from high school. Several others managed to attend college and graduate to pursue other professional careers.

CHAPTER 12

Political Fortunes Won and Lost

*The majority, being satisfied with the ways of mankind as they now are
(for it is they who make them what they are), cannot comprehend why
those ways should not be good enough for everybody.*

—John Stuart Mill

As was widely expected, the Liberal government of Pierre Elliott Trudeau
lost a non-confidence motion in June 1974, 18 months into its mandate,
and an election was called. The economy was in shambles. Inflation
was spiralling out of control, forcing interest rates to exceed 20 percent.
Expectations were also high that the Progressive Conservative Party would
handily defeat the governing Liberals in the general election that was set for
July 8, 1974.

No amount of deficit spending by the government seemed enough to
arrest the downward economic trends. Drastic measures were called for, but
once again Canadians, particularly in the central provinces, allowed themselves
to be seduced by the old master. Trudeau attacked Bob Stanfield's proposal
for a 90-day freeze on wages and prices followed by a somewhat longer period
of minor adjustments to allow for relief in certain circumstances. He called
it a draconian measure that was neither necessary nor justifiable in terms of
the erosion of investor confidence and the deleterious effects it would have on
the economy generally. Stanfield, despite his reputation as a competent leader
worthy of trust, was no match for the more charismatic old pro.

The so-called "natural governing party of Canada" obviously derived
most of its strength from the ignorance and complacency of the Canadian
electorate. People don't like their politicians to confront them with bad
news, even if it happens to be the truth. Liberals, I discovered over the years,

Bob Checkley, a volunteer worker, and Lee Acott working on the 1974 election.

understand that fact much better and tailor their policy manuals accordingly. On July 8, instead of accepting the inevitable, the voters in the industrial heartland of the country not only returned them to power, but gave them a healthy majority to boot.

In fairness, most of the electorate in the western provinces voted heavily in our favour. I won my second election victory by a margin of over 5,000 votes against Allan Bate, a highly regarded Prince George lawyer and very popular candidate representing the Liberal Party. Wendell Smith, the Social Credit candidate, received less than 5 percent of the 40,000 ballots cast. He was the local undertaker and funeral director, and some of my campaign workers decided that his otherwise dull campaign effort could benefit from an injection of a bit of humour, so they set about embellishing the signs his supporters had put up throughout the city, adding the slogan, "I'll be the last to let you down."

Of the 23 federal ridings in British Columbia, Conservatives were elected in 13. Alberta recorded a clean sweep for the Conservatives in all of 19 federal constituencies. But they would be punished severely for it. The Liberal government's response to the so-called energy crisis in the mid-'70s was the National Energy Program which, by some estimates, pilfered 6 billion dollars from the Alberta treasury. With the creation of Petro-Canada, the national oil company that was given a majority stake in all leases on federal lands, and the Foreign Investment Review Agency, established in 1975, Canada experienced a mass exodus of capital, compounding an already critical fiscal situation. It would have been difficult to find anyone in Alberta who would ever again contemplate voting Liberal for the rest of their lives.

Stumping for votes in Prince George–Peace River, I spoke out on the issue of wage-and-price controls. I boldly predicted throughout the election campaign that, regardless of how vehemently the opponents of what we had proposed ridiculed it, should it be our misfortune to suffer them for another four years, they would have no option but to implement our program.

In fact, any delay in doing so would be disastrous. As it turned out, to save face, the new government wasted another 18 months to swallow their pride and put in place wage-and-price controls, causing more small businesses to go bankrupt, eroding even further the meagre savings of people on fixed incomes, and driving thousands of families from the homes in which they had invested their hard-earned life's savings and dreams.

When the measure finally passed through Parliament on October 14, 1975, things had become so desperate that people grasping at straws had forgotten what happened during the election and actually gave the government credit for their far-sightedness and courage in finally tackling the problem.

Another result of the Conservative defeat was a change in our leadership. After the 1974 general election, the majority of caucus members and the supporters of the party generally came to the conclusion that despite the virtues attributed to Bob Stanfield and the respect he had earned for his style of leadership, Canadians would never bring themselves to accept him as their prime minister. The matter was openly discussed at a regular caucus meeting. Stanfield himself raised the issue; lamenting the fact that if the media ever discovered him walking across the Ottawa River they would berate him for not being able to swim. One of his more prominent "loyal" followers suggested that he take up bungee jumping as a means to boost his popularity. The man who was referred to by some as "the best prime minister the country never had" resigned and asked the party to choose a new leader.

If one were to compare politics with hockey, the contest for leadership of a political party would be the annual playoff for the Stanley Cup. Given the near dictatorial powers our system bestows on the prime minister, the stakes during a leadership contest are very high. To support the wrong candidate or even to maintain a position of neutrality would mean being shut out from the inner circle of the new leader and to forgo any future claim to an elevated position in the hierarchy of the party.

The convention took place in February of 1976. If I found myself bored by the procedural debates in the House of Commons, I was even less interested in the no-doubt necessary but tedious and often mindless inter-party political wrangling. I soon discovered that no one, certainly not a party in power, paid even the slightest attention to the resolutions so painstakingly developed, debated, and finally agreed upon at local, regional, and national party conventions. As important as conventions most assuredly must be, if for no other reason than to make the party faithful feel involved and important, I found it difficult to participate in the mind-numbing debates, particularly those having to do with changing the constitution.

The leadership contest was another matter. I considered Claude Wagner, Brian Mulroney, and Paul Hellyer, in that order, as the three candidates with whom I felt most comfortable; Wagner, the MP for Saint-Hyacinthe-Bagot, was not only highly regarded in Quebec, he had earned himself a good reputation with the legal profession in the rest of the country. He ended up as my choice because he had the best chance not just of winning the prize, but also of adding enough party support from his province to take us over the top in another election.

However, the outcome of the 1976 convention could not have been more disappointing. Understandably, Hellyer's chances, as the former Liberal Minister of Defence who was infamous for his efforts to unify the Canadian Armed Forces and for crossing the floor to the Conservatives, were slim. Mulroney, on the other hand, had served as a member of the high-profile Quebec Commission of Inquiry into the Quebec construction industry (The Cliche Commission), and was well known and respected in Quebec. But even though he could also boast impressive business credentials, he had never held any elected position.

To have the prize go to Joe Clark instead is a testimonial to the madness of the process Canadian political parties have chosen to select their leaders.

Only 12 percent of the delegates supported Clark on the first ballot. Of all the contenders, Clark, in my opinion, was least qualified. I respected him for his courage, his energy, and his conviction, but considered him someone whose effort was targeted more at securing for himself a respectable position in the new leader's hierarchy than at the leadership itself. He was sincere and true to his convictions and beliefs, and was a thoroughly honest man. He had certain human qualities that earned my respect, but he was not a leader capable of inspiring a nation of people who had been put into a trance by the charisma and skill of one of the best leaders the country had ever produced.

Claude Wagner led on the first ballot, with Mulroney coming second. But in the end, the two candidates from Quebec split the vote from that province, allowing Clark to come up the middle. It took five ballots to decide the outcome which, for me, could not have been more unsatisfactory. Certainly to some degree, my dislike for the new leader stemmed from the old conspiracy to depose my idol John Diefenbaker, in which Clark was clearly identified as a significant player. For the legion of loyalists in our party and throughout the country it had spelled the end of an era.

Obviously, considering my lack of personal sympathy with Clark's position, it would be an understatement to say that I was nowhere near the new regime's inner circle. In fact, I would eventually join many of my friends and colleagues who were close to the edge of being cast into the outer darkness as rebels.

My suite of offices on the third floor of the West Block of the Parliament Buildings was immediately next to the meeting rooms assigned to the Progressive Conservative caucus. Cell phones were not yet in vogue, so it was not unusual for some of my colleagues to make use of our telephones rather than make their way back to their own offices. I was away in the riding when one day Joe Clark himself knocked on the door to ask Gudrun if it would be okay for him to make an urgent call. As she described the scene to me later, he was half-sitting, half-leaning against her desk, his mind obviously engaged in the phone conversation, but his eyes rolling around the room, presumably to survey the images that were adorning the walls, which reached up to a 10-foot-high ceiling. One of these images, quite prominently displayed next to one of the windows overlooking the Gatineau "mountains," was a reproduction of a cartoon that had previously been featured on the editorial page of the *Ottawa Citizen*. It showed our illustrious leader dressed in a Boy Scout uniform, his head sporting a propeller-driven beanie. He was observing a horde of pinstriped-suit-attired, briefcase-toting specimens hurriedly rushing by him to be absorbed by the distance.

"Here they go," the caption read, "and I must quickly follow for I'm their leader."

Poor Gudrun was sweating bullets. Following his wandering gaze, she had noticed it coming to rest in the general direction of the offending exhibit.

But his parting words were most polite and offered no critique of the decor. I did manage to allay any fears she might have had as to the repercussions that Clark's venture into my domain might produce. I assured her that it was unlikely that anyone fortunate enough to have feasted their eyes on the natural splendour of the Rocky Mountains, let alone as fortunate as Joe was to have grown up and lived in their shadow, would have been distracted by any ornaments on the office walls, given the alternative offered by the view through my window.

Whatever the case, Joe never mentioned the matter to me. Had he done so, I would surely remember, because it would have been the only conversation the two of us had in all the time he served as the leader of our party.

We went into the next election in 1979 with every reason to feel positive about our party's prospects. Joe Clark, while he may have had little more to offer than Bob Stanfield in terms of charisma, nevertheless managed to accurately assess the public's mood at the time and tailor our message to suit it. He also proved himself to be a formidable campaigner.

The election was called for May 22, 1979, and after the votes were in, Joe Clark was the 16th and, at 39, the youngest prime minister in the history of Canada. The results gave the party a minority government, with most of the seats in the western provinces and the Maritimes but, as was anticipated, we were left too short in Quebec and Ontario to form a majority.

My own riding had been reduced in size under the vote redistribution initiative in the '70s that created the riding of Prince George–Bulkley Valley. As a result, I had lost some of the area where, in the previous two elections, we had registered only marginal support. My traditional voting stronghold in the north remained constant, contributing to the comfortable 62 percent of the votes cast for me in Prince George–Peace River in 1979.

Quebec's support, always important, was particularly key. This was a time of Quebec nationalist resurgence. Montreal had hosted the Olympic games in 1976, the same year that brought the Parti Québécois to power under René Lévesque. A year later Bill 101, an act putting serious restrictions on the rights of anglophones to have their children attend English schools, passed through the Quebec legislature. Coupled with these draconian measures was the odious "sign law" and the "language of work" provisions that prompted several major corporation like Sun Life of Canada to move their headquarters from Montreal to Toronto.

The new leader of the Progressive Conservative Party and now prime minister, even less well known in Quebec than he was in the rest of the country, was not seen as counterbalance or guardian of the rights that some Quebecers were thus forced to surrender. Claude Wagner, whom he appointed Minister of External Affairs, appeared to show little interest or inclination to fill the gap or promote Clark's image in his province.

Prime Minster Clark, not overly blessed with humility, did not allow Wagner's lack of interest to get in the way of his ego or become a deterrent to his unbridled ambitions. He had won the leadership of the party with the support of only a few members of caucus. His leadership style, "my way or the doorway," did not endear him to the rest of us, certainly not to those who, like myself, were not labouring under any illusions of being called to the inner circle.

From the time of the election until Clark finally decided to recall Parliament on October 9, ordinary members of the newly elected Conservative caucus had to rely on the media for any official word from the Prime Minister's Office. Nor was there any invitation to submit thoughts or proposals for policy options the new government might wish to pursue.

When caucus was finally called to meet shortly before the opening of Parliament, the members engaged in the type of warfare Conservatives are best known for. They circled the wagons and began shooting toward the inside; the media was having a field day. Clark provided them with a rich menu of juicy tidbits that exposed his shortcomings as a leader and international statesman. Reporters observed the battles from the safety of the press gallery during the day, from whence they descended at night to finish off the wounded.

In November Trudeau announced he was resigning the leadership of the Liberal Party, but before a convention could be organized to replace him, disaster struck. On December 13, just two months into the session, our government was defeated on a motion of non-confidence because no one had bothered to secure the support of the Créditistes, a remnant Quebec offshoot of the western Social Credit Party, vital to carry the vote on our first budget. The six Créditiste members abstained, the NDP's non-confidence motion passed, and the country was forced into another election.

The issue in the election was Conservative Minister of Finance John Crosbie's proposal to increase the excise tax on gasoline by 18 cents a gallon, which the Liberals, of course, decried as a sure recipe for economic ruin. They couldn't believe their good fortune. Trudeau, perhaps reminded of his "greatness" by the generous tributes afforded him by his colleagues from all sides of the House of Commons and Canadians from across the country, and having survived a close call with dying from a laughing fit over what Joe Clark had offered up, rescinded his resignation and led his party back to another majority on February 18, 1980. Then, without missing a beat and before Canadians could awake to the reality of what they had done, they were treated to a replay of the 1974 wage-and-price controls deception. In a dazzling display of political gymnastics, Trudeau succeeded in convincing the masses that while a gasoline tax increase of 18 cents an imperial gallon would have been absolutely disastrous in January of 1980, an increase of more than a dollar just a few months later was just what the country needed to stave off disaster.

It came as no surprise to me at all that the Canadian people so promptly dismissed us just eight months after being elected. No doubt it didn't take them long to discover that Clark and the people he had surrounded himself with would be competing in the same philosophical arena the Liberals had been forced to vacate.

The constant bickering between the right- and left-wing factions sapped us of much of the strength that should have been channelled toward more productive causes. Moreover, it was the dominance of the left under

Frank at the Konrad Adenauer Foundation in Bonn on a fact-finding mission.

184

Joe Clark's leadership that was initially responsible for crowding out those in the Progressive Conservative party, mainly from the west, with a more traditional conservative bent, eventually forcing them to abandon the party altogether to work toward an alternative more acceptable to their own view of the world and the people in their regions. These disaffected souls became the core of the Reform Party under Preston Manning, who was able to take advantage of the situation by attracting most of our traditional western power base to his movement.

It was, in the Reformers' view, our tardiness to address the problems of the deficit and accumulated debt we inherited from our predecessors that allowed the pendulum of political trends swing toward the extremities of the far right. They considered our fiscal situation serious enough to urge upon the government drastic measures to reduce public spending, even if it meant defaulting on our commitments to the provinces to assist with their delivery of certain social programs under their jurisdiction, including health care and education, and the federal government's direct statutory obligation for programs such as unemployment insurance and old-age pensions.

There followed another long four years during which Trudeau, capitalizing on the civil war among Her Majesty's Loyal Opposition, gave Canadians their Charter of Rights and Freedoms. The Constitution Act, which includes the Charter, was passed by Parliament in 1982 and came into force on April 17 when, with all the appropriate pomp and circumstance, the Queen signed the repatriated constitution.

Joe Clark fully supported the social engineers at the helm of the Liberal Party in this effort. Captured by the notion that government can, and therefore must, guarantee delivery of social justice, he tolerated no dissent among his colleagues, some of whom, like myself, saw the role of government in a much different light.

In my view, a nation's character is shaped and defined through enlightened, charitable public attitudes. Morality is the product of faith, custom, culture, and tradition. No matter how virtuous and well intentioned a government might be, it seems naive to think that these are matters that lend themselves to enforcement through legislation. Edmund Burke said, "It is not what a lawyer tells me I may do, but what humanity, reason, and justice tell me I ought to do."

Government's main function, in my opinion, is not so much to guarantee rights, but to limit them. No right can ever be absolute; no freedom, even the freedom of speech, can be exercised totally without restraint. The individual cannot simply demand something that has not been earned. No one, in exercising his or her perceived right, should be allowed to exceed what society, as a whole, is willing to tolerate and accept. By charging the judiciary, as the Charter does, with the mandate to define the limits within which these new rights and freedoms can be enjoyed, the government has abdicated the most essential part of its responsibility.

Though it was clear that even some Liberal members could not bring themselves to vote in favour of the Charter when it was finally put to a vote in the Commons, Clark, well aware that the majority of our caucus had strong reservations about what was included in the bill, insisted on unanimous support from the Progressive Conservative caucus. Any dissent was considered an expression of non-confidence in the leader.

I had just taken my seat in the House in preparation for the vote when Erik Nielsen, Clark's Opposition House Leader at the time, came to see me to deliver the leader's ultimatum.

"If it is your intention," I was told, "to have any future in politics, you basically have two choices. You either vote with the party, or you abstain by watching the proceedings from behind the curtain." Nielsen, my neighbouring MP for Yukon, had long been a good friend and comrade-in-arms and had declared himself opposed to the charter, once characterizing it as "The Lawyers' Endowment Act." I merely told my good friend how disappointed I was in him for judging me a coward capable of doing either.

As might be expected, only the NDP voted unanimously in favour. Some Liberal and Conservative members abstained; I, together with 16 others, voted against the final motion.

In the mad rush to assist Pierre Elliott Trudeau to complete his masterpiece of social engineering, everyone else seemed to have overlooked the fact that the province of Quebec, with 25 percent of the population, had, for reasons of its own, found the Charter entirely too odious to accept.

The aftermath was predictable. The federal forces had already fought one Quebec referendum on separation in 1980. This latest rift would exacerbate the historically strained relationship between the regions, but most of all between the English and French factions in our country. It would sap us of much of the energy that could have been directed toward building on the foundations that the Fathers of Confederation had envisioned for a strong, united Canada. History has proven Erik Nielsen right; only the legal profession can point to tangible benefits. The rest of society, in terms of our dependence on our elected representatives as the guardians of our rights and freedoms, has suffered a grievous loss.

Clark, to his credit, not only accepted all of the blame for the rebuke we received from the electorate in 1979, but also apologized for failing to read the signals. But that was not enough to dissuade those among our caucus members who were not entirely disappointed with the outcome of the election from launching a campaign to depose him. Just as I had declined to join the old Diefenbaker loyalist covert faction in plotting the demise of Bob Stanfield, I was not interested in advancing my political fortunes by carving up our present leader who, even though he had little support in caucus, had been chosen for us by the party faithful at a fair and democratic convention.

In fact, I shared Clark's belief that Canadians deserved to be informed about the state of the nation, as painful as that was at the time, and to be told the truth about our intentions to redress some of the more serious problems. That approach, certainly in my relationship to my own constituents, had proven itself with the strong support I continued to enjoy. We reasoned that any thoughtful person who took the time to evaluate what we were proposing would have no choice but to give us their support. But therein lies the problem. While there were always enough people to reward my efforts in my Peace River constituency, thoughtfulness yielded to expedience and false hopes in most of the rest of the country.

I chose the coward's way, perhaps. Rather than participate in the ongoing family feud, I retreated to my office to concentrate my energy on serving the people who had just elected me for the fourth consecutive time. It was an approach that served me well throughout all the Joe Clark years.

CHAPTER 13

There Are Better Ways
and Other Ideas to Explore

Progress is a nice word. But change is its motivator. And change has its enemies.

—Robert F. Kennedy

As one can imagine, it is most difficult for anyone outside the political establishment to promote new ideas or change old ones. I was under no illusion, given my position in the party hierarchy and my relationship to the leader, Joe Clark, that any suggestion to address issues that had motivated me to enter the political arena would ever find resonance within the structure. People in power during the Clark years, from 1976 to 1983, were much too busy pursuing their own ideas, and none of them addressed any of the concerns I had brought to the job.

There were times when, given my limited prospects for advancement within the ranks of the caucus, I seriously considered finding my way back to the real world. But unlike most of my friends and colleagues who, shut out from the mainstream of activity, found themselves frustrated and bored by the daily grind, I never lost my enthusiasm for exploring new opportunities and new ways to bridge the gaps between the people at home and their government. I stubbornly clung to my hope that, as with Moccasin Flats, I could use my office to promote change and improve people's lives in other ways. I attended most caucus meetings and fulfilled my obligations to the standing committees of the House of Commons and special committees of caucus. In the main, however, I derived most of my satisfaction from my work in the constituency and my own special projects, trying to address those inequities in our system that seemed particularly offensive and discriminatory to me.

I was assisted in these projects by two admirable research sources. Most of the facilities and services the House of Commons provides to private members are channelled through the various parties. But private members, even those without any party affiliation, have direct access to the Library of Parliament. In fact, the research support offered by that resource is infinitely more useful to individual members than that provided by the research departments of the different parties— unless, of course, the research topic is slanted solely toward purely partisan matters. In addition, much of the inspiration for some of the major studies and reports published out of my office during that period came to me through the contacts I had cultivated through the German–Canadian Parliamentary Friendship Group, of which I was the co-founder, together with Volker Rühe, later the Minister of National Defence in Helmut Kohl's Cabinet. The frequent and lively exchanges facilitated by this association, as well the services and contacts offered by the Konrad Adenauer Foundation, helped me and some of my Canadian and German colleagues gain valuable insights into the structures, programs, and services of our respective jurisdictions.

So it was that my most productive period as an Opposition member was during the Clark years, when I had the least influence in shaping the policy direction the party was taking.

Throughout my tenure in Parliament, I was keenly interested in constitutional reform. When I first came to Ottawa, I was astonished at how little actual influence and power was exercised through Parliament itself, and the apparent impotency of the Senate. I soon discovered that the real power is vested in the Prime Minister's Office. Despite the Senate, which in other jurisdictions acts as the guardian of provincial rights, there appeared to be little, if any, formal contact or representation through which the provinces could channel their concerns.

Meanwhile, I found Parliament was hampered by archaic practices and an electoral system that fails to produce anything close to a democratic verdict.

For help, I looked once again to the Federal Republic of Germany. I can think of no other jurisdiction anywhere in the world, except perhaps Australia, with more similarities in terms of its basic laws, its constitutional framework and our respective political legal and social cultures. Before reunification, Germany had 10 provinces that shared powers with the federal government in precisely the same configuration and to the same degree as our provincial and federal governments do. Also, the Germans have a charter of rights that generally parallels our own. And the problems Germany had to address after the war were remarkably similar to those faced in our own country.

We generally regard Europe, with its countries' colourful histories dating back thousands of years, as the origin of our own constitutional framework. It's surprising to learn that, in fact, our constitution predates that of Germany by almost 80 years. True enough, it was at precisely the same time, July 1867, that the Germans proclaimed the *Norddeutsche Bund* as the basis on which the greater German nation was founded in 1871. This, however, led to the Weimar Republic, followed by the Third Reich, which gave way to the two postwar German states: the Federal Republic of Germany in the west, and the German Democratic Republic in the east.

It was against this background that the 1949 constitution was developed. The architects were not only influenced by their own experience of those turbulent years, but were also obliged to consider the advice of constitutional experts and scholars seconded to the process by the Western Alliance, which dictated the terms of the final surrender at the end of the Second World War.

As was the case in Canada, the design of Germany's constitutional framework had to be sensitive to the many diverse and distinct economic and social entities that had manifested themselves in the various regions of the country.

Joan and I had an audience with Franz Josef Strauss, the premier of Bavaria, just a short time before his death in 1988. When Gudrun, by that time my chief of staff, was introduced as Berlin-born, he assured us that no harm would come to her during our stay in Munich, the capital of Bavaria. During his grandfather's lifetime, however, Strauss explained to us, not entirely tongue-in-cheek, it was not only condoned but even encouraged to shoot any Prussian on sight. But in today's world, he continued, to run over one of them on the streets of Munich would invite the risk of having 10 more come to a funeral, of whom nine would apply for permanent residency.

Despite all efforts, Bavaria, one of the most populous provinces, declined to become a signatory to the constitution in 1949, calling itself a Free State within the new federation instead.

No doubt after studying other jurisdictions such as ours, the architects of the German constitution thought it essential to opt for a *Bundesrat* [Upper House] through which the *Länder* [provinces] pool and safeguard their powers and provide important checks and balances to the central government. Unlike Canadian senators, who are appointed by the prime minister, the *Bundesrat* is made up of provincial ministers, including the premiers, who act as presidents of the assembly on a rotating basis. Each of the *Länder* is represented in the national capital by a permanent plenipotentiary of Cabinet rank who keeps his government informed of any activities in the federal Parliament that could potentially impact on their jurisdiction.

This seemed to me a preferable model to our Canadian Senate, which consists of 105 members appointed by the PM, based on their willingness to act in accordance with his and the party's wishes. Also known as the "chamber of sober second thought," the Senate has no real power other than perhaps to delay a piece of legislation and ask that it be reconsidered by the House of Commons, the final arbiter.

The Canadian Senate is an offspring of the British House of Lords. Britain, in the main a unitary state, should have been the last place anyone would have chosen as a model for safeguarding provincial rights in Canada. The Canadian Senate has no political foundation and therefore no acceptable source of legitimacy.

A study produced for me by the Library of Parliament concludes:

> The manner in which the *Bundesrat* [the German Senate] fulfills the recognized criteria for Canadian Senate reform is remarkable. The precedent in Canada of the federal–provincial conference and the proven success of the *Bundesrat* as a modern federal constitutional creation lends a great deal of encouragement as to the feasibility of its adoption for a new Canadian upper house.

The report also quotes Donald E. Briggs, a widely recognized and respected expert in the field:

> If the Senate were to become a sort of permanent federal–provincial conference, it would not be unreasonable to expect that both central and regional governments would, by virtue of the more

complete and continuous information available to them, be in a better position to appreciate the position of the other, and thus the business of both might be facilitated rather than delayed or complicated or blocked.

Prime Minister Mulroney was no doubt in sympathy with this assessment. To his credit, he moved to formalize his relationship with the premiers through regular biannual conferences. More recently, the premiers have formed a Council of the Federation as the basis of their relationships with one another and for dealing with the federal government—a hopeful sign to say the least.

The Germans, rather than frustrating and clogging their regular system of justice, also opted for a separate court, which acts as the guardian of the constitution and the administrator of their equivalent of the Canadian Charter of Rights and Freedoms. Disputes between the provinces and the federal government are adjudicated by this court. Every citizen, regardless of means or status, is entitled to free access to this court, providing that he or she is supported by a committee of peers whose role it is to sift out any frivolous claims. This, too, seems to me a better model than our own, where it is left to the Supreme Court to sort out Charter challenges.

Finally, given Germany's most recent experience with totalitarianism, great care was taken in the design of an electoral system to assure the purest possible democratic results, namely, a system of proportional representation based on a rather simple mathematical formula that allows electors to cast two ballots; the first, which chooses the representative in each constituency, follows the "first past the post" method we use in Canada. The second allows the elector to cast a vote for his or her preferred party. The procedure assures that the number of seats allocated to each of the parties gaining at least 5 percent of the popular vote is proportional to the votes cast in their favour.

The benefits of such a system, were it applied to our situation, should be obvious. First and foremost, as would be the case in any country where the system of proportional representation is used, a party with less than 50 percent of the popular vote would be required to share their power with coalition partners.

In the November 2000 election, to give one example, the Liberal Party earned 41 percent of the vote nationally, but ended up with almost 60 percent—or 172 out of 301—of the seats in the house. Under a system of proportional representation, they would have been entitled to 128 seats, forcing them to either attempt to govern as a minority, or form a coalition with one of the other parties. In most other western democracies with proportional representation, such as New Zealand, Japan, or Germany, party coalitions are common and regarded as positive, because they provide additional checks and balances in the exercise of power.

In Ontario, the results of the 2000 federal election were even more bizarre. Here the Liberals did get 52 percent of the vote, but ended up with 97 percent, or 100 out of the 103 seats allocated to that province. The Canadian Alliance Party scored two seats, with 24 percent of the vote, and the Conservatives, with 14 percent, were shut out completely. Proportional representation would have reduced the number of Liberal seats in Ontario to 54; the Alliance would have received 25; the Conservatives, 14; and the NDP, 6.

B.C. provides us with another example of how the present electoral system deprives thousands of their democratic right to have their political view represented in Parliament. In the 2000 election, the Canadian Alliance received 51 percent of the total vote, but instead of 17 seats, they ended up with 27 of the 34 to which B.C. is entitled.

Is it any wonder that so many people, without whose trust and confidence no liberal democracy can survive, have simply opted out of the process, and that members of Parliament are held in such low esteem? Thankfully, there are some hopeful signs of change. In addition to the recommendations contained in the report by the Law Reform Commission entitled "Voting Counts: Electoral Reform for Canada," several provinces have committed to adopting some form of proportional representation. The commission recommends a "mixed member proportional electoral system" similar to those in New Zealand, Germany, Scotland, and Wales. The report rates the various systems in use throughout the world in accordance with 10 criteria that range from regional and geographic representation and include decision making and accountable government. Only the Scottish and the German models meet all the criteria; our present system falls short in seven of the 10. However, despite such unassailable logic and facts, I fear that it would require much more enlightened and courageous leadership in Ottawa than what has been evident in the early part of the 21st century.

In a sense, it is our misfortune that we are unable to point to such cataclysmic events as the American Civil War, the French Revolution or, in the case of Germany, the two world wars, to rationalize and facilitate fundamental restructuring of government and its institutions. As archaic and irrelevant as they may have become, we steadfastly cling to an 800-year-old British tradition.or

The Gentleman Usher of the Black Rod still stalks the halls of Parliament, delivering messages from the Queen—or in our case, her representative—just as he did eight centuries ago. To gain entry to the House of Commons, he must ram his black rod against the solid-oak door exactly three times. The suspense among the members every time it happens is almost unbearable. What if he loses count? Will the sergeant-at-arms simply deny entry, or will it cause the entire edifice to crumble and collapse around our ears? Fortunately, at least during my 21 years' tenure in office, we were blessed with the best-qualified and well-enough educated people and were never to be put to the test.

Given the deeply entrenched, time-honoured British tradition and the bureaucracy that thrives on its inherently adversarial system that breeds such discord and distrust—not only among practitioners in Parliament, but among the various levels of government as well—it would be foolhardy to expect that the Gentleman Usher will discover the telephone to convey the Queen's message any time soon.

It can be argued that change has taken place. The increasing power of the Prime Minister's Office cannot be blamed on history. While it may not have been intended by the Fathers of Confederation, and it certainly is not part of the British tradition, in Canada, it is the prime minister whose advice Her Majesty the Queen relies on to appoint our head of state, the Governor General. And when it comes to actual governing, it is in the Langevin Block, across Wellington Street from Parliament, where the decisions are made and where the real power now resides. This is where the people who work in the shadows of the great institution have their offices and from whence they fan out to monitor the show written and choreographed on behalf of their master. They have access to the inner sanctions of the Cabinet chambers where, from the fringes of the room, they have been known to offer polite comment to remind committee members of any diversion from the boss's wishes.

During his tenure, the prime minister fills vacancies in the Senate with his choice of people. Our constitution does assure us of the independence of the Supreme Court, but the prime minister is the one who selects the judges whose qualification he thinks are best suited for the job. Likewise, it is an honour to serve on the Queen's Privy Council, but it is the prime minister who makes appointments to it and dictates the mandate assigned to each of his ministers. As with the Cabinet, all the senior appointments in the Privy Council Office (PCO) serve "at his pleasure."

In addition to appointing all ambassadors and senior foreign-service officials, the prime minister's consent is required for the appointments of over 3,000 powerful positions on boards and commissions. Some of the biggest and most influential corporations and cultural institutions in the country are managed exclusively by PMO appointees. It is the prerogative of the prime minister to dissolve Parliament and call an election at any time of his choosing and, incredibly, Canadians seem to tolerate our political leaders interfering with the process of nominating election candidates in the various constituencies. Nomination papers must be filed and signed by the party leaders, who all too frequently assert their influence by giving preference to their own candidate of choice.

Anyone who has ever witnessed a leadership convention of any of our national parties must be appalled to consider that this process—attended by no more than one 100th of one percent of the population representing a particular political party in Parliament—delivers a mandate to a person granting him or her near absolute power. It's a system that breeds corruption and bestows power and privilege where it is neither earned nor deserved.

"You dance with the one that brung you" was one of Prime Minister Mulroney's favourite sayings, and he no doubt expected it to serve as the rule for everyone he blessed with the "magic wand" at his disposal.

Prime Minister John George Diefenbaker made it his practice upon appointing ministers to insist on an undated but signed letter of resignation, which he kept in his desk to be "reluctantly" accepted in the event that any of them ever strayed from the course he had charted. Pierre Elliott Trudeau perhaps best understood the use of these powers to force the social changes of which he was the architect. To solidify and exercise these powers to their full potential, he surrounded himself with a camarilla of advisers and functionaries accountable only to himself. To insulate himself from the tedious proceedings in Parliament, Trudeau physically moved his offices away from the Hill. To him, Parliament was an historic monument, an attraction where tourists could observe and mingle with the trained seals, as he was known to call his backbenchers performing their daily rituals.

The staff and support structure in the Prime Minister's Office is more akin to a presidential system of government than a parliamentary democracy. In 1967 Lester B. Pearson maintained a personal staff of 12 people. By 1972, after four years of the Trudeau administration, that number had grown to 92. Furthermore, the difference between the PCO, whose officials are paid by the civil service as opposed those of the PMO, who are paid by Order-in-Council, have become almost indistinguishable. The combined number of the two offices was 384 in 1972 and has grown ever since.

This all-powerfull cabal of "fixers" functions more like a president's administration than like members of the prime minister's personal staff conforming to the rules of a parliamentary democracy. It is these people, rather than the people's elected representatives or even the Cabinet, on whom the prime minister relies for developing amd executing his major policies and overall strategic plan.

In his book *Shrug: Trudeau in Power*, Walter Stewart quotes one senior mandarin:

> They are not responsible to anyone other than the prime minister himself. They are more or less hatchet men who go around shooting down other people's ideas. Civil servants are continuously looking over their shoulder with everything they do. You don't think, what is the best policy? But what that SOB at the PMO is going to do with it.

It would be naive to think that giving members of Parliament wider powers and greater freedom to promote their own causes, independent from the party position, in the Chamber and in committees would improve the situation of the democratic deficit in the slightest. Members are utterly dependent on the party structure for support of their activities. The bulk of private financial contributions during elections accrue to their central offices, not only to finance the leaders' tours and the national campaign generally, but to supplement the campaigns individual members are able to finance with their own resources.

Through the Whip's office, the party determines membership on the various House committees, the time and order individual members are allowed to speak in the Chamber, and dispenses a great variety of perks, such as trips abroad, appointments to special committees, and the allocation of office space on the Hill. Anyone who dares to publicly challenge or question the party line, even if it should happen to be at variance with the prevailing view held in the constituency, quickly finds him or herself at the bottom of the food chain—shut out, frustrated, and deprived.

Liberal MP John Nunziata, who was ostracized by his party for publicly criticizing his government's failure to live up to its election promise to scrap the GST, comes to mind as an example.

It is said that power corrupts and absolute power corrupts absolutely. Given the situation that evolved during the latter part of the 20th century, Canadians can consider themselves most fortunate to have been blessed on the whole with people in the Prime Minister's Office who, in addition to enhancing their relatives' and friends' exposure to the sun, derived most of their satisfaction from helping others rather then enriching themselves.

It can certainly be argued that it would be foolhardy to expect people with the power to change the world to rely on anyone other than trustworthy friends and persons who share in their vision, and the means by which to achieve it. We should not be surprised to discover that, after a change of government or any other changeover in the PMO, different people emerge to occupy the most powerful positions in the new administration. But it can also be argued that such people in the extra-parliamentary domain of the Prime Minister's Office, given their enormous power and influence, should be known publicly by their background and status and have their duties defined. Indeed, it can also be argued that, if the present structure is allowed to become a permanent feature, Canadians should have the right, as is the case in any presidential system of government, to choose their head of government in a separate election.

It is, of course, not entirely true that our system operates without any checks and balances. The media fills a big part of the vacuum that has been created. But it is the media that has created the perception that the process is corrupt, and that has sown seeds of distrust among the public of their elected representatives and the system generally, resulting over time in the rejection of anything it produces in terms of leadership and public policy.

Perception has a tendency to become reality. Our system of government can not only claim to meet the test of integrity; it must be seen and perceived to do so. Nothing less than the most fundamental changes at the core of the structure and the electoral process will satisfy what Canadians have a right to demand.

These are well-debated issues and, naturally, I was not the first to tackle them. Throughout my tenure in Parliament, I never met anyone among my colleagues aspiring to leadership who did not profess total and sincere commitment to addressing and resolving the problems of regional alienation, federal-provincial relations, and the "democratic deficit" that manifests itself in the lack of confidence and trust Canadians have in their elected representatives. Once elected, however, these colleagues soon discovered that, without fundamental reforms to the electoral process and the ways the various levels of government relate to one another, nothing can, and therefore will, ever change.

During the 2004 election, Prime Minister Paul Martin, to his credit, raised these issues, together with the Native problem, as ones that not only would be dealt with as matters of the highest priority, but would define his government's mandate and his own career.

But why, one might ask, would anyone in their right mind, once elected and addicted to the powers vested in the Prime Minister's Office, allow himself to be persuaded to dilute or divest any such power? Why indeed would one want to accommodate the provinces with a formal and effective role in the development of the national agenda? Why would one allow a shift of some of the power to the domain of Parliament generally and to private members? It must be obvious to anyone who has ever studied our system and compared it with other jurisdictions that provincial governments, given the important mandate allocated to them in the constitution, must not only be allowed some input and control over the national agenda, but must also be required to assume some of the responsibility and accept some compromise to their parochial interest for the benefit of the nation as a whole.

Any prime minister who is sincere in his or her commitment to erase the so-called democratic deficit and improve the relationship between the federal and provincial governments must surely realize that mere tinkering with the rules and procedures in the House of Commons and the committee structure will do little to ameliorate the problem. It's the private domain of the Prime Minister's Office, the very core of the structure, where fundamental change must occur before Canadians can have their trust and confidence in government restored.

CHAPTER 14

Thinking Outside the Box

There are two ways to slide easily through life: to believe everything or to doubt everything. Both ways save us from thinking.

—Alfred Korzybski, Polish-born author, logician, and scientist

During this period on the Opposition benches, I focussed special attention on numerous other major issues, all of them critical to the lives of Canadians. In every instance I found that, with just the slightest effort by the government to look for more practical, common-sense solutions offered by other countries' experiences, Canadians could have been spared much of the pain and suffering inflicted on them by some ill-considered public policies.

Home Ownership (The Revival of the Canadian Dream) is the title of one report we produced with respect to the crisis during the latter part of the 1970s and early '80s, when interest rates exceeded 20 percent, making it impossible for most Canadians to ever aspire to own their own home and worse, forced thousands of families onto the street or into substandard dwellings. Our constituency offices were flooded with desperate pleas for help from families trying to cling to dreams in which they had invested all their savings; now they were facing foreclosure by the banks and other financial institutions. I had to reach back to my memories of my childhood during the war years to imagine myself in such a hopeless situation.

The problem at the time was not unique to Canada, but the effect on Canadians would have been lessened had we been willing to look beyond the narrow scope of conventional programs and consider the solutions developed in other countries to deal with the crisis. We would have quickly discovered a whole array of innovative measures in place in other jurisdictions designed to cushion homeowners against the vagaries of wildly fluctuating capital markets by means of specially tailored financial instruments and concessions. The report, published in June of 1984, touches on the issue of home ownership as a "social right and social utility." It explains why most European countries, despite the scarcity and much higher cost of available land, can boast a significantly higher per capita ratio of home ownership than Canada.

In the course of the 1974 election campaign, Prime Minister Trudeau proclaimed that "Every Canadian family is entitled to be housed in a healthy and satisfying environment … The national government has a responsibility to make this expectation a reality." A conference held by the Canadian Council on Social Development concluded that "decent housing at an affordable cost is a social right." It was all part of the promise of the "just society." But programs aimed at addressing the housing market turned out to be "just" for the Liberals, in that they helped them get re-elected, and "just" for banks, who opened their vaults to finance some of the schemes, scooping up a sizable share of the subsidies for themselves and leaving the government to assume all of the risk. In October of 1981, when interest rates peaked at 21 percent, a leaked Cabinet document suggested that 45,000 Canadian families facing mortgage renewal would lose their homes.

Conversely, the policies in the European countries we studied were structured to channel all resources targeted at the domestic housing sector directly to the consumer, the premise being that any foregone tax revenues or direct subsidies would be substantially offset not only by the myriad of social benefits, but also by the revenues arising from a healthy construction sector and the industries manufacturing and supplying building materials and furnishings.

We found that in both Britain and Germany, the most effective way to entice individuals to set aside a portion of their disposable income and invest in their future homes was to allow such savings to be sheltered from taxes and through the establishment of co-operative credit institutions called "thrifts," building societies," or, in the German case, the "*Bausparkassen.*" As Bruce Stakes of the *Christian Science Monitor* pointed out in 1982: "*Bausparkassen* lend money to prospective home buyers through savings contracts. Depositors (individuals, parents, or grandparents putting aside money for their children) agree to a specified amount at a low rate of interest, in return for a future mortgage commitment at a guaranteed interest rate, which in the late '70s was between 4.5 to 5 percent."

Widely circulated though the report was, I was under no illusion that any of the "experts" or those in a position to do something about the crisis would pay the slightest attention to it. My own party, during the 1979 election campaign, did go so far as to promote the idea of mortgage interest and property tax deductibility, but once the party was in power and in a position to implement such measures, the bureaucrats at Finance convinced the government that the policies were altogether too risky in terms of the tax expenditure they would induce. As well, it was argued, since such tax incentives could be expected to benefit mostly middle-income earners, they would siphon off scarce resources from any other programs aimed directly at social housing.

It must be assumed that some of these expert critics were among those who considered the housing crisis in Canada during that time to be nothing more than a malicious rumour started by some people with no place to live.

"Am I to understand that you have joined the ranks of the Red Tories?" Michael Wilson, our Finance critic, asked me in his response to my paper.

"No," I responded, "but there are certain aspects to governing where the term 'Progressive Conservative' might be considered less of a contradiction in terms." In any event, the basic human instincts to have a place to call one's own and to strive to secure one's future are hardly socialist traits.

Another issue, and one that hearkened back to my own past, was occupational training. Any European immigrant who arrived in Canada after the Second World War must no doubt have been as surprised as I was by the lack of any formal approach to occupational training and the total disregard for those young people who had neither the aptitude nor the inclination to pursue an academic career for which the entire school system still seems to be predicated. Even those who did manage to complete high school were left entirely to their own devices in their attempt to make the transition from school to work.

The report I published on the subject in 1981 (*Toward Solving Canada's Human Resource Paradox: A National Apprenticeship Policy*) focussed on the coexistence of unconscionably high levels of youth unemployment with increasingly high skilled-labour shortages in several key sectors of the economy. Efforts by the federal and provincial governments to offer occupational training to school-aged youth were, and still are, in their infancy and are in the main lacking the essential ingredient of participation by all stakeholders, including industry and labour.

As is the case in most European countries, occupational training is an element of a two-part system of education that commences at Grade 9 or 10 and carries on until a person is either a qualified tradesperson or well launched in the pursuit of an academic or advanced technical career. The various trades are organized in much the same way as the professions are in Canada, setting their own standards to determine different levels of proficiency and performance, from apprentice to master, and acting on behalf of their members to negotiate levels of compensation. The apprentice splits his or her time between the workplace in an industrial setting, and school, which he or she must attend for one day—in some cases two—a week. Industry is obligated by law to supply the required training positions, assuring that no one is left behind, and is also expected to absorb part of the cost, with the help of specially tailored tax incentives or penalties. Most of the larger firms are known to maintain their own in-house but government-supervised schools.

Frank Stronach of Magna International is only one of many high-ranking captains of Canadian industry who are a product of that system. He came to Canada from his native Austria in 1954, with not much more than his training as a tool-and-die maker, which he acquired after leaving school at the age of 14, and of which there was a critical shortage in Canada at the time. He arrived with big dreams, a penchant for hard work, and all his worldly possessions stuffed into one suitcase. He started out as a dishwasher in a hospital in Kitchener, Ontario, and became the founder, president, and CEO of one of the world's most diversified auto-parts manufacturing companies, with over $6 billion in annual sales.

Coming from Austria, he would have been familiar with an entirely different corporate culture, not only in terms of seeking competitive advantage through specialized skills training, but also in the way employers relate to the unions. After reviewing vocational training in the Federal Republic of Germany, a commission of the Organization for Economic Co-operation and Development, of which Canada is a partner, identified Germany's training program as an approach in which individual and national interests converge and are satisfied:

For young people, vocational training is an important prerequisite for their personal and vocational development. Their prospects in work and life are permanently affected by the vocational qualifications achieved. Skills training must also be secured for all young people for economic and social reasons. A well-trained rising generation of skilled workers is considered vitally important for the maintenance of economic strength in the Federal Republic of Germany.

Instead of drawing from the experience of such progressive labour policies, we continue to be perfectly content to address chronic skills shortages by tailoring our immigration policies to suit our needs and relying entirely on government-sponsored institutions and programs for every effort to bridge the gap that separates us from the rest of the industrial world. Industry, on the other hand, remains equally content to rely upon government entirely to forecast the needs and the type of skills the new century will demand, and to have them supplied free of any cost or obligation.

In its conclusion, the report offered a number of recommendations and the statement that, without major reforms of the system, including the participation of industry and labour and a move toward combining the jurisdictions of the provincial and federal governments in the field of education and manpower training, Canada will remain shackled to a resource-based economy, depriving our youth of their much greater potential.

This report too was widely distributed and I reaped a rich harvest of personal satisfaction from the positive response not only from my colleagues in the House of Commons and the provincial legislatures, but also from a wide constituency throughout the country. Even though these reports are still cited in subsequent studies and reports, they also had their critics—mostly "experts" on the various topics who, condescendingly and generously, would have gladly accepted my superior expertise in matters related to German sausage and sauerkraut, but questioned my credentials when dealing with such complex problems. There were even some who offered the opinion, politely of course, that given the praise awarded in these reports to my country of origin, it would perhaps have been better for all concerned had I chosen to pursue my happiness and a career there.

But there was one study about which I felt myself to be on unassailable ground. Given the geographic nature of my area and the people I represented in Parliament, and given my considerable experience living in the north and in some very isolated communities, I felt no need whatsoever to apologize for the report entitled *Equity and Fairness: A new approach to Northern development.* This topic, after all, was among the main reasons I'd chosen a political career in the first place, and it remained a major preoccupation throughout my tenure.

It should come as no surprise that, considering our cultural and social mainstream flows within a 100-mile corridor along the Canada–U.S. border, where more than 80 percent of our people are crowded together and exercise their political power, Parliament pays only scant attention to the concerns of the rest of the population who live in areas where a harsher climate, long distances between settlements and service centres, and higher prices for food and other essentials all add up to a much higher cost of living.

Published in June of 1980, *Equity and Fairness: A new approach to Northern development* profiled the different classes of citizens that make up the demographics of most northern communities in Canada. The most privileged among them are the employees of the federal government and its Crown corporations such as the post office and the RCMP, and the teachers and agents of the Department of Indian Affairs, as it was then known. These people, given their advanced position on the evolutionary scale and, of course, their proximity to the public trough, deserve and therefore enjoy an "isolated post allowance" as part of their remuneration.

Depending on the degree of remoteness and isolation, large companies in the resource sector also find it necessary to offer their employees generous pay supplements, usually in the form of travel and housing subsidies and other forms of incentives, to maintain a stable workforce. The government considers such concessions to be legitimate business expenses that can be deducted from taxable income. Everyone else, presumably the culturally challenged, socially illiterate, or perhaps otherwise afflicted with certain character flaws that made them choose to live in isolation from the rest of the herd, is excluded from laying claim to such benefits.

Given the prevalence of such accepted assumptions, I have always made it a practice to examine problems from a perspective "outside the box." This time my venture took me to Australia, where we discovered a much fairer, more equitable, and more enlightened approach to the treatment of those citizens who make their contribution to the country's prosperity from the "outback" or other places similar to our northern areas. There, the income-tax act is used to provide a quite simple, effective, and straightforward solution to the problem. The continent is divided into three zones each, according to its degree of isolation, with its own formula of calculating personal and corporate contributions. Surely no one would argue against such an approach being applied to our situation in Canada—or so we thought.

Using much the same rationale, it would be a simple matter of drawing a line along the 60th parallel and identifying all the territory north of it as "Zone A." Federal employees in this zone already qualify for and enjoy generous supplements to their pay. An intermediate "Zone B" would start at the 55th parallel in the west, ending at the 50th to take in Newfoundland in the east. Within that zone, a somewhat more modest rate of concessions would apply.

I had managed to persuade another Liberal minister to accept and fund the Chetwynd housing project 10 years earlier, so I could see no reason why Bill Rompkey, the Minister of National Revenue from 1980 to 1982, wouldn't be interested in championing the cause among his colleagues in Cabinet. Rompkey, now a senator, was the MP for Grand Falls–White Bay–Labrador and hailed from the province of Newfoundland. I presented the report to him personally, asking for his support and any recommendations he might have as to how the government might be persuaded to implement something along the line of the report's proposals. He promised to take it under advisement and, as something one would expect any Newfoundlander to do before embarking on any new adventure, he undertook to test the waters.

That was as far as it went. I must assume that the good man either chose to act as a paragon of virtue and defender of the public purse and the integrity of the tax act under his ministry, or that he considered the idea too risky and against his selfish interests, in that it might draw attention to the much more lucrative arrangement already in place in his own part of the country. A good portion of the population there, by means of some not-so-informal "job-sharing" arrangements, managed to not only be excused from paying any income tax at all, but also lived on the dole for most of the year. Whatever the case may be, it must have taken his experts in the bureaucracy no more than a few hours to convince him that if there were such a simple way to solve as complex a problem as the report purported it to be, they would surely have thought of it themselves, and that it would not be in his best interests to allow a member of the Opposition to disturb the tranquility they had worked so hard to maintain in his office.

But I had invested altogether too much time and effort to be so easily dissuaded from taking the idea any further. Somehow Gudrun and her staff in my office managed to produce enough copies of the 50-page report to supply every municipality, Chamber of Commerce, and Rotary Club in the areas that would benefit from the proposals. With the report went a letter urging them to join the crusade by writing to the Minister of Finance and their member of Parliament directly in support of its recommendations. Afterwards, I could easily have spent all my time speaking to dozens of service clubs and organizations in the north that had invited me to elaborate on the proposals and report on the progress in implementing them. The only problem was that we weren't making any progress at all—not, that is, until five years after the report was first published.

It then came to the attention of the new prime minister who, since he had grown up in Baie-Comeau on the north shore of the St. Lawrence River and was now representing that vast northern riding, was all too familiar with the economic hardship and deprivation his constituents were made to suffer. He decided to test his magic wand on giving the idea his blessing.

After making the argument that in Canada only the media provides checks and balances to the power exercised out of the Prime Minister's Office, I now discovered that was only partially true. Prime ministers, after all, come and go, but the bureaucracy remains substantially the same. Naturally bureaucrats would never question or openly defy the supreme authority, but on policies or issues that are at variance with or offensive to the principles of their established order, they have been known to innovatively obnubilate the matter and procrastinate long enough to allow or, if necessary, even hasten another transition.

It was with good reason that Brian Mulroney gave each of his new ministers a copy of a script from *Yes Minister*, the hugely successful BBC television miniseries.

One of my colleagues recounts an incident from a reception, at our London High Commission, to recognize a change in the Canadian government. He overheard a high-ranking British parliamentarian asking one of his Canadian hosts whether he was a member of the new government.

"No," he replied, "I am a member of the permanent government."

In the case of the crusade for preferential treatment of northerners, the "permanent" government had already rendered the opinion that this system, which understandably had caught the imagination of the electorate in those remote areas of the country, would be impossible to administer if it were totally equitable and fair. Ordered to proceed with the implementation anyway, the bureaucracy saw it as a welcome opportunity to stake out some ground and introduce the newcomers in government to a reality check by simply proving their point.

Instead of following my recommendations based on the Australian example, they introduced not two, but 15 different new categories of beneficiaries. Some of the categories were based on distances and types of road that had to be travelled to reach major centres, some on a definition of the essential services they had to offer. It was a masterpiece.

What should have secured us the affection of every single voter in the north for all time turned into a political nightmare. Not only was the system generous to the point that it generated a serious drain on the treasury, but once small, adjacent communities or even individual households discovered that one but not the other would qualify, the negative reactions from those left out were predictably swift and brutal. Clearly something needed to be done to extricate ourselves from this boondoggle. Once the bureaucrats were satisfied that all the blame was firmly placed on the shoulders of their political "masters," they became most obliging and accommodating in helping us fix the problem.

The classic response in such cases is to appoint a commission and give it a mandate to fine-tune the system, with the understanding that the government would not be disappointed if the commission were to conclude—reluctantly, of course—that, in spite of our deep concerns and best efforts, some other means would have to be found to offer relief to those northerners not already compensated for their extra burden and hardship. In the immortal words of Pierre Trudeau, "the universe was unfolding as it should"—for the bureaucracy. In *Yes Minister*, Sir Humphrey Appleby, the quintessential bureaucrat, devises the law of "inverse proportionality"— the less you intend to do about something, the more you have to study it.

The commission was appointed and, even though it took 10 years and 6 months, in this case justice prevailed. The commission members actually studied my report and drew their own conclusion from the Australian experience. With only minor variations, they recommended the system

I had proposed in the first place. When it was finally implemented and enshrined in the income-tax act, the benefits amounted in some cases to as much as $3,000 a year in savings to the taxpayer.

"Frank Oberle for PM" was the front-page headline in the Fort St. John *Alaska Highway Daily News*. The editorial read as follows:

> If a vote were held today on who residents of the Peace would like as their next prime minister, the overwhelming majority would certainly pick our local MP Frank Oberle.
>
> On Friday it was announced that partial Northern Tax Benefits would be reinstated for residents of this area. In Fort St. John and Taylor, this will make living here a little easier; it will free up several million in discretionary income, which will benefit the shopkeepers and will make recruitment of skilled people from the south easier. Thank you, Frank.

Another area I had always felt passionate about was forestry. Even without Mr. Stanfield's instructions and advice, I would have felt compelled to use some of my time and resources as an MP to produce another major study, *The Green Ghetto,* a report on the prevailing forestry practised in our country.

Had I been afforded the privilege of a university education, it most certainly would have been in the field of forestry. As it was, while my love for nature may have been kindled by my father and grandfather, I had acquired a lot of practical knowledge and experience, first as a logger along the coast of British Columbia, and later as a partner in a lumber mill. Given the importance of the industry, any politician, particularly from B.C., would be remiss if he or she did not concern himself with forestry issues as part of his or her education. Warren Everson, an exceptionally bright young man we hired to assist with the research and writing, had earned himself a Bachelor of Arts degree, but was no more an expert on the subject than I was. We both considered this a distinct advantage.

Our Canadian forests are like the proverbial elephant encountered by a blind man—it resembles something different depending on where one touches it. To the environmentalist and the ecologist, forests filter the water we drink and generate the air we breathe. They provide refuges for a myriad of wildlife. Some see the forest as their cathedral—a spiritual domain, a refuge from the tyranny of the outside world, a place to find and connect to one's inner self. The logger sees the forest as a gigantic farm and a source of enormous wealth and employment. From the government, I could only discern a keen interest in our forests as a huge source of tax revenue.

In a search for balance, we sought counsel from experts who seemed to be in open warfare with one another. Their advice ranged from the Paul Bunyan belief that a tree is an obstacle to agriculture and is otherwise worthless until you slice it up into useful products, to the David Suzuki extreme that a tree, if left untouched, will eventually grow all the way to heaven.

Our forests occupy a significant role in our natural history and heritage. We are the custodians of almost 10 percent of the entire planet's forests. They impact critically on the health of the earth's natural systems. We found Canada's forestry practices, at least in the eyes of our critics from abroad, did not live up to the responsibility expected from us as guardians of such a vast and crucial component of the world's forest inventory.

They may have had a point. Only recently had provinces deemed it necessary to oblige the licence holders on public lands to restock some of the denuded areas that were showing no sign of natural regeneration. Nature, it had been assumed in the past, would replenish in ample time what was being harvested annually, except of course that no one seemed to account for the huge amount of mature prime timber that fell prey to fire, insects, and disease as part of the natural cycles as well.

Most of the experts we consulted confirmed what I had long suspected; namely, that we had built an industry based on an annual harvest that was not sustainable with the management practices in place at the time, thus putting in peril the economies of whole regions of the country and over 350 forestry-dependent towns such as Chetwynd.

I was not the first to raise this concern. Our first prime minister, Sir John A. Macdonald, expressed his fears in a speech to the House of Commons in 1871: "The sight of the immense masses of timber passing my window every morning constantly suggests to my mind the absolute necessity there is for looking into the future of this great trade."

He went on to write: "We are recklessly destroying the timber of Canada, and there is scarcely a possibility of replacing it."

Of course, given the exclusive right to ownership of the resource, the issue is mostly one of provincial jurisdiction. However, as the customers for our wood products abroad keep reminding us, the custodianship of our forests affects the integrity not only of our own environment, but also the ecology and natural order of the planet as a whole. Any ill-considered forest practices anywhere in Canada also transcend the artificial political boundaries within our own jurisdictions. Given this awareness, the role of the federal government in forestry management comes into focus.

The Green Ghetto, which came out in October of 1983, pointed to that need and laid out a blueprint for the transition to much more integrated and more intense forest management practices. It also recommended the creation of the federal Ministry of Forests and the Forestry Act that was created and proclaimed by the Mulroney government.

CHAPTER 15

Back on the Home Front

If God would only give me some clear sign. Like making a large deposit in my name in a Swiss bank account.

—Woody Allen

The great secret of successful marriage is to treat all disasters as incidents and none of the incidents as disasters.

—Sir Harold George Nicholson

These were all very ambitious projects and, coupled with the work of promoting the recommendations in the various reports I had authored, they came on top of the regular routine of my constituency work. The burden of this, while stimulating and exciting, tended to absorb all my time and energy, leaving Joan to deal with the more mundane problems on the home front. Bills still had to be paid, family obligations attended to, and some kind of home life carved out of the crowded schedule.

Peter was still at home attending high school; Ursula, too, lived with us for a few months, helping out in the office before her transfer from UBC to Saskatchewan to finish her studies there. Frank, after a year travelling in Asia, had chosen to leave UBC as well to continue his studies at the University of New Brunswick, at the time a school better suited to the specialty he wished to pursue in the field of forestry.

Just before Joan, Frank, and Peter joined me in Ottawa, Isabell had graduated from Chetwynd high school and, as with all our children, we expected her to visit Germany to rediscover her roots. In a hurry to get on with her life, as usual, she was not inclined to waste time on a "useless" trip. Neither could she see any future in getting "bogged down" in Ottawa. She had always expressed a desire to become a nurse, but in her haste to leave school, she left behind a few credits in biology she would have needed to be admitted to college. Finally, we did manage to persuade her to make the trip to Germany in 1973, and we made arrangements for her to attend a private "finishing school," as they were trendily called, in London, Ontario, when she returned. At the time she insisted it was the cruellest thing any parent could subject a child to; but today, upon reflection, she would tend to agree that the not entirely insignificant bundle of money we laid out to afford her the opportunity may have been well spent.

Incidentally, the perfect family we had created—two of each sex, all born within 10 years, one even on my birthday—is healthy and well adjusted. We are, of course, immensely proud of all of them, even though only Isabell is actually certified as "finished."

Back in Chetwynd, after living through another of the troughs in the forest industry's business cycle, Lorne Dalke started to play with the idea of offering our assets in Chetwynd Forest Industries (CFI) for sale. The rough period we had just gone through could have threatened its survival, had it not been for Lorne's infusion of additional capital. Naturally, with my modest House of Commons salary, I was in no position to be much help, although I would have preferred to hang on. Isabell, who had earned her degree in nursing, was now married and allowed herself to be persuaded to return to Chetwynd, where her husband, Gary, an environmental technologist, was hired to help manage the office at CFI. It was also assumed that Frank, after graduation, might likewise be inclined to practise his skills as a professional forester at the company.

But finally I had to agree that we would invite offers from any company, as long as it was willing to carry through with the commitments we had to our employees and had the resources necessary to expand the facility into a wider range of products. Lorne and I also agreed on the importance to the people in town of maintaining some competition in the labour market. From our past experience, neither of us was willing to swallow our pride and allow Canfor to be restored once again as the sole employer in the dominant sector of the local economy.

In the end we could not have found a better suitor. West Fraser Timber, a very progressive and highly regarded company, answered the call. Undoubtedly much more interested in the supply of raw material the government had allocated to our plant than in the facility itself, they made us an offer that not only satisfied our objectives and demands, but also gave us a fair—if not generous—price for the assets. The deal was completed in 1979.

Gary was offered a position with the new owners, and quickly earned their recognition and respect for his loyalty, hard work, and total dedication to the jobs assigned to him. He was eventually rewarded with a senior management position and would spend his entire working career with the company.

To me, though, it meant a postponement of my retirement from politics. I did not relish the idea of being relegated to the backbenches of the House while Joe Clark was in power, being required to defend government policies that I would mostly be at odds with. But Joan and I, not quite ready to retire to the ranch, agreed to commit to another term.

The proceeds from the sale of the mill came in handy for our next venture—finding a more suitable place to live in Ottawa. As Joan and I soon discovered, we were not city people. After the Nepean apartment, we had purchased a house in the same area that, unfortunately, had some major drawbacks. It was eight miles away from the office where, on most days, I would spend 14 hours of my time. It was also situated in a typical suburban neighbourhood that offered little in terms of a view apart from other people's armpits and clotheslines, or ready access to the open spaces for which our free spirits were yearning. It was a comfortable enough place, but we never considered it our home.

We always knew that living in Ottawa would be temporary. For Joan, it was not a happy arrangement. I would only seldom be able to come home for supper, and felt obligated to spend most weekends back in the riding. During the few precious moments we did manage to be together, I was hardly in the mood to rehash my day's experiences, to which she could not in any case relate. It was natural that she would feel remote and shut out from my new life, which, though stressful and at times and frustrating, could not have been more interesting and exciting for me.

Unlike some of the other members' spouses, Joan wisely refused to come to the office unless it was absolutely necessary. No doubt she must have felt a slight tinge of resentment and jealousy, given all the attention I was getting from the "girls on the Hill," who were hogging most of my time.

It was a new experience for both of us. Being used, as she was, to looking after four kids in addition to her hyperactive business career and social commitments, Joan found it difficult to adjust, but she was way too proud to either mention the subject openly or burden me with her problems. Perhaps we should consider finding a place closer to the office, she suggested as a solution to what both of us were sensing would, over time, develop into a problem.

On those rare occasions when I was home for the weekend, Peter and she acted as tour guides to the city, showing me all the hidden treasures they had discovered. The National Arts Centre had just recently been built and even though the Museum of Civilization, across the Ottawa River in Hull, and the National Gallery, today recognized as world-class attractions, were still in the concept stage, there were nevertheless plenty of other attractions and amenities: the War Museum and the Museum of Science and Technology, spacious, well-laid-out parks, ample green spaces bordering the Ottawa River, the Rideau Canal, Dows Lake, and of course the pomp and ceremony around the precincts of Parliament, which was such a magnet for tourists. Taken all together, all of these attractions shape our capital city's unique character and the modern image of which Canadians can truly be proud.

As always during such outings, we would—only by chance, of course—drive by sites Joan and Peter had investigated as potentially more suitable residences. Since we spent most of the summer months in the west and were not able to do the maintenance chores associated with a conventional property, they thought it wise to shop for a high-rise condominium in the centre of the city.

Given my obsession with a view, Peter speculated that one place appeared particularly well suited. In response to their inquiry as to the direction of the view the place had to offer, the sales agent had promised not just a southern exposure, but also one to the east, the west, and the north. They discovered upon closer inspection that, true to his word, there was nothing in the place to prevent anyone from looking out in all four directions—except for the walls, only one of which had a window in it.

Finally, just before the 1979 election, Joan did coerce me into inspecting a condominium that had just been advertised as a private sale in the local paper. In terms of its proximity to the Parliament Buildings, the quality of construction, and the amenities it offered, it was, next to the Sussex—a very prestigious high-rise building in close proximity to City Hall and the prime minister's residence—perhaps the most desirable address in the city.

This was getting a bit more serious. When I called for an appointment to view the apartment, located on the 16th floor of Number 20 The Driveway, I was relieved at first to be told by the owners that an offer had already been received, but they didn't object to us looking at the place. It was love at first sight. On the way over, I reminded Joan with all the sensitivity I could muster that considering our present state of affairs, with a house in Chetwynd, one in Ottawa (both with mortgages), and an election no more than a few months away, we would hardly be wise to make yet another commitment to a temporary home.

However, with great eloquence and commensurate sensitivity, she reminded me of the many times when I had thrown all caution to the wind in a gamble that could well have gone sour and been ruinous to our fortune.

This is what's so great about our partnership—we can switch our respective roles at will without losing stride. So, as it turned out, Joan was the architect of our last big financial gamble. The vendors, a nice young couple who had opted for a house in the country to raise a family, much preferred our offer because we were not interested in taking possession until after the election and our return from a trip to Europe that was planned for the fall.

It turned out to be not much of a gamble at all. The proceeds from the sale of the sawmill, together with what we had set aside from the sale of our other real estate, gave us the security for which we had been striving for so long and with such total commitment. We had been fortunate. Normally a career in politics in not recommended for anyone whose goal in life is to be wealthy. Like Scarlett O'Hara in *Gone with the Wind*, I too had sworn to God that I would never, ever be hungry again, but there remained, no doubt ingrained in our consciences, enough of the faith into which we were born to prevent us from worshipping the wealth we had now accumulated as our new God.

Some much-needed changes to the parliamentary calendar after the 1980 election and a generous allotment of additional resources to members of Parliament, together with the move to our new address at Number 20 The Driveway allowed us, for the first time, perhaps, to live what most people would consider almost a normal life. There were still the regular late-night sittings, but I was now in a position to monitor the proceedings from home on television and get to the House in time to attend any unscheduled votes.

There was the occasional dinner together at the parliamentary restaurant, and even the odd visit to the art centre, just a short walk along the canal from the apartment. Peter, now the only one left at home, attended Lisgar Collegiate right next door.

Things had changed for the better in the office as well. Denise had manoeuvred herself into a position where she had to choose between her job and a new husband, who wanted to settle on a small farm property 60 kilometres outside of Ottawa. To no one's surprise, she chose the latter.

Gudrun stepped into the breach. She brought with her much more than her Prussian instinct for *Ordnung* [order]. She took charge of the place, and never once in all the years we worked together gave me cause to question her loyalty or her judgement. She was very demanding with the staff, challenging everyone to rise her own high standard of integrity and performance, but she was also tactful, sensitive to personal problems, and fair. The staff in the constituency offices referred to her as the "wicked witch of the east," but it was respect and affection more than anything else that earned her that title.

Gudrun immediately assumed most of the mundane administrative problems, routine inquiries, and constituency demands, leaving me free to focus on the larger picture and our special projects. Both she and her husband, George, a senior executive with Eldorado Nuclear, could not have been more generous in offering highly valued advice and counsel. George became our English-language consultant, editing some of my more important speeches, correcting my grammar, and adding the odd word or phrase not yet registered in my vocabulary.

I also afforded myself the time to broaden my horizons in world affairs by accepting some of the invitations regularly extended to members of Parliament by foreign governments seeking to project a better-focussed, more positive image of their countries' international standing than that offered by an often ill-informed, opinionated world press. Some of these invitations were extended to members' spouses as well. In such rare cases, Joan and I combined the trips with a short vacation, something we still considered a luxury and for which we would otherwise not have taken the time. We count some of these adventures among our most memorable experiences, including a trip to Taiwan and the Philippines in 1976, where we spent time with one of Joan's cousins, a Catholic missionary, and a three-week trip to South Africa and Namibia at the end of October and the first part of November 1978.

In South Africa, much to my amazement, we were shown extensive forest plantations that were feeding vibrant domestic and even export markets—in addition to providing a base for some much-needed employment in some of the homelands. I felt immensely proud to be told that it was mainly thanks to the efforts of Canadian foresters, sponsored by our government, that these plantations were established and cared for in the first place. A two-day visit to Krueger Park served to enrich our love for the natural world and heightened our sensitivities and consciousness for its care and protection. There are few areas in the world that offer up a greater variety of wildlife and a more diverse, spectacularly beautiful natural setting.

I actually made several much shorter trips to Taiwan where, on one occasion in January of 1982, I was featured—along with Senator Frank Murkowski of the United States, former Argentine president Roberto Levingston, and Dr. Feigenwinter, a representative of the Swiss government— as one of the main speakers at the annual World Freedom Day Rally. The Taipei Municipal Stadium, where the event was staged, was attended by 60,000 wildly enthusiastic fans, who were treated to an exhibition of military prowess and discipline and a spectacle of acrobatic skill that no doubt would have rivalled the scene in the Berlin stadium during the 1936 Olympics.

Carried away by the cheering masses and my own enthusiasm for the occasion, I was almost hoping that God could arrange for certain deceased relatives of mine to look down and see just how utterly false their assessments of my character and my future prospects turned out to be. Foremost among them would have been my grandfather Leibold and my uncle Wilhelm, the memories of whose behaviour after the war still conjure up for me the worst images of my childhood. However, I had to assume that God might have little jurisdiction over the domain to which their tortured souls must have travelled.

CHAPTER 16

Conspiracies

Anyone who is capable of getting themselves made President should on no account be allowed to do the job.

—Douglas Adams

Winston Churchill once said: "The Conservative Party is not a party but a conspiracy." The loss of the 1980 election triggered a general feeling in the party that it had been a crucial mistake to elect Joe Clark as leader in the first place. Even before the final results were proclaimed, several contenders from the previous contest made it known that they could be persuaded to try again if "by chance" the job were to become vacant. For those among my colleagues to whom politics was a blood sport, war preparation once again became their major preoccupation. The problem with political wars, as Joe Clark would soon find out, is that they tend to be much crueller than the regular kind. You can die more than once.

Unlike the Westminster Parliament, where to a large extent it is left to the caucus itself to retire leaders who have outlived their appeal, in Canada that power rests with the party membership as a whole—unless, of course, the leader can be persuaded to leave voluntarily. That, however, did not dissuade any of my honourable colleagues from organizing the conspiracy, choreographing the play, and deciding the roles everyone had to play (including that of Brutus) to liberate us from the yoke the party had placed on our shoulders during the 1976 leadership convention. Clandestine meetings, lasting long into the night, produced mountains of top-secret notes and memos, most intended to be leaked to the press.

Meanwhile, those aspiring to replace the king—both inside and outside caucus—shifted into high gear the campaign they had started the

221

day after he was first elected. The rules for this stage of the game were written in the 15th century by the Italian bureaucrat and diplomat Machiavelli, and are therefore well established: First, the aspirants leave no stone unturned in drawing attention to themselves, planting rumours with the press that are sure to lead to rampant speculation regarding their ambitions for the leadership. Having done this, they are then seen on television and in the newspapers vehemently denying any interest in the matter, certainly not as long as the party is blessed with such a popular leader and one so worthy of their support. Dropping helpful hints to the media to focus its attention on the present leader's shortcomings, their real intention is to fuel and support the conspiracy being executed behind the scenes by their agents, who are busy travelling the country, organizing support for the impending campaign.

If honourable members were to channel the same kind of energy and ingenuity into the business for which they are elected as they tend to contribute to the internal warfare of party politics, they would be assured of their constituents' loyalty in perpetuity. It could be quite confusing for those who, like myself, chose to watch these proceedings from the sidelines, taking pleasure in being entertained and solicited by the various factions to embrace their cause.

One devious scheme involved collecting signatures from caucus members on a petition indicating the lack of confidence evident throughout the country that would make it impossible for the leadership to carry on. Several volunteers selflessly offered to bell the cat, but only after a clear majority of the members had contributed their signature to the document. Another, more gentle, version proposed that a majority of caucus members write a personal letter to Joe, praising him for his selfless service to our country and the party, but also expressing the opinion that Canadians could never be persuaded to restore him to the Prime Minister's Office. The letter was to suggest—reluctantly, of course—that we were appealing to his sense of duty to sacrifice his personal ambitions for the good of the country. To ease the deposed leader's transition from the fast lane back to the real world, it had been suggested that members and well-to-do supporters of the party contribute to a trust fund.

Clark was never given the opportunity to consider these "heartfelt" sentiments since neither the document nor the letter was ever presented, because the committee had overestimated either the number of traitors in caucus or the generosity of any potential donors.

Clark himself should have taken the hint when some of the key players in the party, who usually preferred to operate in the backrooms of the organization, began showing up at every Conservative meeting throughout the country to proclaim their loyalty to him. Clark, as we know, had a big enough ego to think that he should have been able to take that for granted. The aspirants for the job, on the other hand, were simply observing the golden rule: Never cast the first stone at someone you wish to replace once he has been assassinated.

There was, of course, the party's constitution to fall back on. It provided for a leadership review after every election, so the attention shifted in that direction. The situation finally came to a head on a cold January day in Winnipeg at the 1983 biennial Conservative Party convention. Given the way the media had treated Joe Clark during the entire time of his leadership, and having observed all the efforts from within to dethrone him, I was absolutely stunned by the outcome of the vote. What seemed like an eternity may only have been a couple of hours between the time the ballot boxes were sealed and the announcement of the result. The atmosphere in the Winnipeg convention centre could have been carved with a knife. Clark received just a fraction below two-thirds of the votes cast, plenty enough to legitimize his mandate.

But then he stunned everyone by doing something only a person with his peculiar sense of pride and arrogance could do: he rejected the verdict and called for a leadership convention anyway.

By that time, I had given up any hope that the Progressive Conservative Party could ever penetrate "Fortress Quebec," which the Liberals had managed to stake out as their domain ever since Metis rebel Louis Riel's untimely death at the end of a rope in 1885.

In the leadership contest that followed, I did use my head by urging such senior members of my staff as Lynn Belsy to support Brian Mulroney as the most likely person to succeed. (Belsy was rewarded with a position on Mila Mulroney's personal staff.) But my own decision was to support John Crosbie, and it came from the heart.

I felt the campaign of John Crosbie, a typically colourful Newfound-lander, with a long history in politics, would undoubtedly provide the most fun and entertainment and since he was the first to approach me with an offer to serve as one of his western lieutenants and a role in choosing the menu for the policies he would defend there, I signed on. Despite his appeal throughout the country, his humour, and his impressive intellect, I was never under any illusion that Canadians were ready for a prime minister from Newfoundland.

Brian Mulroney, probably because he had every reason to consider me among his supporters, was most disappointed when I told him of my commitment to Crosbie. I realized that he was our only hope for a breakthrough in Quebec, and also that I owed him a debt of gratitude for the interest and support he had invested in some of my work. Perhaps I was not quite honest with him when I told him, during his visit to my office, that I was nervous about some of his corporate connections and the fact he had never held an elected position. That he had appointed, without consulting me, Tom Siddon, the MP for Burnaby-Richmond-Delta, as the man to carry his banner in British Columbia may have been another reason for my decision to support Crosbie.

I got what I had bargained for. The campaign was a lot of fun. I accompanied John and his wife on their western tours, which included trips to Prince George and Dawson Creek. John, keeping everyone in stitches with his dry Newfie humour, never disappointed anyone among the masses that attended the meetings, more for the entertainment value no doubt than for the political message we had scripted for him.

I either blame (or give credit) to God himself for his intervention in the affairs of our party. The cold ice fog he'd used to shroud the Winnipeg convention centre clearly must have been a factor in Clark's decision, perhaps decelerating his metabolism to a state of temporary hibernation. Six months later, on the day of the Ottawa leadership convention, one had difficulty breathing, much less thinking clearly, in the sauna-like atmosphere inside the hall that exacerbated the stifling heat and humidity outside. I can only assume that the Catholic Brian Mulroney, who was the beneficiary at the Ottawa proceedings, had a stronger claim to favour by divine intervention than Joe Clark, who was to be chased from the Garden of Eden.

The heat on that June 11 day certainly must have been a factor in my thought process as well. My parochial interest compelled me in the end to cast my first ballot not for John Crosbie, but for my good friend John Fraser from Vancouver who, despite his sagacity and what I consider a talent for leadership, was given the least chance to succeed. But I had promised Brian Mulroney my vote on the second ballot, and ended up betraying him on that as well.

There are but few occasions in the affairs of men that can compete with the high drama of a leadership convention, particularly during the final days. People whose entire lives have been consumed with the burning ambition to be the focus of the lights and cameras recording the contest's final outcome must endure absolute torture, having to watch the frenzy and insanity visited upon the scene during the final hours of decision.

After just a few short words by some stranger announcing the verdict, the chosen one will find himself blinded by the glare and attention now focussed on him. In an instant, his or her life will have changed forever. The others, once their eyes become adjusted to the dark now descending around them, will wonder where everyone who had pledged unreserved loyalty and support has gone. Only their spouses, members of the immediate family, and perhaps one or another of their closest friends will be left to share in the utter disappointment and despair.

The final act for them is to make their way to the stage in the pretence that politics is a team sport, and to render a commitment to support the new monarch which, with only a few notable exceptions—Joe Clark being one of them—none of them ever intends to keep.

I did manage to redeem myself in the end. As it happened, the Crosbie and Mulroney camps were situated side by side on the west side of the arena. Clark led by 217 votes after the first ballot. Only three of the eight candidates were left standing after the third: Clark, Mulroney, and Crosbie. Clark's lead had shrunk to 22 over Mulroney, with Crosbie trailing by 200 votes, but still a stronger finisher, with valuable votes at his command. I was sitting a few feet behind him as every one of the 6,000 eyes in the place now suddenly focussed on the person who would either come up the middle to claim the prize, or put the crown on the new king. It was pandemonium.

Frantic efforts were underway in the backrooms to convince the Clark camp to join us in the final ballot as the only means to stop Mulroney. Given his history, it was not unreasonable to expect Clark to once again do the unexpected and comply; John Crosbie had left no doubt in anyone's mind that, having to choose, he would reach for Clark as, in his perception, the lesser of the two evils. I in turn left no doubt in his mind that if that should happen, I would lead an exodus across the barricade separating us from Mulroney. To his credit, in the interest of the party and out of respect for those of his supporters leaning toward

Mulroney, he would have preferred not to signal his personal intentions and endorsement of either of the two remaining opponents.

Some of my friends in Mulroney's box were already frantically trying to get my attention. Everybody was shouting at once. I was tugging at his sleeve: "John," I bellowed into his ear, "I'm not asking you to move. All you owe me is a friendly wave in Brian's direction." But when he turned to oblige, Mulroney's arm and upper torso, seemingly having stretched to twice their natural length, reached over the divider, making it impossible for Crosbie to avoid the handshake.

The Progressive Conservative Party had its new leader.

CHAPTER 17

A Close Encounter

Idealists are foolish enough to throw caution to the winds. They have advanced mankind and have enriched the world.

—Emma Goldman

The ascension of Brian Mulroney to the leadership of the party in 1983 did little to improve my status among my colleagues in caucus or in the House of Commons. It would have been most unreasonable for me, of course, to expect to be considered for a position in the new leader's shadow Cabinet. It was nevertheless a disappointment, and it made it awkward for me to explain to my supporters back home, who weren't as familiar with the rules of the game, why I was overlooked.

My good friend Tom Siddon, who certainly had both the political and academic credentials to claim one of the prizes, offered to put my name forward to serve as the party whip. It would have been a prestigious enough position because it meant regular contact with the new leader, who relies on the party whip's office to monitor the mood of caucus and dispense some of the perks that keep dissident members in line. But aside from a fancy office and some additional staff and salary, this idea had no appeal to me at all. I certainly had no interest in positioning myself in the middle of all the petty bickering among my colleagues, and even less in being shackled to the office on the Hill with little time for the constituency, from which I still derived my greatest satisfaction. In any event, with work on *The Green Ghetto* still in progress, I had little trouble settling back into the old routine that had given me the stimulation, satisfaction, and inducement to consider what was now shaping up to be a career in politics. Major developments and events in the constituency also served to dispel whatever resentment I might have felt at the time.

The new riding of Prince George–Bulkley Valley was relieving some of the pressure on both my own and the Skeena constituency, which in terms of geography ranked among the four biggest in the country. I still retained a portion of the city of Prince George, but lost all the communities along Highway 16 from Vanderhoof to the Alberta border. On the other side of the equation, some interesting new challenges were posed by the massive influx of people seeking employment at the new coal-mining project south of Chetwynd. This and several other major industrial developments had created new opportunities—and new challenges—in meeting the demands for services and infrastructure associated with these developments.

The town of Mackenzie, which had been carved out of the bush a few years earlier to house the workers and families of several new wood-converting enterprises, was by now well established. But like all one-industry towns in the north, it still lacked the stability that comes from greater diversity in business and job opportunities, and the more integrated social structure that is built on a multi-generational family unit.

Of the towns northeast of the Rocky Mountains, Hudson's Hope, the site of the Peace River power project, ranked as one of the oldest in British Columbia. While the dam, particularly during construction, brought with it the most profound changes in the living conditions and character of the place, most people accepted them as positive and welcome. At the other end of the spectrum, there was Tumbler Ridge, about 95 kilometres south of Chetwynd. It became the newest of the "instant towns" that would accommodate the workforce at the two coal mines under development.

I had argued strongly that the project be integrated with the existing communities; that the workforce commute to the site from Chetwynd or Dawson Creek; and that a rail link be built to Chetwynd to join up with the BCR track already in place, all of which would not only have saved taxpayers millions, but would also have brought much more tangible economic and social benefits to the entire region.

But this was to be a megaproject, grandiose enough in scale to elevate the status of B.C. premier Bill Bennett Jr. (William R. Bennett, or "mini-WAC," as he became affectionately known) to his illustrious father's level. Leading the Social Credit party, he had won a minority government against Dave Barrett's NDP in June 1974. Don Phillips, my former business partner and by now a key minister in the new Social Credit government, was himself no slouch when it came to hatching big ideas. Spurred on by the Japanese clients and customers who were craving the 15 million tons of high-quality metallurgical coal the site was to yield annually, only the sky was to be the limit to the quality and scale of the community and transportation infrastructure that would service the project, and to its prospects for longevity.

The experts had a field day. The most prominent architects, town planners, and civic engineers (and every other kind), all of them working out of high-rise office towers in downtown Vancouver, descended on the place with their very own expert opinions and visionary plans of how to create a "model town." Money was no object, in that both the federal and the provincial governments—with good intentions, certainly—had offered to make the necessary investments in housing, public buildings, roads, and other infrastructure to avoid the social stigma usually attached to a typical company town.

In less than no time, the site had been cleared of trees and brush, streets had been laid out and paved, and houses and commercial buildings were soon springing up like mushrooms. The older established communities in the area could only dream of some of these amenities, such as the town-centre complex complete with a library, hockey arena, and aquatic centre, all served by underground electrical wiring that was in place even before most of the workers and their families had arrived.

They even took a page right out of the constitution Loophole Lewin and I had drafted for our fictional "Principality of the Peace River" during our long road trips between Dawson Creek and Prince George, when we had considered—frivolously, of course—separating our region, so richly endowed in natural resources, not only from British Columbia, but from the rest of Canada as well. My good friend Pat Walsh, a former mayor of Fort St. John and a prominent Liberal, was appointed as commissioner of the new town and invested with the powers normally exercised by an elected town council.

In addition to the model town, which was finished in the early 1980s, hundreds of millions of dollars were spent on the development of a port facility at Prince Rupert and a direct rail link requiring a seven-kilometre tunnel through some of the most rugged terrain in the province. When it was discovered that the tunnel could not be ventilated over such a distance, the engineers designed the system to accommodate electrically powered engines.

People can be strange when it comes to dealing with an overabundance of personal happiness and contentment. In recruiting their workforce, the two mining companies wisely gave preference to married couples and their families. Certainly no one could have made a greater effort in making them welcome as they arrived from all parts of Canada, attracted by better-than-average wages, good working conditions, ultramodern subsidized housing, and all the other amenities offered by the town. People in the recruiting office were even thoughtful enough to advise successful candidates to inform the town's administration of the date of their arrival so that the heat and lights would be turned on to make the new arrivals feel welcome and comfortable in their new homes.

I had found it hard at first to generate any enthusiasm, questioning the rationale of such elaborate and massive investments of public money in a place whose life span was entirely tied to the volume of coal the mines could yield. Drawing on my experience of living in other single-industry resource towns, I could see trouble coming.

Only the natural beauty and splendour of the town's surroundings outshone its architecture. All in all, one might think such a place would be what every young person would dream of—the ideal place to raise a family and yet, somehow, it didn't turn out that way. Something seemed to be missing. Not that most of the boys had any difficulty getting assimilated. The workings at the mine were nothing like those I had experienced during my time as a hard-rock miner at Pioneer in the Bridge River Valley. It was all above ground, highly mechanized, and well managed to assure a safe and healthy environment.

The surrounding area is a paradise for the outdoors enthusiast. Soon one could see snowmobiles and high–powered boats parked in front of every house. To occupy people's spare time, there was the hockey rink together with all the other indoor recreational facilities; but there wasn't a grandma or grandpa within a thousand kilometres of the place to liberate young mothers from their children for a few hours a week, or to provide the moorings to which a young family could anchor their relationship with one another.

In many of the rural settlements and farming areas throughout my riding, where people had carved a small acreage out of the wilderness and spent a lifetime improving it, the most primitive living conditions were still the norm. Having invested most of their energy and scarce resources in developing their land, they were left with little else to invest in their homes. Even if they had access to cultural or recreational facilities, they would not have been able to afford the time to indulge in the frivolities the facilities would have been designed to host.

Strangely, however, apart from the farming community's persistent efforts to urge the government to improve the potential of the farming sector, the farmers' demands for services or my intervention in other matters paled in comparison to the workload generated by the residents of the model town. Since they were tied to longer-term planning and budgets, such direct, senior-government services as the post office, policing, and health service facilities were slow in coming. After moving from locations at the other end of the country, most families felt entitled to recoup moving expenses under the Canada Manpower program. Women who had given up jobs to follow their husbands to a place with few, if any, prospects for work felt cheated when they found out they would not be entitled to unemployment insurance benefits. Working with some of the more enterprising individuals, I helped champion initiatives to attract other industries to the area and enable locals to access federal-government programs intended to assist small businesses to become established as a means to diversify the job market.

Fifteen years later, it seemed that all the best-laid plans had been for nought. The resource was still plentiful, but the demand for it had declined, and the price coal fetched in world markets fell below what was needed to keep mine operations viable. The workers and their families, once again on the move, were fighting to recoup the investment they had been encouraged to make in their homes. Fortunately, with the emergence of China in the 21st century as a major industrial power starved for raw materials to fuel its growth and expansion, the cycle appears to be reversing itself once again, giving the place another lease on life. However, the industry and the people earning their livelihood from it are much more cautious now in making longer-term commitments.

I was reminded of Tumbler Ridge by another megaproject I had occasion to become involved with during this period.

Among the more stimulating and memorable experiences Joan and I had was participating in the Canada–United States Inter-Parliamentary Committee. An equal number of committee members from the houses of Parliament and the Senate, together with their spouses, meet annually to address matters of interest or concern and to exchange ideas on how to improve the working relationship between our two countries. The committee met alternately in some of the most exclusive places our respective countries had to offer, allowing the participants sufficient time to develop and foster personal, friendly relationships.

On one occasion, during the great pipeline debate in 1979, the group decided to study the pros and cons of a land route to deliver oil from Alaska to the lower 49 states. Stopovers were organized at strategic points along the Alaska Highway to meet with people in the communities that would be affected by the project. We in the Canadian contingent strongly favoured a land route for a pipeline, which would not only produce significant benefits in terms of construction jobs and throughput services, but could potentially secure us access to our own reserves along the Mackenzie Valley.

Regrettably, the Americans eventually opted for a project that would combine a pipeline, already in place, from Prudhoe Bay to Valdez, with an ocean-tanker delivery system to the lower 49 states. Several of the witnesses we had lined up to promote the Canadian position cautioned against the potential risks of a spill along the route which, some argued, was entirely predictable. The fact that they were proven right is of little comfort to anyone who had to deal with the calamitous consequences of the *Exxon Valdez* disaster in 1989, or for the rest of us who still live with the risks today.

At Prudhoe Bay, the central point of the development, the Americans reached even deeper than the engineers in Tumbler Ridge could ever have imagined to provide habitats for the project's workforce. We were afforded a VIP welcome to a town that would not have looked out of place on the moon. This oasis on the frozen tundra was covered by a vast array of glass domes stretching over an area large enough to host not only the living accommodations of hundreds of people, but also a forest of palm trees and lakes, with fountains and flower gardens that God himself would have found suitable for inclusion in his paradise.

The social engineers who helped design the place must have had nothing less than that on their minds. Like the expert planners at Tumbler Ridge, they did not discourage married couples, as long as the women could be placed among the service staff. But unlike at Tumbler Ridge, women were required to live in comfortable but separate quarters from the men. Several times each year, the company would grant their employees a two-week vacation in the south. In the meantime, anyone discovered engaging in sexual activity was summarily dismissed.

As the company's public-relations representative, who had flown in for the occasion of our visit, explained, "Our rules are very strict, even for married couples living on-site. Sex is a misdemeanour, and it certainly shows because the longer they miss it, the meaner they get." Not for the first time, I wondered what the experts were thinking, creating such an artificial environment and playing God with people's lives.

Back in Ottawa, Mulroney's star continued to rise. Everybody, even Prime Minister Trudeau, considered it a foregone conclusion that the next election would result in a change of government. In February 1984 Trudeau resigned for the second time and set in motion the events that led to John Turner's election as the leader of the Liberal Party and, in June, made him prime minister.

I liked John a lot. Not one of all the people in positions of real power that I'd met during my career proved more generous and decent in dealing with their colleagues, or displayed more love and respect for the institution to which we were elected. He never made any distinction between members of the different parties when taking a few moments and an extra step to pat someone on the back and offer a few kind words of encouragement and advice.

I got to know him more intimately just prior to his ascent to the "Front Office" during a personal encounter that might well have had tragic consequences.

Both of us were close friends of the late Peter Bawden, who had built a fortune in the energy sector for himself and was operating a fleet of executive jets out of the Calgary airport. For a time, he also represented a Calgary constituency in the House of Commons, but with his conflicting business interests and his personal dislike of Joe Clark, he decided not to compete in the 1979 election. In later times and among people in other parties, concerns over conflict of interest between private business and public duties appeared to be much less of an impediment to anyone's ambitions or political aspirations.

Peter missed his friends in Ottawa and looked for any excuse to engage us in some of his escapades.

"It's a tough job, I know, but someone has to do it," he said to me over the phone late one evening at home. "Just watched you on the tube and decided you look tired, and we need a break. I want you to be at the usual place at the airport at 6 a.m. Friday morning. Tell the Hun [his nickname for Gudrun] that you will be back on Monday. Seeing that the survival of the free world lies in the balance, I cannot take no for an answer." It would have been useless to ask where we would be going or who else was to join the party, but the dress code was "Chetwynd bush" and, since it was late fall, warm underwear.

John Turner had boarded the Lear jet in Toronto and was already nestled in the back seat when I arrived. He knew little more than I did about our destination, other than that Peter would meet us there after we picked up one other passenger en route. It turned out to be old Mr. Congeniality himself, Don Jamieson, who had served for many years in Trudeau's Cabinet. The last time I had a personal encounter with him was over a few scotches in Pretoria, South Africa, where he was representing Canada as the Minister for External Affairs at the same time that Joan and I were visiting.

Only after we left St. John's, Newfoundland, did the pilot share with us our final destination. We were heading to former premier Frank Moore's fishing camp on the Labrador coast. The rest of the party was waiting for us at Goose Bay, where a helicopter was standing by, blades already in motion, to take us to our rendezvous with some of the most spectacular fishing in the world.

I had expected Labrador to be a barren place, but was surprised to discover significant volumes of prime timber all along the valleys that were carved through the high ground by the force of the rivers cascading over the rocky terrain on their journey to the great ocean. My mind's eye could visualize this resource supporting several major wood-conversion facilities, providing employment for hundreds of people on a sustained basis. But, at the same time, I couldn't help thinking that like so many places along the coast of British Columbia, the wealth of this great natural asset could be even more enhanced were it left in its natural state and measured by a different yardstick.

It wasn't hard to imagine why Frank Moore had fallen in love with the place he had built for himself. His cabin, safely tucked among some stately trees that looked respectable even by B.C. standards, provided all the comforts of home for the party he had invited to share in this particular adventure. Every board, every fixture, every nut, bolt, and nail had been transported to the site by helicopter and was fitted together with care so as to not offend the pristine surroundings.

As we were to find out the following day, this was where one could feel the embrace of the spirits that roam in such special places; it was a place to explore one's inner self, to be in touch with one's soul. But it could also be a harsh, unforgiving place and a reminder of one's own mortality.

The following morning John Turner and I were given the use of the helicopter to access some of the better fishing spots further up the coast. We had just settled in at a promising site when the pilot was recalled to attend an emergency at an industrial site near Goose Bay that required the evacuation of one of the victims.

"It's a routine assignment," he assured us. "I'll be back in plenty of time to get you back to camp before nightfall."

It was a spectacularly bright, sunny fall day, the air clean and brisk, no cause for anyone but the fish to worry. After lunch we headed out in different directions along the riverbank, testing the equipment Frank had supplied us with. Here we were above the treeline. The water along the shore of the river was shallow, tempting us to venture further out to play the line over the main stream, which was used by spirited Atlantic salmon to make their way back to their place of origin. Throughout most of the time, we maintained eye contact, occasionally hoisting a fish above our heads to boast our success. In the excitement, neither of us paid much attention to the sun heading for its daily rendezvous with the horizon in the west.

It had been some time since I'd last seen John when I decided to make my way toward the area where he had been fishing from. I found him sitting on a large boulder, his arms crossed over his chest, soaking wet, and obviously suffering from the onset of hypothermia. Having lost his footing, he had been caught by the current of the icy river, forcing him into a desperate struggle to keep from being swept away. The only sign of shelter was far off in the distance, where a small clump of conifers seemed to have withstood the harsh environment that had deprived the area of any other sort of vegetation. Pointing to it, I pulled him upright, urging him to collect his strength so that we could make our way over there to find shelter among the trees. The sun dipped below the horizon before we got there. In the interval the temperature must have fallen by at least 20 degrees.

Our lives may well have been saved by John's insistence on bringing his own tackle box, which was not only spacious enough to accommodate a good-sized bottle of Scotch whisky, but was also stocked with such absolute essentials as matches. I managed to appropriate some dry moss and small dead branches from the scrubby trees with a gaff hook, which helped us to start a fire.

John was drenched through. His hip waders were filled with water, and he looked a miserable sight without the clothes we had struggled to take off him to wring out and dry over the fire. With no implements other than a knife it was hopeless to gather enough wood to keep the fire going, leaving us with no option but to light the entire clump of stunted growth in the hope of being rescued before whatever fuel it contained was exhausted.

Not even libations from the bottle were sufficient to relieve John's misery and violent shakes, or me from worrying what would happen after the fire had consumed whatever flammable material was left. It is situations like these that test and reveal a man's character. Throughout the ordeal, we tried to cheer each other up, and John even made some attempts at humour, speculating on the next day's newspaper headlines, after our frozen bodies had been discovered and salvaged.

It was close to 10 o'clock in the evening when I first heard the faint, unmistakable sound of a helicopter rotor. While it seemed to be coming closer at first, to our horror, it soon started to fade off into the dark void. What may have only been minutes seemed like hours before we heard it again; this time it got louder. Soon after, we could make out the strobe light mounted on the ship's nose coming toward us. Because of the terrain, the pilot had been unable to ground the machine when we had arrived at the site, requiring us to disembark from a hovering position. Now, to get into a position low enough for us to scramble aboard—in the dark among large boulders—would undoubtedly test the pilot's skills to the limit. It took all of John's remaining willpower and strength and whatever assistance I was able to contribute to get him safely inside. But in the end, the only visible injury he sustained was from being hit by one of the tackle boxes I'd thrown in after him before hoisting myself aboard as well.

No one was more relieved than the pilot himself, as he adjusted his coordinates guiding us back to the cabin. He had been searching for us for over an hour and was running low on fuel before he spotted our fire. Back in the cabin, the rest of the boys whom Frank Moore had recruited for the adventure had anticipated the worst. It turned out to be some reunion. Eager hands deposited John's frozen bones into a bathtub filled with steaming water. Dr. Frank Moore counselled that the medication for the victims should be changed from scotch to hot rum, laced with lemon and butter, and the dosages increased to a level of total saturation. The rest of the crew, good companions that they were, sacrificed themselves in sympathy with the afflicted by joining and keeping pace with us in imbibing the medicine.

Most people who had the privilege of knowing Don Jamieson would agree that he missed his calling by not pursuing a career in show business. He kept us entertained with his unique blend of humour for the rest of the night, dispelling any thought or danger of becoming afflicted with post-traumatic stress syndrome. I had never laughed harder in all my born days. Recalling some of his hilarious anecdotes the next day even helped relieve the worst of our hangovers, which, fortunately, were the only after-effects anyone suffered.

CHAPTER 18

Success at Last

It is frequently a misfortune to have very brilliant men in charge of affairs; they expect too much of ordinary men.

—Thucydides

The pundits and Trudeau were right. The election of September 4, 1984, my fifth, resulted in a massive majority for Brian Mulroney and the Progressive Conservative Party—the largest in parliamentary history, with the Conservatives winning 211 of 282 seats. It gave us the majority of ridings in all of the provinces, including Quebec. When the votes were counted in Prince George–Peace River, I ended up with 62 percent—a 13,000-vote margin, the highest I had ever received—over Jim Best, the candidate representing the NDP.

I must confess to feeling an ever-so-slight tinge of sorrow for John Turner personally. The Liberals had invested such high expectations in his ability to produce a seamless transition from the Trudeau era to a more traditional phase of dominance, yet saw his party reduced to just 40 seats instead.

I did whatever I could to tone down everyone's expectations regarding my own prospects for an appointment to Cabinet. Secretly, I could see a remote chance, and during the first few days of transition I never ventured too far from a telephone. Both before and after the announcement of the new executive council, I was pestered by reporters, both in Ottawa and the riding, inquiring about my expectations and testing my reaction to being overlooked. As he had promised, Mulroney appointed a minister of state for Forestry with a mandate to rebuild the Canadian Forestry Service and discharge the federal government's responsibility in this critical area of our national life. The recommendations in *The Green Ghetto*, which had been adopted by my colleagues in the caucus committee, were to be the new minister's guide. In response to one testy reporter hoping to identify some early discord or dissension in the ranks of the new government, I confessed my disappointment in having built a church wherein I wouldn't be allowed to preach, but I assured him it would not cause me to denounce my religion.

Nor should it have. Most of my friends to whom I felt close and who had earned my respect did get appointed to Mulroney's first Cabinet. All of them were familiar with my work and were attached to the same principles that had shaped my political orientation. Even though I felt remote from the new leader himself, I felt much closer to the current of central power, which soon shifted in a new direction much more to my liking.

Brian Mulroney, in contrast to his predecessors, wasted little time establishing himself as a strong, decisive leader. His style quickly earned him the respect of friend and foe alike. Only on the rarest of occasions did he fail to attend our weekly parliamentary caucus meetings, and no member wanted to miss his spellbinding pep talks. Compared to Clark's supercilious style, he was a virtuoso.

One of Mulroney's first priorities was to mend the strained relationship that had developed with the United States. By the end of March 1985, he had invited U.S. President Ronald Reagan to what became known as the "Shamrock Summit," which laid the foundation for improved U.S.–Canada co-operation on missile defence and free trade.

The newly created Minister of State for Forestry was Jerry Merithew of New Brunswick. John Crosbie became Minister of Justice, and Tom Siddon was in the Cabinet as Minister of State for Science and Technology. Several of my other west-coast colleagues were also in Cabinet: Pat Carney, MP for Vancouver Centre, was busy dismantling the Liberals' National Energy Policy as the Minister of Energy, Mines and Resources. John Fraser of Vancouver South was Minister of Fisheries and Oceans. David Crombie, the former mayor of Toronto, was sworn in as Minister of Indian Affairs and Northern Development.

Desperately trying to get acquainted with his job, David Crombie called upon my brief experience as chairman of the parliamentary committee on Indian Affairs. David was interested in my views and suggestions regarding a review of Native treaties, and on how to fill the gaps in places such as British Columbia that were not covered by them, thus adding to the complexity of the claims process, which he wished to accelerate. He asked me to head a commission to study the subject, interpreting the treaties in both historic and modern contexts to determine and better define any rights and unfulfilled obligations inherent in them.

I eagerly accepted the offer because it allowed me to be away from Parliament for extended periods of time and gave me the excuse I needed to reject any other offers to appoint me to committees, which in the main exist to keep members busy and focussed on matters that don't interfere with the real agenda of the Prime Minister's Office and the government. I insisted on Walter Rudnicky, a good friend of both Gene Rheaume and Louise Hayes, as my deputy and consultant. Walter was a former senior civil servant who had won a wrongful dismissal suit against the federal government, which had fired and blacklisted him as a member of a revolutionary "extra-parliamentary opposition" group that was intent on destroying the existing political and social structure in Canada. Now there was a man after my own heart, particularly when it came to dealing with our Native people and their problems.

Walter shared my conviction that nothing less than fundamental change in the relationship between the Native population, the government, and the rest of society would ever result in breaking the cycle of poverty, deprivation, and mistrust to which they still feel shackled.

Our report would attempt to dispel the great myth that social and economic equality with the non-native community can ever be achieved as long as Natives insist on clinging to their traditional pursuits of hunting, fishing, and gathering as their sole sources of livelihood, and persist in their traditional ties to collective forms of self-government. We would expose some of the flaws, false assumptions, and contradictions by which the treaty commissioners allowed themselves to be influenced. We would recommend a process that would lead to the development of separate political and social structures, ones that would allow Natives to guard against cultural assimilation, but would remain harmonious with the democratic principles and charters of rights by which the rest of us govern ourselves. It was agreed that Treaty 8, which covers parts of Saskatchewan, most of Alberta and all the area in my constituency of northeastern British Columbia, would be used as a model.

Walter and I travelled extensively throughout the area meeting with Native leaders and their representatives. The report, which recommended a formal structure and process that would eventually replace the Indian Act, was presented to the minister on January 31, 1986. It died shortly after the department experts, who would no doubt be burdened with the guilt of past neglect and have their jobs threatened, managed to convince the minister of the wisdom of the status quo. The report has been dead ever since.

I also found myself occasionally filling in for colleagues who, given the additional demands on their time as ministers from British Columbia and members of special Cabinet committees, found it exceedingly difficult to discharge political duties in their constituencies. This explained my attendance one year at an annual Italian festival in Vancouver.

The larger metropolitan centres such as Toronto, Montreal, and Vancouver, with their heavy concentrations of immigrant communities, pose both a problem and an opportunity for any politician with an instinct for survival. Our predecessors in government were masters at tailoring their political message to the demands of those ethnic communities whose patriotism for their home countries remained as strong as that for their new homeland. While Germans chose to assimilate as quickly as possible, other immigrant groups such as Italians, Greeks, and Asians preferred the comfort of the best of both worlds. They also tended to respect the guidance of their own leaders during an election. Catering to their peculiar demands still ranks among the highest priorities of every one of our political parties.

It was no doubt my special attributes that prompted Pat Carney and my other Vancouver colleagues to give me the honour of representing them and the government at the Italian community's annual ball, which was held at the city's Italian Cultural Centre. The disappointment of not having a person of higher rank, perhaps even the new prime minister, respond to the invitation was quickly dispelled with the revelation of my impressive credentials. Who other than an immigrant whose parents had chosen Francis of Assisi, the 12th-century Italian saint, to lend him his Christian name, could possibly be better qualified to convey the prime minister's personal greetings and message of recognition for the unparalleled contribution the Italian community had made to Canada, and to represent their special concerns and needs in Ottawa, where a new government had just been installed? The best indication of how well my speech was received was to be given the rare honour of acting as one of three judges of the beauty contest, the highlight of the festivities.

For most of the evening, I was the target of every member of the contestants' extended families, who insisted on acquainting me with the special skills, attributes, and exceptional character of their entrant. Even the mothers got into the act, extricating me from the throng of petitioners to test my skills on the dance floor.

"Atsa my girl," said one amply proportioned lady, beaming with pride and pointing to one of the candidates—after she had literally carried me to the front of the hall, where the contestants were now gathered in preparation for the big event.

The rules by which the judges were to be guided appeared to be very basic in that the outcome was pre-ordained. Even before the ladies, every one of whom Michelangelo would have been proud to have as a model for a fresco adorning the ceiling of the Sistine Chapel, had finished displaying their exemplary skills and impressive physical assets, it became clear that my fellow judges were working from a script that limited them to a single choice. Ever the champion of the underdog, my own preference was a young lady whose hidden beauty required the special skills of a beholder to discover. By confessing my disappointment and surprise at having been invited to preside over such an important event without being able to exercise my judgement, I forced my fellow judges to choose between the wrath of the community's president and his council and the blessings that might be anticipated from the new government in Ottawa, about which I had created such high expectations.

After prolonged and serious discussions, during which I remained the only one paying any attention at all to the proceedings on the stage, they were still inclined to favour the former, but finally offered to support my candidate on the condition that I make the official announcement and present the lucky contestant with the prize. From the corner of my eye, I could see my two judicial colleagues leaving the stage through a back door just as I was making my way to the microphone.

The tearing of the envelope shattered the silence. The reaction to the announcement was similar to what one might hear from a gallery of thousands watching Tiger Woods miss a two-foot putt for a birdie that would have won him the Masters Tournament. The rest was a blur. Those seated at the head table were on their feet. Stern-looking, moustachioed faces were elbowing their way toward them. Several others, including the president's wife, had the presence of mind to escort me off the stage and toward the exit. I met with no resistance at all to my suggestion that, given the advancing hour, it might be wise for me to be on my way back to my hotel.

I had barely entered the room at the weekly meeting of our British Columbia caucus when the Honourable Pat Carney, now Minister of International Trade, blurted out, "How could you have been so stupid as to allow yourself to be conned into being a judge at an Italian beauty contest?" Even before I could muster my thoughts to formulate a defence, the Minister of Fisheries, the Honourable John Fraser, warned our Vancouver colleagues to brace themselves for the next election, since we had just lost four-fifths of the Italian vote. Indeed, it's entirely possible that some of the 42 seats and 7 percentage points by which our majority was reduced between the 1984 and 1988 election could be attributed to such blunders.

Members of Parliament ignored such important voting blocks and special-interest constituencies at their peril. In my own constituency, aside from the Sudetan communities, several other tightly knit, mostly religious communities who traced their roots to Germanic culture and traditions considered the prospect of a German immigrant aspiring to become a member of the Canadian Parliament quite a curiosity.

Noting that the Progressive Conservative Party might form the next government following the 1984 election, our friends in the Hutterite community outside Fort St. John had thought it prudent to invite Joan and me for a visit. We considered it quite an honour. Of course, the reason for the invitation would have been to discuss some of the election issues, and to be shown the most impressive assets in terms of modern, state-of-the-art farm equipment, buildings, and tools the commune had acquired and assembled.

However, the visit also meant being subjected to the scrutiny of the elders, whose assessment of our background, character, and principles would determine our eligibility to be included in their prayers and be exclusively supported by their menfolk at the polls. The leaders of the group, who were highly regarded throughout the area, could be counted on to exert great influence—even beyond their community—in choosing the right person to represent their interests in Ottawa. Mainly of Swiss–German ancestral origin, they were delighted to learn that both Joan and I spoke a familiar German dialect and were still conversant with the old, Gothic script we were taught in our first two years at school, still in vogue as an adjunct to the basic provincial curriculum taught in their own school.

Another group we got to meet in our riding was the Mennonites. Unlike the Hutterites, who like to keep themselves geographically isolated and resist interaction with the outside community in order to preserve their religious values and identity, the Mennonites in the area are not nearly as averse to engaging the world around them. Also, given that Joan was specifically mentioned in the invitation we had received from them to attend a pre-election meeting at the home of one of their leaders, it appeared that the women among that group might have a say in selecting the candidate worthy of their support.

As it turned out, there were actually two meetings. One, at which only the men participated, dealt with the somewhat more conventional issues the various parties had staked out in their platform such as free trade, the economy, and national unity. The other, at which Joan was the principal guest, was conducted in the kitchen and turned out to be much more focussed on things that really matter: the values we attach to our family and the quality of our spiritual moorings.

The Mennonites are known to take their civic duties very seriously—so much so that two of the leaders even accepted our invitation to a reception to celebrate the splendid victory that they helped us win at the polls. They also showed themselves to be exceptionally forthright and humble by admitting they had attached less weight to my conversancy with some issues than to my skill in avoiding others, such as capital punishment, abortion, and other controversial social policies obviously of greater importance to them. However, they confessed, it was the proceedings in the kitchen that swayed them to overcome some of their reservations.

There is no need to explain why none of my Vancouver colleagues ever again solicited my talents to the service of their ethnic constituents, but that was just as well because it was soon thereafter that my life took yet another dramatic turn that deprived me of the time it would have taken to do justice to such important assignments.

I was in my office on November 19, 1985, attending to some correspondence when I received a call from the prime minister's secretary inquiring as to my whereabouts and whether I would be able to meet with Mr. Mulroney that evening at his residence.

My personal relationship with Brian Mulroney had been cordial and friendly, but nothing led me to expect an invitation to the residence at such short notice and late hour. Of course, there had been John Fraser's resignation from Cabinet shortly after the "Tainted Tuna" affair, in which he had authorized the sale of canned tuna condemned by Fisheries inspectors. The issue centred around a disagreement between Fraser and the prime minister over the involvement of the PMO. Fraser was forced to resign shortly after the affair becoming public on September 17, 1985. It created a vacancy in Cabinet for B.C., but I had long ago resigned myself to the fact that any hopes I might have had for a Cabinet position were misplaced.

Nevertheless, my heart was in my mouth when, shortly thereafter, I received the call from Paul Tellier, the clerk of the Privy Council: "The prime minister has asked me to call you about a matter of outmost secrecy," he said. "You are one of the candidates he has chosen for a Privy Council appointment and he wishes to conduct an interview with you tonight. I am merely calling to tell you that you must not discuss this with anyone, other than perhaps your wife, and to inform you of the procedures the successful candidate will be asked to follow during the swearing-in ceremonies scheduled for 9 a.m. at Government House."

I knew how much Joan thought me deserving of promotion and how disappointed she was for me when it hadn't materialized. It took me some time before I regained enough control of my emotions to speak to her over the phone. She had promised our friends, Reinhold and Erika Herr, that she would help out with the launch of a new branch of their delicatessen stores in Hull, where I now reached her. Trying to be as casual as possible, I told her to make no commitments for the following morning, because she might have to accompany me to an important function at Government House. It didn't work, of course. She knew at once that something out of the ordinary had happened and needed no explanation as to what it might be.

"I will be home waiting for you when you get there," I managed to choke out. "Please promise me that you will not say anything to anybody in the meantime."

As I herded our five-year-old Nissan Stanza through the gate at 24 Sussex Drive, the RCMP officer on guard needed to be assured that I was the person the prime minister was expecting. Inside, I was ushered to a small study where he would join me shortly. He let me stew in my sweat for another 20 minutes before he delivered the second bomb I was hit with that day.

Frank becomes Minister of State for Science and Technology in the "fish and chip shuffle."

"How are you, Frankie?" he wanted to know.

"Can I wait a while before I answer that?" I replied, as nonchalantly as my state of excitement and anticipation permitted.

"I would like you to join us in the Cabinet; does that allow you to put a definition on how you are?"

"I am stunned," I said. He then told me that he expected me to take over Tom Siddon's responsibilities as the Minister of State for Science and Technology. (The press would dub it the "fish and chip shuffle." Siddon would assume the role of Fisheries minister that had been vacated by John Fraser.

I could feel myself getting dizzy, my blood obeying the law of gravity. There had to be a mistake. Surely he must be aware of my background, and must know that a Grade 8 education is hardly the right qualification for what he had in mind for me to do.

"You'll do a great job," he said, obviously sensing my distress. "Don't worry. I intend to take personal interest in this portfolio and you can call on me for support."

There was only one other thing he required from all appointees to Cabinet.

"I will not follow Diefenbaker's lead of insisting on an undated but signed letter of resignation from all his ministers upon their appointment," he said, "but I must ask if there is anything at all in your background that could potentially imperil the integrity of the government or conflict in any way with the oath you'll be required to deliver."

Father Dorer, the village priest back in Forchheim, came to mind, which quickly restored some colour to my face. He would certainly have had a long list of items that he could have thrown in to question my eligibility to sit anywhere near the right hand of the Heavenly Father. However, even though my life had been anything but dull, apart from my arrest and brief incarceration in Forchheim by Ernst Meier as a 13-year-old after the war, I could not think of anything that I needed to confess to this particular deity.

This time the constable stood at attention and offered a smart salute as I aimed the Nissan through the gate, thinking perhaps that, like the blessing of a new priest, a friendly first response from a new minister might carry some special magic.

"This is it. There will be no more surprises," I managed to tell Joan as we embraced and tasted each other's sweet tears. I had reached the pinnacle of a career to which only a chosen few can ever aspire. At age 53, 34 years after a Canadian customs and immigration agent at Pier 21 in Halifax harbour had stamped "Landed Immigrant" in my German passport, I was a member of the Queen's Privy Council of Canada.

It would take both of us some time to come to terms with this new reality. Neither of us got much sleep that night. Surely it was all just a dream, I thought every time I woke up during the night. I remember how excited we both were in the morning, assembling the right clothes and getting ready for the event that would change our lives forever. But, as we soon discovered, we would be given precious little time to savour the moment.

The ceremony at Government House was sombre, dignified, short, and sweet. Madam Jeanne Sauvé, our Governor General, whom I had befriended during an official visit to Germany in September 1981, was most sincere in offering her best wishes. The Clerk of the Privy Council administered the oath and, aside from Madame Sauvé and the prime minister, only Tom Siddon, his wife, Pat, and, of course, Joan, attended.

As we stepped outside Government House to face a solid wall of cameras and reporters, the reception was anything but sombre, dignified, short, or sweet. I didn't have to wait long at all for the obvious question and, as it turned out, I didn't need to worry about having to enlighten anyone in this crowd about my background. A press release had been circulated moments before, so everyone was aware of what had happened inside.

As usual, Tom was not at all shy about stepping up to the microphone that had been positioned in the centre of the front yard, but it seemed that for the moment, people were more interested in testing my mettle for the first time. Everybody talked and shouted at once, but finally a consensus emerged that yielded to perhaps not the loudest, but certainly the most cunning of the questions being floated.

"Mr. Oberle, how do you intend to respond to any questions the science community could legitimately ask about your competence or qualifications to head such an important portfolio, given your sparse educational background?"

Fortunately, I could reach back to some basic rules taught us by the likes of George Hees and some of the other old pros. You lower your head for just a few seconds to give the impression that the question merits a thoughtful response and then slowly raise your eyes to the level of the inquisitor and pretend to be as sincere as possible, even though you lie by telling him that you are glad he asked the question.

"I am glad you asked this question," I responded. "In fact, it's much the same question I asked the prime minister when he offered me the job. His response was that he wouldn't be asking me to either design or build the spaceship that would take us to the moon or even be involved in figuring out the flight plan. Instead, he said, he needed me to help arrange the priorities of the government and shape public attitudes suited to an environment in which the science community can flourish."

It seemed to go over well, but I knew I wasn't off the hook. The next question was the zinger. It came from Harvey Oberfeld, a CTV reporter from Vancouver. He had done his homework well.

"Tell me, Mr. Oberle," he wanted to know, "how do you intend to reconcile the responsibility inherent in the oath you have just sworn to Her Majesty the Queen of Canada with your background in the Nazi party?"

There was a stunned silence, as if someone somewhere had turned off a switch. It wouldn't have been so bad if, instead of lowering my head, I hadn't glanced over to the sidelines, where Joan was watching the proceedings. I could see her horror-stricken face, tears welling into her eyes, and couldn't think of any way to comfort her. My first instinct was to go for his throat, but good old Tom, who was standing beside me, had the presence of mind to take charge of the situation.

"I don't think," he said as he grabbed the microphone, "that anyone here believes that Frank will grace such a stupid question with a response." To my surprise they all seemed to agree.

As we climbed into Tom's staff car for the trip back to the Hill, I instructed his driver to drop me off at the entrance to the East Block, where Erik Nielsen's office was located. I knew the prime minister was already on his way to Toronto, where he was scheduled to deliver a luncheon speech. Erik, who was serving as the deputy prime minister at the time, would likely be the only person able to get in touch with him to convey the good news that his new Minister for Science and Technology had just made history by having established the dubious record of the shortest time in service to her Majesty the Queen's Privy Council.

Erik, whom I knew had recommended me for a Cabinet appointment, was beside himself.

"How old were you anyway when the war ended?" he wanted to know. "I'll deal with that son of a bitch," he said, "and in the meantime I want you to concentrate on your new job. You may at best have 48 hours to become a 30-second expert on everything there is to know about your portfolio." He also promised to be in touch with the prime minister as soon he got off the plane in Toronto and before he had a chance to listen to a newscast featuring the debacle.

Somehow I couldn't believe that that was the end of the affair. I found it difficult to concentrate and become immersed in the mountain of briefing material that was already piled on my desk when I got to the office. There was that doubt again, that feeling of being haunted by the ghosts of my past, but it soon passed. Gudrun, Lynn, and some of the staff in the adjacent offices had arranged a reception to which no ghosts were invited. Gudrun, in particular, had every reason to claim for herself a portion of the credit for what we had achieved. The phones were ringing off the hook, but the most important call came late in the afternoon from the prime minister himself. He congratulated me on how I had handled the media scrum in front of Government House and, no doubt sensitive to the torment it must have caused Joan and me, offered thoughtful words of encouragement to put my mind at ease about his own reaction to the news.

Joan was back at work in Erika's shop when I called her with the good news. We decided to have dinner at the parliamentary restaurant before going home to make some calls to share the good news with the rest of the family.

The reception we got as we entered the restaurant was overwhelming. Colleagues and friends from all sides of the House and the entire staff of the restaurant came to the table, generously sharing their thoughts and offering good wishes. But nothing prepared us for what we found as we got off the elevator at Number 20 The Driveway. The full length of the 16th floor hallway was covered with bouquets of flowers and ribbons, many from friends in the German community, as well as their clubs and associations. The cards expressed deep and profoundly personal feelings of satisfaction and gratitude in having one of their own recognized and appointed to such an important public office.

Frank and Joan in his ministerial office in the Confederation Building with the Peace Tower behind them.

Back in Forchheim, Erich made sure no ink was spared in printing the headlines in local and regional papers highlighting the event.

As I took the new seat assigned to me on the front benches the next morning, I was greeted with a standing ovation and a steady stream of well-wishers. Two of them, John Turner and Ed Broadbent, the leader of the New Democratic Party, expressed their outrage at Harvey Oberfeld's behaviour the previous day, both offering to propose a motion of censure that could have resulted in his losing his credentials for the parliamentary press gallery. Erik Nielsen and I counselled against such a move on the grounds that, given the source and that none of the media outlets had picked up the story, any further reaction would give the story a buoyancy that it didn't deserve.

As soon as we got our feet back on the ground, Joan arranged a reception for all our B.C. colleagues to celebrate the event. Several among them no doubt had high expectations of claiming the prize for themselves, since most of them had much more impressive credentials in terms of education and loyalty to the party and its leaders. Yet it was their unreserved offer of support and continued friendship that gave me the confidence to tackle my new assignment.

MINISTER OF STATE FOR SCIENCE AND TECHNOLOGY AND MINISTER OF FORESTRY

1985–1993

CHAPTER 19

Fencing with Bureaucrats

Guideline for Bureaucrats: (1) When in charge, ponder. (2) When in trouble, delegate. (3) When in doubt, mumble.

—James H. Boren

Perhaps it is wrong to claim that I was denied the privilege of a university education. It's just that I pursued my advanced studies in a rather unorthodox fashion, entering university by way of the president's office and the faculty clubs—not as a student, but as Minister of State for Science and Technology. The deans of the various departments generously offered their private tutorship on my new responsibilities, with the emphasis, of course, on their peculiar interests and expertise, thus sparing me the trouble of attending tedious lectures. Such are the perks for people in public office who happen to be in charge of an annual budget of over $4 billion of public money, a good share of which was allocated to the universities.

I quickly discovered there was no shortage of advice from a great variety of sources. The department presented me with volumes of reports and policy directions, some at variance with the material supplied by my predecessor and his political staff. My schedule during the first two weeks in office was crowded with departmental briefings and delegations representing the agencies that would be reporting to me, such as the National Research Council, the Science Council of Canada, three councils in charge of the peer-review process that aids in funding disbursements to universities, and some of the other major science establishments.

The theme of these discussions, it soon became apparent, was as consistent as it was universal. Canada, relative to our GDP, spends far less money on research and science-related activities than every other modern industrial nation in the world. My first priority, therefore, given the personal interest expressed by the prime minister, was to insist on a massive infusion of new money.

The other consistent message each of the practitioners conveyed to me was the urgent need to refocus the government's priorities to favour their particular discipline of science over all of the others. I had to discover for myself that in every other modern industrialized country in the world, it is the private sector, not the government, that contributes most of the money for research. One must keep in mind that in all of these discussions, I was dealing with experts whose minds had been narrowed to focus exclusively on their work. George Christoph Lichtenberg once said that "People who read a great deal rarely make great discoveries. I do not say this in excuse of laziness, but because invention presupposes an extensive independent contemplation of things."

I discovered quite early in life that to make the world a better place, one has to look beyond the established order and the rules governing it. I am also of the view that in the quest to remake the world, one must first learn to avoid the counsel of experts, who are perhaps best defined as people who are trained and disciplined to work within certain clearly defined limits of their particular profession.

Well, nobody can ever be perfect, except perhaps for taxi drivers and barbers who, according to George Burns, are usually way too busy driving taxicabs or cutting hair, which is really too bad, given the wise counsel generously dispensed from such sources.

I am reminded of an experience I had on my way from downtown Edmonton to the Nisku International Airport in a taxi one early morning. Just to make conversation with the driver, I inquired why it was that, given all the perfectly suitable land much closer to the city, the airport ended up about 25 miles away.

"I suppose," was his prompt reply, "that's where all the airplanes land."

In the face of such unassailable logic, one can't help but speculate how many hundreds of millions of dollars the government could have saved the Canadian taxpayer had the era's transportation minister whose decision it was to build the Mirabel airport 60 miles outside of Montreal weighed the advice from his experts against that of my taxi driver. The latter would at least have told him that all the airplanes were landing at Dorval (now the Pierre Elliott Trudeau International Airport). Mirabel was the world's biggest airport when it was opened in 1975 at a cost of $500 million. It is still the biggest in Canada—boondoggle, that is. It was closed to passenger traffic altogether by November 1, 2004.

Unfortunately, when experts are confronted with new ideas that don't fit their parameters, their narrow minds instantly engage to produce arguments for why they can't be implemented. It stands to reason that if there were better ways to do things, the expert surely would have thought them up himself.

"If you are so smart," I usually responded to any expert critical of the way I was managing my affairs, "why aren't you rich?"

That is not to say that successful people in business and industry should not seek out expert accountants or lawyers for advice, but to give these people the mandate for overall management, as it is common practice with larger corporations, is not always the best choice.

The same holds true in government. Most senior bureaucrats are hired for their expertise. All too many politicians, even if they are bereft of ideas themselves, can rely on their constituents and a whole host of other individuals and organizations to supply them with a steady stream of great new ones against which to balance their in-house advice. Sadly, rather than championing some of these causes and ideas, they find it more convenient—and certainly, as was demonstrated with some of my own projects—less time-consuming to rely on their experts to provide reasons why they should be discarded.

As a result, very little ever changes, except that the heavier our reliance on bureaucrats to run the country, the greater the justification to hire more experts. That, too, is an unwritten law.

I was fortunate. Among the first to present themselves in my new office was Dr. Stuart Smith. In 1982 he had been appointed president of the Science Council of Canada, after serving five years as the leader of the Liberal Party in Ontario. But it wasn't his political credentials that caused me a tinge of anxiety as I prepared for the meeting. Stuart Smith had been the president of the student society at McGill University, graduating in medicine and pathology and winning the school's top honours. He had been a professor of psychiatry at McMaster University's medical school before he was lured into politics. I can only imagine what he thought he would find after having studied my credentials.

I should not have worried. Here was one of those exceptionally gifted people who understands the important relationship between science and society—the critical balance that must exist between the all-important, curiosity-driven basic science and the applied research targeted toward the country's industrial needs and priorities.

On the advice of the bureaucracy, my predecessor, Tom Siddon, had cut the budget allocated to the Science Council in half. Since previous governments had not paid the slightest bit of attention to its recommendations in the past, Stuart Smith suggested that I might wish to heed the advice I was given to phase out the Science Council altogether. In line with our government's overall priority of bringing spending under control, this was the kind of advice I was looking for. But I was also curious and suspicious enough to delay my decision until I'd had a chance to review the advice offered by the council in the past and to ask Stuart to present me with his case to justify their existence into the future. I soon discovered that the reason for the lack of affection the bureaucracy had shown the Science Council was that the eminent people who served on it had the effrontery to openly challenge the bureaucrats' expertise.

The council, for example, had pointed to the fact that while there were over 20 departments and agencies in the government engaged in research and science-related activities, no one was comparing notes or making any effort to avoid duplication. The major players, such as the departments of Agriculture, Energy, Transport, Communications, and National Defence, were all in competition with the National Research Council (NRC) for scarce resources. The NRC itself was still operating according to the original mandate it had been given in the early part of the 20th century, long before the universities were well enough established throughout the country to generate much of the intellectual capital on which Canada thrives today.

In the comparisons we made to assess our performance, we tended to look at countries such as Germany and Japan for the proper spending targets, with no regard for the fact that as a resource-rich and resource-dependent economy, we might well have different priorities.

Stuart Smith also pointed out to me that it was costing the government over a million dollars a year to sustain the Canadian Patent Development Agency, whose main objective, aside from acting on behalf of all government departments involved in research to register their patents, should have been to diffuse or commercialize some of the ideas generated. Instead, they appeared to have interpreted their mandate as carte blanche to shelter and protect any patents resulting from the government's in-house research and science efforts from the light of day.

So one of my first major decisions as the new Science and Technology minister was to ignore the advice to phase out the Science Council and instead commission it to organize a major national forum, involving not only the science community but also private-sector industry, labour, and every other stakeholder as well.

The National Forum on Science and Technology was held in Winnipeg on June 9–10, 1986, and would become the basis for a national science policy that promoted excellence and established a balance between curiosity-driven research and targeted, applied research. The conference would afford us the opportunity to reflect on the accomplishments of the past when, through focussing on our peculiar need to bridge distances and tame the harsh environment of the north, we became world leaders in the development of certain communications and transportation technologies. When properly focussed on Canada's great potential, we positioned ourselves among the leaders in the world in those natural sciences targeted at our agriculture, energy, and mineral sectors.

My remarks at the conference in 1986 were scripted with the aim of reminding the private sector of the advantages of funding some of their own research activities. The new policy was to be designed to build on our strengths and expose any weaknesses that needed to be addressed. In my opening address to the conference, I said: "What is required of us is not genius. We do not need another think tank, nor just some more consultation. We need clarity. We need to set priorities. We need to develop links with one another. We need to discuss our differences and arrive at mutually acceptable accommodation. We need to understand the role each of us must play."

Most importantly, the conference was designed to build new partnerships with the provinces, business, and labour, so as to identify and focus on the priorities that would keep us in the mainstream of the science and technological revolution rushing us toward the 21st century. The new policy would be promoted even in the lowest grades of the public school system, and alert every citizen to the challenges of the new age. It would become part of our culture, and the exceptionally gifted among our scientists and researchers would be celebrated and rewarded like pop stars and hockey players.

The entire process was preceded by series of round-table discussions involving the various sectors and stakeholders in the science community. Once again, I found the study of other jurisdictions yielded valuable insights and ideas applicable to our situation.

The equivalent of the National Research Council in Germany is the Frauenhofer Institute. The most revealing aspect in comparing the two agencies is the average-age difference of 20 years in their research staffs. The Max Planck Institute, Germany's most prestigious science establishment, which concentrates entirely on pure basic science, also looked to me like the model we ought to adopt to recognize and give a home to some of our own particularly gifted scientific minds.

Such were my hopes and the aims that guided my policies. The enthusiasm and support flowing from it gave us the mandate and confidence to proceed with a series of innovative programs, earning us praise and respect at home as well as abroad. The prime minister, true to his word, agreed to personally chair the National Advisory Board for Science and Technology, a council made up of prominent scientists as well as industry and labour leaders.

Carried away with my own enthusiasm and supported by a cadre of my own trusted experts—having forced some much-needed change at the top level of the bureaucracy—I gradually won the respect and confidence of my staff, most of whom were diligent workers and highly regarded among their peers in the science community.

I had come a long way from working as a baker in the Green Lantern in Halifax, and as a novice logger and hard-rock miner, astonishing myself more than anyone else by the impressive accomplishments and good fortune I had earned and the circles in which I was now moving. Aside from the PM's group, I met regularly with a number of key people in the science community on whom I could rely for impartial and sound advice.

Key to any minister's success is a department's deputy minister. He or she, in the Canadian system, is the link between the political sphere of responsibility and the department's public mandate. My deputy minister was cast in the mould of Sir Humphrey Appleby of *Yes Minister* fame. He was not in the least impressed by my intrusion into his private domain.

"It is my responsibility, Mr. Minister," he told me on one occasion, "to keep you out of trouble and, as long as you insist on going outside the department to question my advice, you are making it very difficult for me."

Only about 240 people were attached to my headquarters in Ottawa, and none of them was allowed any direct contact with my office without the deputy minister being present. Right at the beginning, I had requested a "walkabout" through the offices to be introduced to at least some of the key people. After six months, during the deputy's absence, Gudrun and I decided to venture out on our own. The next morning, he stormed into my office in a highly agitated state.

"I must assume that you no longer have confidence in my judgement and that you are working to undermine my authority," he blurted out. "You have put me in an impossible position, leaving me with no option but to report the incident to the Privy Council office."

I almost felt sorry for the poor man. He had no doubt been briefed on my lack of qualifications for the job and had been instructed not only to keep me out of trouble, but also in line as well. In fairness, it cannot be easy for the bureaucracy to deal with the unbridled enthusiasm with which new ministers promote new ideas, and accept major budget cuts at the same time.

I assured my friend that he could not lose my confidence, since he never had it in the first place, and if he felt that the breach was irreconcilable, I would be prepared to bring his concern to the attention of the prime minister himself.

It took me another nine months to have the good man promoted to the position of special advisor to the government, a type of bureaucrat's purgatory where no one is ever bothered for advice.

When the prime minister called me to suggest Bruce Howe as his successor, I was euphoric. What I lacked in skepticism about senior bureaucrats, Bruce more than made up for. As a former president and CEO of MacMillan Bloedel and several other high-profile private positions he was very much accustomed to getting his way. Fortunately, his style matched my own, and the occasions were few when our assistants had to be sent out of the room in order to spare them the bilingual dialogues in which we chose to settle serious disagreements—mercifully so, at least in the opinion of Gudrun and Lynne Ree, Bruce's own executive secretary, whom he had brought with him.

Bruce had other assets to boast of, as well. His wife, Ann, had gone to school with Brian Mulroney in Baie-Comeau, Quebec, and the prime minister himself had recruited Bruce. No doubt it was much closer to perception than to reality, but this personal relationship with God had allowed my new deputy minister to immediately become invested with the rank of St. Peter among his peers in the bureaucracy. The structural changes and new programs that we hatched, with the help of our consultants and some absolute gems we had discovered among department staff, were perceived to be sanctioned and guided by the hand of God himself. The department soon blossomed into something akin to a central agency.

Since Bruce and I authored the agenda and laid out the topics for discussion at the high-profile meetings with the prime minister and his advisory board, the endorsement of our ideas became routine procedure once we had planted the seeds. Among the major new initiatives we embarked on during those years between 1985 and 1989 were the Centres of Excellence Program, the Canadian Institute for Advanced Research (CIAR), the Canadian Scholarship Program, the Mobile Satellite Program (MSAT), RADARSAT (the Earth-observation system incorporating Synthetic Aperture Radar (SAR), the latest, state-of-the-art technology), and, of course, the space program.

At this time, both the Soviet Union and the U.S. were actively competing in space, sending up craft and launching satellites and probes. We in Canada had concentrated our efforts on the development and launch of ever more sophisticated communications satellites and on the more narrow niche of space robotics. Canadarm, the Remote Manipulator System, was

With Canadian astronauts Bjarni Tryggvason and Steve Maclean at the announcement of Maclean's mission.

first deployed on a U.S. space shuttle in 1981 and 1982. Canada became established as the undisputed leader in the field, earning us the invitation to participate in the Space Station Enterprise.

A year before my appointment as Minister of Science and Technology, Marc Garneau, aboard the *Challenger*, had become the first Canadian in space. By January 1986, the Russians were ready to put up the first element of the space station Mir, the shuttle *Columbia* was orbiting the earth, and the *Voyager 2* probe was investigating Uranus. It became clear that space exploration would undoubtedly yield the modern equivalent of the glory and power the great explorers of centuries past had earned for their respective countries. It would provide the modern-day focus for mankind's inherent instinct for adventure and curiosity.

However, given the tight fiscal situation in the late '80s, when every department was forced to reduce their budget by at least 10 percent, the space program proved to be the greatest challenge to maintain, since it required over $1 billion in new funds. It was hard to convince my colleagues in Cabinet that passing up the opportunity to partner with the United States, Japan, and the 12 countries of the European Union in embarking on this new frontier would deprive future generations of Canadians of their rightful place among those shaping our destiny. My colleagues had to be reminded of an earlier time in our party's history, when the Diefenbaker government scrapped the Avro Arrow program and triggered the exodus of some of our country's brightest stars in the science and engineering fraternity to the United States, as well as exacting a political price we were still paying a quarter of a century later.

Nonetheless, in 1985 we had signed a preliminary agreement under which we would contribute an array of robotic remote-control manipulators, including an advanced version of the Canadarm, as an integral part of the Enterprise station. Lucrative tax incentives were offered and tied to a private-sector matching formula, allowing us to stretch our scarce recourses and attract new money to support research leading up to the project.

In the middle of all this came a day I will never forget: January 28, the day of *Challenger*'s fateful mission, when a spectacular and catastrophic explosion seconds after the launch destroyed the shuttle, killing all seven astronauts on board, including civilian teacher Christa McAuliffe.

After I broke off a meeting with my senior staff, we all stood in stunned silence as the drama unfolded on television before our very eyes. As the

Touring a mock-up of the space shuttle at the Kennedy Space Center.

tragedy began to sink in, I placed a call to Larkin Kerwin, the head of the National Research Council, home of our space program and the astronaut corps, so that we could share some time with the people whose life and work were so closely linked to the crew members who had perished and with whom they had forged such solid bonds of intimate friendship and trust. We met in the boardroom, each of us groping for words that could express the pain and sorrow we felt for each other and for those whose lives the disaster had claimed. Our original corps of astronauts were all there: Roberta Bondar, who eventually became the first Canadian woman in space, Ken Money, Bob Thirsk, Steve MacLean, Bjarni Tryggvason, and Marc Garneau—the people with the "right stuff." We all just stood in silence, holding each other's hands, shedding tears.

Two days later, Senator Pat Carney and I represented Canada at the memorial held to honour and celebrate the lives and achievements of the crew of the ill-fated mission. President Reagan gave the eulogy, quoting the line from the poem by Second World War poet John Magee: "They have slipped the surly bonds of earth to touch the face of God."

Naturally, there were those who felt that we had overreached: space exploration was entirely too risky and ought be restricted to robotic probes.

But others—the astronauts themselves, most of all—became even more determined to overcome the barriers that stood in the way of the "last frontier" left for us to conquer, including some last-minute ones.

Just a few days after we had celebrated the final approval by Cabinet for the space program, I was told by my officials that a serious misinterpretation of the space-station agreement just negotiated would add another $200 million to our cost. We had wrongly assumed that the Americans would absorb the cost of the shuttle flights necessary to deliver our contribution to the space station. It was pointed out to us that in fairness to the other partners, who had all agreed to absorbing their own costs, and in view of its own budgetary problems, NASA could not be persuaded to move from its position.

I knew that any attempt to persuade Cabinet to reopen the file and consider boosting our contribution even further would be utterly futile and would strip me of whatever little residue of credibility and support among my colleagues I had in reserve. Knowing that our backing away from the project would not only cause serious delays, but would force us to vacate the world-dominant position in space robotics we had worked so hard achieve, I instructed my staff to arrange for me to meet with Bill Graham, the chief science advisor to the president of the United States. I was going to test my skills at high-stakes poker.

As I walked into Graham's office in Washington, I felt the same tinge of nervousness with which I had walked into the coffee shop at Bralorne Mines 25 years earlier to seek permission from Charlie Cunningham to bring my bride to Canada. I offered my sincere apologies to Graham for the misunderstanding but stated categorically that, as a result, we had come to the painful position of withdrawing from the partnership. Unless NASA could be persuaded to hoist our system to the site without charge, Canada would not be a partner in the enterprise. I hinted that in the hope of retaining the human resources that had been attached to the project in Canada, we would reallocate our finances to the pursuit of other, perhaps equally important, science projects to bolster the strategic position we had already established in space. I did offer some continued support to Spar Aerospace, the lead Canadian company in space robotics, if the remaining partners wished to engage them as a contractor for the project.

Bill Graham was not impressed, but he had to conclude that without our contribution, which was part of the very first stage of development, the project would fall far short of everyone's expectations in terms of timing and it would exacerbate their own budgetary difficulties. He agreed to engage NASA in discussions to find a way out of the dilemma. The Americans blinked first and we were back in business.

I remember that moment during Emil and Berta's visit to Canada when astronaut Neil Armstrong descended from his space capsule on July 20, 1969, to step on the moon. All of us were glued to the television, mesmerized by the event. Emil, I recall, considered it entertaining, but no more so than any other Hollywood-inspired science-fiction movie. He didn't wish to spoil our fun and excitement, of course, but I am certain that he never really believed it actually happened.

Had I been able to look into my own future to see myself, I would have been no less skeptical of the belief that such a "giant step" as I was now a part of was anything more than just another of my impossible, crazy dreams. But there I was, 18 years later in a room in Washington, D.C., with my counterparts from the U.S., Japan, and the 12 European nations, representing Canada as the signatory to our partnership in the Space Station Enterprise.

The timing of the event was curious because it was scheduled for the morning of the same day—September 29, 1988—as the launch of the shuttle *Discovery*, the first flight after the long hiatus following the *Challenger* disaster. My colleague Robert de Cotret, then Minister of Regional Economic Expansion, and I had flown that morning to Washington, where we joined our counterparts from the other signatory nations on a military flight to Cape Canaveral to witness the launch—a most memorable experience.

There were other personally gratifying or astonishing moments from my work on the space program. During his first flight on October 5, 1984, Marc Garneau was equipped with an IMAX camera, a major Canadian contribution to the world of cinematography, bringing us as close to being part of an adventure in space as most people could ever hope to be.

Had he been able to view the resulting documentary, *The Dream Is Alive*, even Emil would have had to accept that perhaps we were on our way after all to God's universe, which, hitherto, apart from Jesus Christ himself, of course, no mere mortal had visited.

Marc Garneau accompanied me to Los Angeles for the premiere of the film; it was just close enough to Hollywood without actually being there. As the sponsor and guest of honour at the gala event, I was asked for a list of people I might wish to invite as my personal guests. Two came to mind immediately: our good friends, Rudi and Poldi Reibenschuh, who had moved their beauty-salon business from Vancouver to greater Los Angeles. Somehow we had kept in touch with each other over all the years since leaving the Pioneer mine, where Rudi and I had toiled and shared the experiences of the first years in our new homeland together, including the great pig-buying adventure. Though it may have been just a little bit intimidating for them, I could not think of a better way to repay them for the friendship and support they had given Joan and me during a difficult phase in an earlier stage of our marriage.

I also managed to invite several of the astronauts I had befriended to visit the good burghers in my Prince George–Peace River constituency. Roberta Bondar spent several days there, motivating young people at various schools and addressing service clubs in the cities. Joe Engels, the American astronaut who commanded space shuttle *Columbia* on the 1981 mission, during which the Canadarm made its space debut, is an ardent hunter and outdoorsman. He accepted my invitation to visit, hoping to combine a bit of business with pleasure.

Astronaut Roberta Bondar visits Chetwynd.

A gifted speaker and storyteller, he kept everyone, particularly his young audiences, mesmerized with his real-life stories of drama and adventure. He spoke of the difficult task it had been to liaise between the Canadian and NASA crews during the installation of the first robotic arm onto the shuttle. Miraculously, everything seemed to fit together just as the engineers had intended. The delivery of the various components was meticulously timed to coincide with NASA's critical time schedule, all except for a six-foot section of the insulating blanket that protected the hardware from the extreme

240-degree temperature fluctuation in space.

The Canadian contingent appeared not to be too alarmed, assuring everyone that the missing part would be retrieved and installed by the time the critical phase of the countdown commenced. Frantic phone calls were exchanged during the last few days, when it appeared the mission would have to be delayed. The way Joe Engels told the story, it was nothing less than a well-timed devious plot by

Otto Jelinek, Minister for Fitness and Amateur Sport, and Frank pose with the torch for the 1988 Winter Olympics as it passes through Ottawa on its way to Calgary.

the Canadians to highjack the entire mission and turn it into a Canadian enterprise. When the Canadian crew had finally installed the missing part and, with just hours to spare, stepped back to admire their handiwork the reason for the delay was no longer a mystery. Several cameras had been installed to monitor the Canadarm's performance, so there it was, in sharp focus: The Canadian flag was proudly displayed and, lest someone among the American and worldwide television audience should not recognize it as such, the word CANADA was there, to boot. The rascals!

In desperation, Joe and one of his crew, unable to locate an American flag anywhere within the space centre, finally found a specimen in a downtown hardware store, but neither its size nor the location in the shuttle bay where it could be mounted could compete with the Canadian symbol, and their effort did little to mitigate the damage.

Canada's accomplishments in space ought to be a great source of national pride. Next to the United States and the USSR, we were the third nation to establish our presence in space. In fact, with the launch of the Anik-series satellites in 1972, we were first to establish a commercial, space-based communications system. The next-generation Hermes satellite was the most powerful of its kind in the world, capable of direct-to-home transmission.

We should never miss an opportunity to honour those among us who have become world leaders in the various disciplines of science and have made it possible for Canada to compete with the best and brightest in the new frontier. People like Marc Garneau are true Canadian heroes. A brilliant scientist, he is now president of the Canadian Space Agency, after following his historic *Challenger* flight in 1984 with two more flights in 1996 and 2000. In total, he has logged 677 hours in space.

My own involvement, modest as it was compared to those who dared believe that Canada had the right stuff, fills me with a sense of pride, personal accomplishment, and deep satisfaction.

CHAPTER 20

Measuring Success

Fame has also this one great drawback, that if we pursue it, we must direct our lives in such a way as to please the fancy of men, avoiding what they dislike and seeking what is pleasing to them.

— Benedict de Spinoza

Despite the wise counsel and generous support I enjoyed from some of the country's luminaries in the science establishment, not everything we set out to do during my tenure in the science portfolio met with success. Given the government's tight fiscal situation, perhaps the most notable achievement was the 44 percent increase in our budget allocation, from $4.1 billion in 1984 to $5.9 billion in 1993.

Projects and new initiatives, for which there was never any shortage of ideas, had to be carefully selected to fall within the purview of the science and research strategy adopted by the Winnipeg conference and to help address the government's other major priorities. The prime minister's National Advisory Board played a key role in this process. Aside from our commitment to the space program, there were several other major initiatives that proved to be of lasting benefit. One of them was the Centres of Excellence program. The centres provide generous funding to support networks and partnerships among scientists, both at home and abroad, who have already earned recognition for leadership in their respective scientific disciplines.

The Canadian Scholarship Program answers the need to entice more young Canadians to shift their aspirations away from the arts and social studies toward the study of natural sciences and engineering. Half the funds allocated were earmarked for women. By the end of my mandate, over 12,500 Canadian students had benefitted from the program.

Brian Mulroney and Frank at the National Conference on Technology and Innovation, January 13–15, 1988.

The Canadian Institute for Advanced Research (CIAR), is another unqualified success story. It was the brainchild of Fraser Mustard, another of those very few exceptionally gifted people who understand the relationship between science and society, and between knowledge and wisdom. Fraser promoted CIAR as a university without walls that could attract young scientists who were committed, adventurous, and courageous enough to think outside the box, challenging the experts and working in an interdisciplinary environment toward the opening of new frontiers.

I liked the idea right from the start and managed to free up some seed money to help get it launched. CIAR operates much like the Max Planck Institute in Germany where, through a rigorous peer-review process, both people and fundamental, untargeted research projects are selected and funded. Perhaps its biggest accomplishment, in the short term at least, was the attraction it held for a number of young Canadian scientists who had left the country for more hospitable research climates but had now returned home.

The MSAT and the RADARSAT programs were part of the overall space initiatives. MSAT, the first Canadian mobile satellite service, was launched in 1993 with the aim of providing what has become an indispensable mobile telephone service, operating anywhere in Canada and using small and inexpensive terminals. RADARSAT is a uniquely Canadian success story; for 24 hours a day, unimpeded by cloud cover, it provides timely global geographic information, satellite imagery, and remote sensing that is used in crop monitoring, ocean surveillance, and a myriad of other services.

The National Research Council of Canada (NRC), the most important of the agencies reporting to me, was another story.

The NRC sees itself as being singularly responsible not only for keeping our scientific community in step with the rest of the world, but also for the leadership Canada enjoys in certain key technological developments and scientific discoveries. But there is also no army in the entire world better trained in the art of bureaucratic turf war than the NRC. Resting on the laurels of its glamorous past, it considers itself beyond reproach. Working at arm's-length from the government, it relies on its outside clientele and other departments of government for its defence against hostile forces threatening its independence. My attempts to persuade the council to reorient itself to meet the new challenges of the age of technology, and my polite suggestion that the Frauenhofer Institute in Germany might be looked at as a model, were immediately classified as hostile acts.

The Frauenhofer Institute has much to recommend itself, in my view. It is only partially funded by the government, and relies heavily on the private sector and joint-venture partnerships for its financial needs. Most of its work, therefore, is focussed on applied research with specific commercial targets and opportunities. As one of its prime functions, the institute attracts from universities and technical colleges some of the most gifted people in the various natural science and engineering disciplines, honing and developing their knowledge and skills with the chief purpose of making them available for secondment or recruitment for permanent positions by the private sector. Sadly, my best efforts to steer the NRC into a similar direction failed miserably.

My meagre head-office staff was no match at all against the guerrilla warfare that was launched in the media against the government, and me, in particular.

At a press conference on July 18, 1987, I hinted at my desire to reorient the NRC's mandate in order to capitalize on research performed in government labs, recommending more effective private-sector linkages and a greater emphasis on skills development. The headlines in the *Ottawa Citizen*, the *Toronto Star*, and the *Montreal Gazette* read: "Ottawa Ready to Sell Labs to Private Sector."

A relatively modest cut to the NRC's budget in October of 1986 sparked a torrent of headlines. "NRC Budget Axe Fells World-Famous Scientist," blared the *Ottawa Citizen* on October 16, 1986. "Research Council Cuts 200 jobs" was the headline in the *Calgary Herald*. The *Globe and Mail* took the prize for the most outrageous rumour emanating from the council: "Draft R&D Plans Ask Ottawa to Cut Thousands of Jobs." The offices of the prime minister and my colleagues were flooded with letters and phone calls demanding a stop to the "senseless attack" on the country's most important research establishment, with some suggesting that I be relieved of my duties.

This disinformation campaign resulted in the only major altercation I had with the prime minister throughout my tenure in his ministry. He gauged the political heat much too intense for us to absorb if I insisted on forcing the issue. We settled on a classic compromise: a commission to review the NRC's mandate and make recommendations to the government—within the time it would take to make room on the shelves, where the report would share space along with all the others that would never be read or receive the slightest bit of attention.

I was not the first or only one to identify the lack of interest and commitment shown by the private sector in getting involved in research, promoting innovation, or gaining competitive advantage. The multimillion-dollar compensation and bonus packages the CEOs of some of the larger companies appropriate for themselves at the expense of their shareholders are not based on their farsightedness or their commitment to research and development, which might secure the longer-term future of their enterprises, but rather on the bottom line of the balance sheet recording the results of the last quarter's business.

It has always seemed very curious to me that a country as dependent as we are on our natural resources such as mining and forestry must depend mainly on foreign imports of equipment and technology to harvest and process our trees and minerals. I remember the miners in Pioneer using

Swedish drill bits and air drills exclusively to carve their way through the rock. The power saws we use to cut our timber are imported from the U.S. or Europe. We were even importing the paper on which we printed our postage stamps. A single company in the U.S., Weyerhaeuser, allocates more money in its annual budget for research than the combined effort of all Canadian companies and the government. Why bother with innovation? Why spend money and resources to build expensive facilities, increasing the labour costs associated with refining and adding value to the resource, when the whole world is clamouring for it in its most primitive form? When the resource runs out and shareholders look for greener pastures, the CEO can always rely on his just reward in the form of a golden handshake for having guided the company through the good times.

Our predecessors in government attempted to address this issue with the implementation of the Science and Research Tax Credit (SRTC) program in January 1984. The purpose of this infamous program, well intended as it may have been, was "to attract investors to science and industrial research projects and to overcome many of the uncertainties in more conventional tax incentives that were perceived as impeding development." Anyone, regardless of history or experience in science or research, could apply. There was no project review or any assessment of the applicants' intellectual capabilities. The money was paid up front and could be passed through directly to the investor.

Almost immediately, the creative activities this program was to unleash were diverted from the research laboratory to the corporation's accountancy office. Instead of attracting investors interested in long-term projects, it attracted ones who were interested only in quick profits, and the "quick flip" was born. For every dollar invested, individual shareholders netted a rebate of $1.25. People couldn't believe their good fortune. The government did issue a moratorium on quick flips in October 1984, limiting tax credits to the issuance of qualifying shares in the company, but the scandalous abuse of the program continued unabated. This was one case where the bureaucrats who conceived and were to monitor and attest to the legitimacy or value of the research projects were no match for the innovative skills of the crafty bean counters in the private sector.

In the end, after the enormity of the fraud had revealed itself, it was discovered that even if the companies had intended to conduct any research, most of them, since they had passed the windfalls through to their shareholders, wouldn't have had the money to pay for it. There was some effort to recoup part of the money, but it merely resulted in bankrupting otherwise healthy enterprises and in having to host some of their directors in jail at additional taxpayers' expense.

The SRTC program was finally eliminated in the May 23, 1985, budget, but not before it had bled $3.5 billion out of the treasury, with little in terms of research or science-related activities to show for it. It has the dubious distinction of being termed the biggest boondoggle ever to come out of the Finance department.

Upon my arrival in Science and Technology, against all advice from the department, I managed to persuade our Finance minister to let me try another approach. Still aiming to lure private-sector industry into getting involved in research, we would commit to a modest increase in funding allocations to colleges, universities, and other research establishments, but tie all of it to a dollar-for-dollar private-sector matching formula.

Naturally, given the recent experience, the idea was met with skepticism and outright rejection. I reasoned, however, that if the bureaucrats in Industry,

From left: Stan Hagen, Barbara Brink, Frank, Flora MacDonald, Gordon Campbell, and Grace McCarthy during ceremonies dedicating the Expo Centre as Science World in October 1987.

The Queen talks with then mayor Gordon Campbell at the dedication of Science World in 1987 in Vancouver, with Frank and Joan in the background.

Trade and Commerce, who had termed the scheme "harebrained," were right, we could actually reduce research spending and deflect the negative political fallout resulting from it onto the short-sightedness of the private sector. On the other hand, should my assumption prove correct, we could claim political credit for doubling our contribution to the sponsorship of industrial research and innovation.

My colleague Michael Wilson, our Finance minister, had no difficulty at all grabbing onto that idea. Soon university professors, their students, and the instructors in our technical colleges were scouring the country in search of strategic partners in the private sector. They had little trouble selling the idea that since the government allowed them to deduct legitimate research expenses from taxable income, it would cost them just 50 cents to benefit from two dollars' worth of professional research. In just over three months, the program was oversubscribed. There was no need for an army of government auditors either. The private sector made certain that their investment yielded the expected return.

For me, these were fun times. There was that extra bounce in my step as I made my way to the office in the mornings. In comparison to my Cabinet colleagues, whose jobs were mostly routine, tinkering here and there with the tax rate or improving or cutting back on certain social programs, I was positioned to do things that were new and exciting and, better still, I was making progress, creating institutions that would have a lasting impact on the lives of future generations of Canadians.

Oddly enough, as my influence and effectiveness rose in Ottawa, it fell in my home riding. It wasn't long after my appointment to Cabinet that my popularity in the constituency began to wane. For one thing, it became increasingly difficult to keep to a schedule of regular visits. Sure, there was now a well-staffed ministerial office in Prince George and sufficient resources to maintain an office in both Dawson Creek and Fort St. John, but people rightly sensed that my personal priorities had shifted elsewhere—away from looking after their special interests and concerns. No longer could I afford to spend most of the summer months during the parliamentary recess travelling the Alaska Highway, showing up at every country fair and rodeo, and riding in every parade.

People have a tendency to ask their federal representatives where they make their home. In my case, it would not have been far-fetched to say that I spent most of my time on airplanes and in airports. It was not unusual for me to wake up in strange surroundings, confused about my whereabouts. There are not nearly enough hours in a day to allow anyone to responsibly discharge the duties of a minister with a busy portfolio and, at the same time, cultivate important contacts in a constituency 6,700 kilometres away. People living on the Prophet River or the Fort Ware Native reserves, who relied solely on my office for any improvement to their squalid living conditions, could not be expected to appreciate the importance of my being away at some international conference when they desperately needed my help. They did not understand how it benefitted them to have me travel halfway around the world to accept invitations to banquets and conferences.

As Science minister, I was now in demand to speak at every science convention throughout the country and abroad, requiring an extra member of staff just to cope with the increase in my travel schedule—and my next visit to Germany reached new levels of eminence.

Frank greets Richard von Weizacker, president of the Federal Republic of Germany, as he arrives in Ottawa.

In early October of 1988 I was invited to a banquet in my honour by the premier of Baden Württemberg in Germany. It actually was not a special trip at all, but the tail end of an extensive mission that started in Oslo, Norway and took us to Hamburg, Köln, and Bonn before we touched down in Stuttgart. It was billed as a private affair designed to build on the friendship that had developed over time between Premier Lothar Späth and me.

However, after our Lufthansa jet touched down at the airport in Stuttgart and the captain requested that passengers remain seated until the special delegation from Canada had disembarked, I knew that Klaus, my nephew, who was charged with organizing the event, had much more elaborate things in mind. He had worked himself to the top of the provincial hierarchy in the Christian Democratic Party and was well entrenched in a brilliant career with Lothar Späth's administration. Neither of us was too shy to trade on one another's prominence.

After a hearty embrace, Klaus introduced me to Minister Herzog and the rest of the reception committee that had gathered on the tarmac. A fleet

The 1988 official visit with Lothar Späth, *ministerpräsident* of Baden Württemberg, in the *Neuen Schloss*, Stuttgart, Germany. Standing from right to left are Minister Kleinert, Minister Herzog, Lothar Späth, Frank, Joan, Mrs. Späth, Mrs. Herzog, and Mrs. Kleinert.

Frank and Premier Lothar Späth meet in Stuttgart on October 4, 1988.

of Mercedes-Benz limousines took us to our hotel. Klaus kept hinting that despite the premier's wish to keep the affair casual, I would nevertheless be expected to treat the invited guests, which included most of the members of Cabinet, to a few words of wisdom. The next major clue came when, after a brief respite, we arrived at the front steps of the *Neuen Schloss* [New Chateau] to be greeted by the premier himself. I also spotted my brother Erich near the front entrance, recording the scene on his movie camera.

It wasn't my first visit to the facility, which dated back to the middle of the 18th century. On an earlier occasion, when I was leading a delegation of

Joan and Frank and a delegation of Canadian parliamentarians, including Duncan Edwards and Bob Coates, meet Stuttgart Mayor Manfred Rommel, son of the famed Second World War general.

Canadian parliamentarians, we were guests of Lord Mayor Manfred Rommel, son of the famous Second World War general, Erwin Rommel. He gave us an exposé of the proud history of Stuttgart, one of Germany's older cities. It was also another one of the places for which "Bomber Harris" and Winston Churchill must have shared a particularly deep affection during the last phase of the Second World War.

The good burghers of Stuttgart, it was deemed, needed to be liberated not only from the "Nasty Nazis," as Churchill called them, but from their homes and their attachment to a proud cultural heritage and its infrastructure. The *Neuen Schloss*, together with some of the churches and other cultural icons, the theatres, libraries, and art museums, some dating back to the 10th century, were totally obliterated. I recall how astounded we all were at the attention to detail that had guided the architects and builders commissioned to restore all of these facilities to their original splendour.

It would no doubt be difficult for someone with a North American mindset to understand how, in a post-war Germany, where millions had lost their lives, most families had lost everything, and most of the industrial infrastructure was totally destroyed, it was possible to generate the resources and attach such great priority to the costly reconstruction of these cultural edifices. To me it was no surprise at all. How could the German people ever dispel the ghosts of the past and their experience with barbarism unless they could first discover a way to reconnect to their moorings and find their souls?

Deep emotions, both of humility and pride, stirred within me at the sound of the choir singing "Ave Maria" and the realization that great leaders—the kings of Wurttemberg, whose residence this was; the Prussian kings, who came to pay homage to them; and Count Otto von Bismarck, who came to seek support for a constitution that would unite the German people—had all walked these steps before me. As we ascended to the great hall, Joan and I were surprised to suddenly find ourselves among a throng of people all wearing familiar faces and applauding as we entered the hall. I recognized my siblings and their spouses: Ludwig and Hilde, Lina and Reini. Erich was still taking pictures, but Edith was there as well as Rudi, Joan's brother, the priest. Almost every one of our old classmates from Forchheim was there, too, together with several members of the town council and the full choir of St. Martin's Church.

This was anything but a casual affair. Klaus was having a heyday. He had thought of everything, except the predicament I would be in as I tried desperately to ransack my mind for some thoughts and phrases suited to the occasion. I have always found it a good rule to substitute humour for lack of profundity, but having once again made the mistake of looking at Joan for inspiration, even that proved difficult. Mercifully, it wouldn't have mattered what I said in response to the generous remarks of the premier and the representatives of the Forchheim's town council. Conspirators in the planning of such unexpected surprises are usually willing to extend the victims generous poetic licence as well.

There were many other memorable occasions and experiences of this kind, but none perhaps as alluring as the thought that people in privileged positions, such as the one I was given to occupy, are actually deserving of the kind of accolades showered on us that night. However, Joan and I both take great pride in never allowing these events to impinge on our humility or divert us from wanting to stay in touch with the real world.

CHAPTER 21

A Bittersweet Reunion
with My First Love

There is nothing that fails like success.

—G.K. Chesterton

My days as Minister for Science and Technology were too good to last. Successful though they were, for the senior bureaucracy and the geniuses in the Prime Minister's Office, it was a different matter. From their perspective, here was a typical case of a minister with way too much time on his hands interrupting the orderly function of government and generating too much interference from the outside. Wasn't the public already pointing to the fact that government was too big and needed to be scaled down to a more reasonable size? In a sense, the outcry was a good measure of the success and recognition we had earned throughout the country and, most of all, from the science community. It certainly got us the bureaucracy's attention, which manifested itself in open warfare.

Even Bruce Howe, my deputy minister, by now well enough positioned to expect a promotion to a bigger, full-line department, offered the opinion that the Ministry of Industry, Trade and Commerce, on which he had set his sights, could perhaps serve as the new home for a scaled-down science and technology department. Soon the chorus organized by the Ottawa mandarins, harmonious and with sufficient volume, was assaulting the prime minister's ears.

My ministry did survive the November 1988 election, but soon after we had won our second majority mandate it became clear that anything working that well had to be fixed. In January 1989, the Ministry of State for Science and Technology was phased out and its functions relegated to departmental status under the Minister of Industry, Trade and Commerce. Bruce Howe did get his well-deserved promotion, and I finally got to be Minister of Forestry.

After being appointed Minister of State for Forestry by Order-in-Council on September 15, 1988, I served in a dual capacity for a while. On January 30, 1989, Mulroney, undoubtedly sensitive to my disappointment with his decision to phase out the science portfolio, kept his promise to elevate Forestry to full departmental status. On February 23, 1990, I was sworn in as the minister.

Historically, the Canadian Forest Service has been concerned with forest conservation. In 1899 Sir Wilfrid Laurier appointed Elihu Stuart, a former land surveyor, as chief inspector of timber and forestry. Stuart is widely regarded as the father of the Dominion (later Canadian) Forestry Service. In later years, with the provinces assuming full control over the resource, the federal role, aside from the management of the remaining forests on federal lands, reverted mainly to science and research.

Not since the Diefenbaker years had the Canadian Forestry Service had any direct representation in Cabinet. It had been shunted from pillar to post without any clear definition of the role it was to play and the responsibility it was expected to discharge. Successive Liberal governments considered forest-related activities, like agriculture, to be rural primitive occupations that had earned us the image of "hewers of wood and drawers of water." Instead, particularly in Ontario, where the trees were gone anyway, we were mainly preoccupied with cultivating a more modern industrial image. The fact that over 10 percent of Canada's forests grow on federal lands, that over 350 towns and small cities throughout the country depended solely on the forest industry for their livelihood, and that the industry earned more foreign trade for the Canadian economy than mining, fishing, and agriculture combined seemed to matter little.

Both the provincial and federal governments treated the industry as a cash cow, competing with one another to get their hands on the teats. The bulk of the resource belonged to the provinces, of course, and they tended to guard their jurisdiction jealously. The more royalty or stumpage they charged the industry, the less money was left for the federal government to skim off in taxes. Neither of the two senior governments appeared to show any regard for the impact our forestry practices were having on the environment and the ecology. The 19th-century poet Alexander McLachlan would have had every justification to compare us with his neighbour, John, about whom he wrote:

> Speak not of old cathedral forests their gothic arches throwing,
> John only sees in all these trees so many saw-logs growing.

Unlike the reception I had received from the officials on my arrival at Science and Technology, the people at Forestry Canada, who had *The Green Ghetto* as a guide to my personal agenda, were downright co-operative and friendly. As a result, we were able to get a lot done.

The new Forestry Act, which I guided through Parliament in 1990, requires the minister to table an annual report on the state of Canada's forests. Naturally, such a report would be meaningless without the input of data that could only be supplied by the provinces. To my pleasant surprise, I found the provinces, even Quebec, most co-operative in sharing information that would allow us to quantify and catalogue not only the economic values of this great resource, but the social, cultural, and environmental assets as well. The annual report has become a highly regarded standard feature of what remains of the federal presence in Forestry today.

In 1991, the parliamentary forestry committee, under the able chairmanship of my good friend and colleague Bud Bird, the member for Fredericton–York–Sunbury, issued a 140-page report entitled "Forests of Canada: The Federal Role." It was endorsed by Gordon Baskerville, Dean of Forestry at the University of New Brunswick, and his colleagues from the University of Toronto, Université Laval, Simon Fraser University, and also by Les Reed of the University of British Columbia, who had been a valuable source of data, information, and support in the development of *The Green Ghetto*. The all-party-committee report highly praised the government's initiative to create a full ministry and made a number of recommendations that formed the basis for the reorganization of the service.

In Canada there are seven major research establishments strategically positioned in every geo-climatic and economic region of the country; these were asked to embrace the principles of much more integrated management practices, biodiversity, and sustainable development as the new focus for their work. We also worked to harmonize the new policies with the provinces.

A tree-planting ceremony for a cloned tree at Government House with Jean Pigott, chairman of the National Capital Commission and, on the right, the Right Honourable Ray Hnatyshyn.

At the National Forest Congress sponsored by the Canadian Council of Forest Ministers, representatives from Aboriginal, environmental, labour, industrial, professional foresters', and educational organizations joined us in signing the first Canadian Forest Accord on March 4, 1992. My former sparring partner, the legendary Jack Munro, was among the most enthusiastic supporters of this initiative. The accord states as its goal: "To maintain and enhance the long-term health of our forest ecosystems, for the benefit of all living things both nationally and globally, while providing environmental, economic, social and cultural opportunities for the benefit of present and future generations."

In 1991, with *Canada's Green Plan for a Healthy Environment*, our government made a major commitment toward environmental causes that provided my department with the resources to launch the Model Forest Program, the Urban Tree Plant Program, and several other significant forest initiatives.

Under the Model Forest Program, we got the provinces to agree to share their management role over vast areas of forested land in all nine of Canada's distinct major geo-climatic zones, with a management board chaired by the federal government and consisting of representatives from the various special-interest groups with a legitimate stake in the forest. Each of the nine model forests encompasses an area large enough to sustain the integrity and diversity of the entire ecological structure. It is in Canada's model forests that the latest, most advanced forest management techniques are tested, demonstrated, and applied. The self-explanatory Urban Tree Plant Program puts as much work into promoting public awareness and understanding of the importance of trees to our national psyche as it does into the health and aesthetics of our urban landscapes.

All of these new initiatives were on display at the Rio de Janeiro "Earth Summit" in June 1992, where Canada took a strong lead, especially on sustainable forestry. Today there are Canadian-sponsored model forests in several other countries, including Russia. The program, together with the other commitments embraced by the Forest Accord, has gone a long way to repair the negative image and bad reputation we had earned as a result of our past misdeeds.

Despite all this new enlightenment and the attention given to our forestry policies and programs, my colleagues in the trade and economic portfolios could not be persuaded to consider any factors other than those related to our foreign-exchange earnings, which were threatened by the

Brian and Mila Mulroney visit the Chetwynd primary school after the area was designated as the Forestry Capital of Canada in 1992.

American imposition of a duty on our softwood lumber. Not the slightest interest was shown in the proposal I had advanced as a solution to the pernicious treatment by the United States.

In the dispute, which is still ongoing, U.S. lumber producers claim that their Canadian counterparts are unfairly subsidized—this despite the Canada–U.S. Free Trade Agreement, which went into effect on January 1, 1989. Given that our share of the U.S. market in these products is proportionally the same as their demand for Middle East oil, I suggested that we should simply take a page out of the trade manual used by OPEC to similarly control the price of lumber in the U.S. market. Of course, the industry could hardly be persuade to take such an initiative on their own, so it would be up to government to adjust the annual allowable cut to satisfy the objective. A 25 percent reduction of shipments from Canada could be expected to result in a price increase of us$100 per 1,000 board feet of lumber, which would satisfy our U.S. counterparts in that it would guarantee them a return for their product closer to its value, and, even more importantly, it might bring us much closer to an annual timber harvest that can be sustained over the longer term.

My response to the argument about the job losses this might precipitate is also simple. With the extra money earned by the industry, it should make it easier for the provinces to enforce their respective forest practices codes, with the intent of shifting surplus manpower from the mill to more intensive, more integrated management practices in the forest. As an example, I pointed out that Sweden, one of our major competitors in world markets, employs one professional forester for every 15,000 hectares of forest land. The ratio for Canada is one in 450,000 hectares. With similar climatic conditions to our own, the Swedes not only manage to grow almost twice the volume of fibre per hectare of land, they also achieve double the value in terms of finished products from every cubic metre of wood harvested.

It remains a source of frustration to me that even with all the obvious signs of timber shortages, here in British Columbia the experts insist that in the Interior and the northern part of the province, there is still an ample supply of old-growth timber to last us through the next 60 years. Even if one overlooked the fact that it takes 80 to 100 years for trees to grow to maturity in these regions, there is still no allowance made for losses to insects, fire, and disease, all part of the natural cycle as well.

According to the latest federal report on the state of our forests, in 2003 the Mountain Pine Beetle epidemic in British Columbia alone claimed 4.2 million hectares of pine forest, double the area claimed in 2002. It is optimistically estimated that of the 500 million cubic metres of timber affected, 300 million might be salvaged,

Brian Mulroney and Frank visit Dawson Creek.

leaving a shortfall of 200 million cubic meters, the equivalent of 2½ years of the annual allowable cut in British Columbia. The area in the province denuded by fires in 2003 amounts to 266,412 hectares. Perhaps we might consider refocusing our science and research activities to teach pine beetles to change their diet to grass, or find ways to redirect lightening strikes away from the forest toward vacant parking lots in the cities as a solution to the crisis.

Of course, the need for me to occasionally vent these frustrations stems from a strong sense of personal convictions and no doubt some romanticism. Preserving the forests has a special place in my heart and reminds me of my childhood. It is linked to my own sense of spirituality. There are times when I manage to block out my painful memories of Grandfather Leibold and think of him fondly as the one who, in my early childhood, spawned my interest in the forest. I remember him quoting the German poet Eichendorff: "*Der Wald, der Wald! Dass Gott ihn grün erhalt. Gibt gut Quartier und nimmt doch nichts dafür.*" ["The Forest, the Forest! May God preserve it ever green. It gives good shelter and asks nothing in return."]

He had been the patriarch of the family, someone to look up to, someone who was respected by his family and peers alike. I recall the few occasions when he took me on his rounds through his forest, riding on the crossbar of his bicycle, securely cuddled between his strong arms. It was he who first taught me to understand, love, and respect nature, and to feel at peace among the spirits that reside in the forest. If he wasn't among the architects of the concept of sustainable development and integrated forest management, he was certainly a wise practitioner. He no doubt inspired my

289

own dad's love for the forests. To satisfy his spiritual needs, Dad very much preferred his Sunday-morning walks through the forest over joining the rest of the family at church. He was careful never to speak ill of Father Dorer or the church, but it was he who taught me to discover my own spirituality and liberate myself from the dogmatism of the church.

I know I should be proud of my grandfather, but instead I hate myself every time my subconscious conjures up these early childhood memories and makes me wonder whether he would have approved of and shared some of my personal satisfaction and pride in the accomplishments during my tenure in the Forestry Ministry. What makes the memory of Grandfather so painful, therefore, is not the neglect and cruelty he made me suffer after the war, but that earlier memory of him.

I was never one who sought to be recognized for my work, but I must confess to feeling some vanity and pride when I received the annual Canadian Forestry Achievement Award sponsored by the Canadian Institute of Forestry. I was the only politician ever to be recognized with this prestigious award.

It is highly unlikely that any future politician will ever share this honour with me since the Ministry of Forestry, just like the Ministry of State for Science and Technology, did not survive. The portfolio officially lasted only from February 23, 1990, until June 24, 1993, and there has not been a federal Minister of Forestry since. The great spirits that roam the upper regions in those intellectual galaxies of the Prime Minister's and Privy Council offices decided that the department of Forestry, now that all the nation's forest problems were solved, would best function under the umbrella of a combined Natural Resources portfolio, where a minister could be entertained and kept busy, relieved of the urge to disturb the order and tranquility that prevails not only in our country's great forests, but within the realm of the federal bureaucracy as well.

CHAPTER 22

A Full Agenda

We have set a new course; it's not a path—it never was and it never will be—for the faint of heart. But this country was not built by timid souls. This is a path for the daring, the innovative and the nation builders who are now called upon to make a firm decision on behalf of a strong, prosperous and united Canada.

—Brian Mulroney

Trudeau's departure left Canada with a lot of unfinished business in terms of the economy and the constitutional changes he had engineered. In fairness to him, he not only brightened Canadians' images of their own identity, he also positioned us among the handful of the most advanced and progressive nations in the world. He knew how to exploit the weaknesses in the constitutional framework we had inherited from the British by building a power structure around the Prime Minister's Office that is unparalleled in any other liberal democracy. But he had no time for "bean counters" and when we came on the scene after 17 years, with only a few months of interruption, it was high time for a reality check.

We found ourselves replacing an administration that, in the opinion of the auditor general of Canada, had lost control of the public purse. The nation was carrying a crushing burden of debt that threatened the integrity of the most basic social programs and benefit structures. It would take the same kind of strong leadership that Pierre Elliott Trudeau, to his credit, had given us, to repair what he had neglected in his headlong pursuit toward his Just Society.

Brian Mulroney was just the man for the job. It saddens me that Canadians still have such a poor opinion of their 18th prime minister, but history will no doubt reflect his true stature in the light of the man he is and the work he accomplished.

In any event, the Progressive Conservative Party of Canada finally had another strong leader. Exceptionally bright, articulate, and sensitive but firm in his dealings with his caucus colleagues and fair to our opponents, Brian most certainly had what one might expect from the leader of a political party aspiring to form a government.

It has been said that the best way to judge a man's character is to give him power. Only a very few among all the people I had the honour to serve with in Parliament used their office and their power with more dignity and responsibility than did Brian Mulroney. Shame on all those who, during his tenure, abused their own positions of power and privilege, whether in the media or in the political arena, to seek recognition and fame for themselves by promoting and broadcasting malicious rumours and baseless innuendo to attack not only him personally, but his family as well. How unfortunate it is that most Canadians, given the poisonous atmosphere created by the press, never got to know Brian Mulroney.

Rumour mongering is an art form in Ottawa. The slightest whiff of smoke is turned into a towering inferno by some overly ambitious scribe,

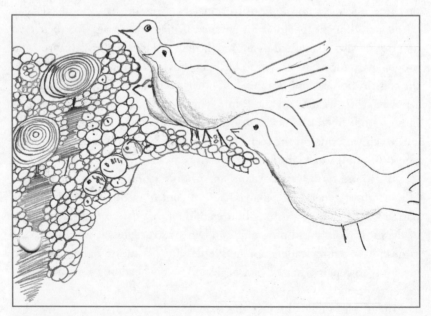

Frank was known for his elaborate doodles. Here's one begun in a Cabinet meeting.

usually with the help of an Opposition backbencher wagering his soul for a newspaper headline. It starts innocently enough and can work both ways. Protected by his parliamentary immunity, the intrepid MP, either on his own initiative or at the suggestion of the reporter, goes on a fishing exhibition during the daily Question Period.

"Mr. Speaker," he might innocently plead, "I have learned from a most reliable source that the Minister of External Affairs, during a recent visit to Bangladesh, was accompanied by his wife, who upon their return to Canada relied on her husband's diplomatic privilege to protect what has been described as "mountains of luggage, bags, and containers" from the curious eyes of our customs officials. My question, Mr. Speaker, is twofold: Can the minister confirm or deny that he is making it a practice of taking his wife on such foreign junkets at taxpayers' expense and could he also inform the House of the disposition of some rather expensive gifts and contraband she brought back upon her return?"

Hansard will report some honourable members as saying, "Shame, shame!" The minister will normally reply by pointing out to the Speaker that he surely could not be expected to grace such a preposterous accusation with an answer. *Hansard* will then record his colleagues' agreement: Some honourable members: "Hear, hear."

The source is now established and the tabloids are free to exploit the juicy affair for all it is worth, without ever bothering to check whether there is any substance to the story. The headline in the next day's papers will read: "The Minister's Spouse Brings Down the House." To the media it matters little which of the political parties are in power. As Claire Hoy, a member of the Ottawa press gallery, once put it, "We have a government to defeat."

I feel compelled to relate one particular story—they are legion— to show just how terribly distorted an image Canadians have of Brian Mulroney and his family and how privileged Joan and I feel to be counted among their friends.

One of my privileges as Minister of Forestry was to host the presenta- tion of a Christmas tree to the Prime Minister's Office every year. The event had an additional charm for me in that there was a distant German connection. General Baron von Riedesel, the commander of the German Brunswick and Hessian regiments that were on loan to the Queen of England during the American Revolution, settled at Sorel, Quebec, after his four-year internment by his American captors. He arrived in Canada with his wife and four children just days before Christmas in 1781. The baroness insisted on a traditional German Christmas and is thus credited with lighting and decorating the first Christmas tree in the New World.

Today, in parts of the Maritimes, Christmas tree farming is a major industry. Every year the association of producers selects one of their members to present a Christmas tree to the Prime Minister's Office in Ottawa. Mila Mulroney and the couple's children usually attended the ceremony, and it was in regards to one such occasion that she suggested how much more meaningful it would be if the ceremony could be held at the Ottawa Children's Hospital instead. Her suggestion was taken up and the results were memorable.

Mila and the kids were already there when Joan and I arrived to be introduced to the doctors, nurses, and other staff of the hospital. Mila knew everyone, including the terminally ill children and their parents, by their first names. She appeared to know everyone's medical history and, together with her own children, who were obviously frequent visitors to the hospital as well, was treated as part of the family. When Brian arrived and made his way through the crowd, shaking hands with every one of the children and

One of the annual Christmas tree presentations.

offering thoughtful words of comfort to them and their distraught parents, he was treated more like a kind uncle than a prime minister. For some of the children it would be their last Christmas, and I found it most difficult to stay composed and find the right words for the occasion. What an honour it was for Joan and me to share this experience with such thoroughly genuine and decent people.

No one could ever accuse the new government of being timid or faint of heart. The Mulroney era of 1984 to 1993 was a time of extraordinary change. The Canada–U.S. Free Trade Agreement was negotiated in 1987, the same year as the stock market's "Black Monday" happened, on October 19.

There was Bill C91, the patent-drug bill that was viewed at the time as a cave-in to American drug companies, but which is recognized today as the reason we enjoy the lowest prices in the world for pharmaceutical drugs. The creation of the Canadian Space Agency in March 1989 was another important milestone, as was the passage of the Goods and Services Tax Act in December 1990. And, of course, there was the 1987 Meech Lake Accord. The last two, full years were equally busy with Canada's participation in the first Persian Gulf War in 1991 and the negotiation of the Charlottetown Accord and the North American Free Trade Agreement (NAFTA) in 1992.

The debates centring on the constitutional amendments we had proposed were particularly engaging and bold. Given the fact that no

Gudrun, Joan, Frank, and Brian enjoy a lighter moment at an Ottawa reception.

A breakfast meeting at Meech Lake.

Canadian government can ever enjoy a majority in Parliament without a sizable contingent from Quebec, Mulroney had managed to convince a group of prominent people on the fringes of the separatist movement in Quebec to join his personal crusade toward constitutional change that would satisfy the legitimate aspirations of the francophone community, correct the omission in the 1982 charter, and guarantee their rightful place in the Canadian federation.

Much has been written about these historic events, but clearly no one has ever come closer than this government did to depriving Canadians of one of their favourite pastimes, a tradition that even predates hockey: the bickering between the French- and English-speaking factions in our country. The Meech Lake Accord was negotiated and agreed to at a premiers' conference in May 1987. It satisfied Quebec's aspirations by defining it as culturally "distinct" and giving it the necessary guarantees to protect the French language. The arrangement agreed to by the premiers depended for its enactment on ratification and the consent of Parliament and the 10 provincial legislatures within a time frame of three years.

However, at the end of that period, the Accord fell victim to the curse of an eagle feather fanned over it by Elijah Harper, a Native member of the Manitoba legislature who filibustered the motion past the deadline. It also fell victim to the petulance of some of the old Trudeau loyalists among the Liberal leadership, including Clyde Wells, the premier of Newfoundland, and of course Jean Chrétien, who had replaced John Turner as leader of the federal Liberals in 1990. Over their dead bodies would they allow anyone to solve our country's most vexing problem, which they themselves had failed so miserably to do. After passage failed in Manitoba, the Newfoundland legislature also abandoned debate on the Accord. The almost unanimous passage by the other eight provinces and the federal Parliament was to no avail.

The Charlottetown Accord, Mulroney's second attempt at constitutional reform, did finally get the blessing and acquiescence of everyone involved in negotiating it, except those for whom it was intended and to whom it mattered most—the Canadian people. The package of proposed amendments was released with all provinces on board on August 22, 1992; it was rejected in a national referendum October 26. Its failure must be attributed to a crucial mistake that could easily have been avoided, had someone only asked me for my opinion on putting the matter to a referendum.

My advice would have been based on Otto von Bismarck's 30-year effort in the 19th century to formulate a constitution for the first German Reich, to which the various and disparate entities of German fiefdoms eventually surrendered some of their sovereignty.

"The German people," Bismarck once remarked, "must never be burdened with the knowledge of how their sausage and their constitution is made." Considering the outcome of the massive effort that was made to prepare Canadians for the referendum, and my not-inconsiderable expertise at sausage making, Bismarck certainly had a point.

Mulroney relied heavily on Joe Clark to champion and steer the constitutional files over some of the hurdles. In addition to serving our government as Minister of External Affairs, Clark shouldered the lion's share of responsibility in forcing the necessary alliances and consensus around the principal components of the Accord, of which he was one of the architects. Here he served with great distinction. No one could attach any blame for the eventual failure of the proposals to any of the efforts Joe contributed to the cause. His name might not feature very prominently in the annals of history as the most gifted leader the Conservative Party ever produced, or as Canada's most successful prime minister, but his custodianship of the constitutional files during the Charlottetown debates and the recognition and respect he earned for himself and the party in Quebec, were no doubt factors in saving the country from the demise that might well have followed a positive outcome of the Quebec referendum on sovereignty in 1995.

Besides the constitutional repairs, our party's first priority had to be boosting our economic prospects by expanding our trade horizons and removing some of the serious obstacles that were stifling growth and expansion. Dismantling the National Energy Program, deregulation, major efforts toward privatization, the removal of the manufacturers' sales tax, and the free-trade deal with the United States were just some of the highlights. As a means of dealing with the large annual deficit and crippling debt left from the Trudeau years, we opted for these measures as a means to stimulate the economy. Coupled with policies to unburden industrial activity from the yoke of excessive overregulation, changes in the tax structure and in fiscal and monetary policies would successfully ease inflation pressures and the high rates of interest Canadians and their governments paid on debt. There was, after all, a profound difference between servicing a $40 billion national debt, with interest rates hovering at 20 percent, and the interest rate of 4 or 5 percent we left behind for our successors to finish the job.

To offset the loss to the treasury from scrapping the manufacturers' sales tax, we opted for a consumption tax, or the so-called Goods and Services Tax (GST).

While this measure was undoubtedly essential to stabilize the country's precarious fiscal situation, one should not have assumed that the Canadian people could be persuaded to accept it without a fight. In fact, during a rather stormy public meeting in Prince George in 1990, I feigned astonishment at learning of a survey showing that only 87 percent of my constituents opposed the new tax. Challenged by the audience to indicate what I would do in response to such a convincing verdict, I promised to seek out the errant 13 percent of our fellow citizens and suggest to them that they seek counselling. After all, who in their right minds, given the choice, could possibly support such a measure? The fact that there was no other option never entered people's minds.

It was a particularly grievous mistake on the part of Finance to think that Canadians would ever accept the tax in the form it was proposed, or that business people would ever understand why they had to hire an army of accountants just to claim back the tax on goods they bought for resale, a tax they should have never been required to pay in the first place. The Opposition parties and the media had a field day. Jean Chrétien promised that as soon as Canadians came to their senses and elected him prime minister, he would not only get rid of the odious tax but also tear up the free-trade agreement, which, in his opinion, was threatening the sovereignty of our country and was sure to have the most deleterious effects on our future economic prospects. How can one blame the Canadian people when even some of the more prominent members of the Liberal Party, such as John Nunziata and Sheila Copps, were gullible enough to believe that he ever had any intention of doing either.

The major initiatives of Mulroney's nine-year administration placed greater emphasis on what was good for the country than on what best served the party or any special interest group. In retrospect, our experience showed that this approach is recommended only for statesmen. Politicians interested in longevity are advised to always put the party and their special friends first. The Liberal experience proves that a well-lubricated political machine will rise from the ashes, no matter how devastating the people's verdict against the government at any given time. The unpopularity of our policies began to take its toll.

Toward the end of the referendum campaign on the Charlottetown Accord, I began to sense that I might be failing the will of my constituents. The Reform Party under Preston Manning had been making steady gains in the opinion polls and was mounting a vicious campaign against the proposed constitutional changes. In all, I spoke at over 40 meetings in the riding—and in many other places throughout the country—explaining the historical context for the negotiations and how the provisions were structured. I urged people to consider the logic of the arguments and the need to give the people in Quebec the assurance and comfort that Canadians, generally at least, recognized their distinctive language and culture and were willing to make the accommodations necessary to guarantee their protection in the constitution.

It was no use. Our voices were drowned out by the crusaders in the Opposition, whose message was crafted to exploit people's ignorance and appeal to their most primitive instincts. The debate became less focussed on the constitution, which, of course, nobody understood anyway, and more on issues that may have in the past, perhaps legitimately, given rise to feelings of alienation from the centre of decision making, and on some of our government's unpopular agenda.

When Canadians rendered their decision on the Charlottetown Accord in October 1992, Alberta and British Columbia registered the highest rejection rate of all the provinces. My own constituents rejected it by a margin of more than 70 percent. Not even the prospect of the total disintegration of the Canadian federation seemed to concern the advocates for principles enunciated by the new Reform Party. When it came to making even the slightest concession to the people of Quebec, western Canadians seemed to shed the tolerance and compassion Joan and I had enjoyed as we made our way among them, and with which they had always shown themselves willing to treat one another. Had I lost my own election, I could not have been more devastated. I sensed that not only had I lost the trust in my judgement and confidence I had enjoyed from my constituents for the 20 years I had served them in Parliament, but I had also failed to live up to the trust and confidence invested in me by the prime minister.

Of course, Joan was not at all disappointed when, on the night of the referendum, I told her that, given the verdict, I would find it exceedingly difficult to hide my bitterness and disappointment or find the enthusiasm to fight another election campaign.

I took the first opportunity I could in the new year to share my thoughts with Brian Mulroney and to tell him of my preference not to compete in another election, unless of course he insisted that I do. As I was told by him later, he had by that time come to much the same conclusion regarding his own future.

"Frankie," he said, "no one could ever ask for more than what you've given in terms of service and commitment to your people and the country."

His only request was that he be allowed to decide on the timing for the public announcement of my decision. Finally, on March 4, eight days after Brian Mulroney had announced his own retirement from politics, I gathered my supporters in Fort St. John to tell them of the decision Joan and I had made.

The timing of Mulroney's announcement was, of course, tailored to produce the optimum advantage for party supporters in recruiting a successor. Once it became public, the party apparatus shifted into full gear and began the search for a new leader. Given that my good friend Kim Campbell, MP for Vancouver Centre, had indicated her intention to compete for the job, I felt not only obliged, but keen, to offer her my support. She won the leadership convention on June 13, 1993, and was sworn as Canada's 19th prime minister on June 25, becoming Canada's first woman to occupy the office. On the following day I handed in my official letter of resignation from Cabinet.

Kim Campbell would no doubt have made a great prime minister for our country, but it wasn't her time. When I met her to offer her my resignation and best wishes, I also told her that any advice I might have to offer her government, from time to time, came free from any obligation on her part. I never had any interest in serving in the Canadian Senate or in accepting one of the hundreds of political appointments sponsored by the Privy Council. Naturally, I was flattered by her suggestion that she might wish to consider me for the post of ambassador to the Federal Republic of Germany, but I was ready to cut my ties to the worlds of politics and diplomacy that exist in defiance of the paradigms of the real world outside.

The party faithful in my riding had chosen a prominent Dawson Creek businessman, Ted Sandhu, to carry their banner in the election. He didn't stand a chance. The fact that he was of East Indian descent was the least of his problems. He was competing against Preston Manning's populist reform movement, which had captured people's imaginations with the most outlandish promises, some of which bordered on outright fraud. The member of Parliament, for example, would owe loyalty to no one other than his constituents. Canada would be like Switzerland, where any issue affecting people generally would be decided by referendum. Members of Parliament would resist any temptation to profit from their position or accept special privileges such as trips abroad at the taxpayers' expense, or a pension at the end of the mandate. Any member found to be in breach of a promise made to his constituents could be recalled. Manning himself, once elected, would set an example by refusing a chauffeur-driven car and the official residence to which the leader of the Official Opposition and the prime minister are entitled.

How could anyone resist a man so totally committed to his cause, and one willing to be judged by the fundamental principles of the Christian faith to which he proclaimed his obedience? The fact that a sufficient number of Canadians in western Canada allowed themselves to be seduced by his sermons is a testimonial to the clarity of vision and the astuteness of the average voter. No doubt Preston Manning had no problem at all finding the appropriate passage in the Holy Book that commanded him, after the election, to take up residence in the Rockcliffe mansion after all and to commute to his palatial office on Parliament Hill in a chauffeur-driven limousine.

The October 25 election was a disaster. The Conservative Party was reduced to two seats, with the separatist Bloc Québécois forming the Official Opposition and Preston Manning's Reform Party coming a close third. It had been difficult at times to keep up a good front as I travelled with the new PC candidate throughout the riding, speaking on his behalf. I had asked to be excused from taking part in election-day activities, fully conscious that his chances were slim. I wanted to be with Joan when the Canadian electorate delivered its judgement on the record we had established during the nine years of our administration. It could not have been more scathing. Ted Sandhu received less than 5 percent of the popular vote. The best I could have hoped for, had I competed myself, would have been to split the vote with the Reform Party candidate, Jay Hill (whom I had defeated in the 1988 election), thus giving the riding to the NDP.

It was very hard to accept the verdict Canadians had rendered, especially since I had no regrets whatsoever over what we had done generally. I could only find fault with the way some of our major policy decisions had been promoted and implemented. Knowing how hard the election defeat was on Kim Campbell, Brian Mulroney, and many of my friends who had chosen to carry on, Joan and I were devastated. The pain and frustration were certainly not eased when, as with the 1974 election, the Liberals immediately reneged on their promises to rescind the key elements of our obviously unpopular measures and instead wasted no time at all in appropriating for themselves all the credit for the benefits flowing to the economy from these initiatives.

Perhaps Canadians ought to be grateful for a government capable of such intellectual dexterity. The consequences of actually keeping some of their promises turned out to be costly indeed. The cancellation of contracts negotiated by the our government for the replacement of Canada's aging fleet of military helicopters and for the upgrading of Pearson International Airport was staggering. It cost taxpayers over one billion dollars in penalties to get out of these commitments, not to mention that more than 10 years later, we still spend millions of dollars every year just to pretend that the now-50-year-old fleet of Sea Kings can still be patched up enough to fly.

I am reminded of Hannah Moore's observation: "So weak is man, so ignorant and blind, that did not God sometimes withhold in mercy what we ask, we should be ruined at our own request."

Occasionally, when I accepted an invitation to address a political science class at a university, I would—much to their disappointment— point to the fact that politics is more of an art than it is a science. Unlike some of my former colleagues, I was never under any illusion about the outcome of the 1993 general election. It wasn't Kim Campbell's fault. People may say that they prefer a government unafraid to commit to an agenda and dedicated to the long-term welfare of the country rather any short-term political objectives. But in truth, people like to be sheltered from harsh realities and the daily challenges that must be faced, referring any nagging problems to others to solve at another time. Canadians needed to catch their breath for a while. Politics, if anything, is the art of timing. I feel privileged to have been chosen at an opportune time, and wise enough to know when to quit. I have no regrets, and make no apologies for my support and contribution to the policies and programs of the Mulroney government.

In retrospect, among the highlights I treasure in my memory are the rare occasions when important world leaders were extended the high honour of addressing Parliament, usually in a joint session with the Senate. Ronald Reagan, Margaret Thatcher, Indira Gandhi, and Nelson Mandela are among the people who brought the place to life with their perspectives and particular views of the world. Chancellor Helmut Kohl of Germany reminded us of the important contribution that German immigrants, among others, have made to Canada in all areas of human endeavour, and he ascribed to those who left Germany after the great wars much of the credit for restoring the more positive image Germany once again enjoys around the world. It was most generous of him to point to my own career as an example.

Given what had become a full career in federal politics for me, it is remarkable how seldom I was reminded of my past or how rarely it was thrown in my face. Despite frequent references to my ancestry in formulating my speeches and in my publications, I can't recall a single occasion when someone reminded me that it was Canada that had offered me a new life and Canadians who had elected me to Parliament. I never once had cause to feel inhibited in any way. During a Cabinet meeting, and after a particularly depressing report given by the Chief of the Defence Staff on the sorry state of our military, I asked the prime minister after a pregnant silence: "Am I to

Frank greets German chancellor Helmut Kohl in 1991.

assume from what the General has just told us that in the event of another war, I am going to be on the losing side again?" It broke up the House.

But there were a few painful occasions, like the time when, in the final days of an election, we were making our way late in the evening from Chetwynd to Prince George, and came upon one of the larger election signs our supporters had put up beside the highway. Someone among my special fans had taken the trouble to climb across a barbed-wire fence to modify the sign's message. Across the entire surface of the four-by-eight-foot display of my handsome image someone had painted a swastika.

Joan saw it first and tried to persuade me to keep my eyes on the road rather than seeing it and becoming upset, but it was she who suffered the most. Tired and exhausted from the gruelling schedule we had kept, she wept inconsolably for the rest of the trip and spent another sleepless night being haunted by our unhappy memories. Still, I can't bring myself to wish, even on a shameless, ignorant person capable of such a cowardly act, that he should ever have to live through the horror of our childhood experiences. I managed to console myself by thinking that while it might have taken just one person to deface the sign, four people had worked to put it up.

Of course, I couldn't help but be conscious of what might be going through people's minds as they watched me, particularly on the occasions when I was invited to stand on the reviewing platform in front of the Prince George Legion Hall with an RCMP inspector and the commanding officer of the military base, taking the salute for the Remembrance Day parade. And I know of one view expressed by Sandy Allen, a long-serving president of the Prince George branch of the Royal Canadian Legion.

After a particularly bitterly cold November 11 morning, the official Remembrance Day party had reconvened in the boardroom so that we could revive ourselves with the aid of several stiff hot drinks, when Sandy gave his customary address.

"As always we are deeply honoured," he said, "by the presence of all of you here this morning, braving the cold to be with us as we show our respect for those of our comrades who have paid the supreme sacrifice in the cause of freedom. I do, however, wish to specially thank our member of Parliament, Frank Oberle, not only for the special effort he makes every year to be with us on this occasion, but also for doing it despite the fact that he is a Kraut. I say this because if you really think of it, if it weren't for the Krauts, we wouldn't have a Legion."

"Sandy," was my only reply, "now I really need another drink."

On another occasion, it was my own demons that inflicted the pain. Even though I participated in at least one official parliamentary mission to Europe as a representative to NATO, I certainly wouldn't have been considered among the hawks in Cabinet when it came to military matters. Of course, I readily accept that Canada has the responsibility to contribute to the collective security and defence of the free world, and I recognize the importance of our military alliances in pursuit of these objectives, but just the thought of war sent shivers down my spine.

It wasn't that I questioned the rationale for the Gulf War, for example. After all, Iraq, seemingly without any provocation, had invaded Kuwait, adding to the instability of the Middle East and threatening legitimate interests the western alliances have in the region. Nor could I fault the prime minister and my good friends and colleagues whose responsibility it was to tailor the Canadian contribution to the response against Saddam Hussein's imperialist adventures. Mulroney deserved most of the credit for making sure that, unlike what took place in the second chapter of the war against Iraq, the United Nations and not the Americans alone took on the aggressor. The issue was clear, as was our responsibility to play a part in the conflict that was about to ensue.

It was just that, apart from one or two colleagues in the room, none had ever been anywhere close to a war, whereas I, burdened with the experience of my childhood, was fully conscious of the horror our action would help to unleash on millions of innocent women and children. As just another item on the day's agenda, the decision was treated no differently than the upgrading of a section of the Trans-Canada Highway would have been. But I, all of a sudden, was back in Dresden, in Lengenfeld, in Poznań. I felt the room closing in on me as I stumbled out the door and ran all the way back to my office, trying to avoid contact with anyone. I found myself pacing my office, trying to control my emotions, but it was no use. Finally, unable to shut out images of the blood-soaked woman clutching her decapitated child to her breast, the ghostly figures stuck in burning asphalt engulfed in the flames of the firestorm in Dresden, or the hungry, pleading, horror-stricken eyes of my friend Joachim on the back of Aunt Johanna's bicycle, I just sat there and cried until there were no more tears.

Such were the memories of my career that accompanied me after my resignation as I left Kim Campbell's office for a long nostalgic walk along the corridors of the Centre Block. Down I went to the Senate Chamber, past the picture gallery of all the distinguished people who had served the institution in important capacities and had graced the place with their presence. Conscious of the prospect that some day my grandchildren, or their children, might visit these halls to discover what role I had played in this great theatre, I strolled through the library for the last time.

It is the most spectacular part of the building; it miraculously survived the disastrous fire of 1884 that destroyed the rest of the original structure. I stopped in to say goodbye to the many fine people and friends I had made among the guards and the rest of the service staff, whose exceptional sense of duty had made life so much easier to bear. I even climbed up the bell tower for a last look over the city. I stood there among some tourists for the longest time, reflecting on the last 20 years, still suspicious that some morning I might wake up to discover that it was all just a dream. Then I walked out through the main portal, down the steps toward the eternal flame. There I turned and walked away toward yet another phase of my life, determined never to look back.

AFTERMATH

1993–2005

CHAPTER 23

The Home Stretch

God gave us memory so that we might have roses in December.

—James M. Barrie

When I announced my retirement from politics, the family was overjoyed, happy with the prospect of once again sharing a normal life together. Thought had to be given to where we would relocate. None of us in the family had ever considered Ottawa as our permanent home. For Joan, the Ottawa experience was a form of "capital punishment."

Ursula and her husband, after prolonged stints as teachers at Fort McPherson in the Arctic, had established themselves and their family on a nice property in Lantzville on Vancouver Island. Every time we managed to stop over for a short visit, she insisted on taking us on tours of the area, hoping that we could be enticed to settle nearby. Like her, I had also fallen in love with the incredible natural beauty of the coast—in my case, during my logging career—and, aside from the old dreams and the lure of the Pine River Valley outside Chetwynd, it wasn't a hard sell. Even though full retirement was never an option, I considered my age a factor: 62 years old was hardly the ideal time to start an entirely new career, particularly one as demanding as ranching. Also, the deep disappointment and disillusion we'd felt over my constituency's overwhelming rejection of my efforts in support of Mulroney's constitutional initiatives made the decision to finally settle on the Island much less painful.

Other than to get busy with building a new home, we had made no future plans. Stuart Smith, after his retirement from the presidency of the Science Council, had been chosen for a number of important public assignments and had joined a private-sector group of brilliant young scientists and engineers involved in research. They had developed and patented a process to convert any carbon-based biomass to a liquid product, yielding an environmentally friendly fuel and a rich menu of commercially attractive chemicals. Dr. Graham, the head of Ensyn Technologies, and Stuart invited me to join their group to help them explore the prospect of applying the technology as a substitute for the archaic and environmentally hazardous method of disposing the mountains of wood residue generated by the forest industry. Given the real and exciting promise of this process, I had no difficulty accepting at all. The fact that I would be able to liaise with the principals in Ottawa from a new home in British Columbia made the offer that much more attractive.

The hectic pace we maintained in the month leading up to the leadership convention and the '93 election allowed very little time for us to manage the transition from the fast lane we'd been travelling for most of our lives in the real world. By this time, Peter was married and had completed his university training. Both he and his wife, Alexandra, had graduated from Queen's University, and Peter had earned himself a master's degree in psychology at York. Pressed into service and testing his skill as a real-estate agent, he was charged both with selling the apartment that had been our home in Ottawa and as someone to help with winding down our personal commitments there.

Once the condominium in Ottawa was sold and the furniture securely stored with a moving company, we relocated to a hotel. That is, Joan relocated to a hotel; I was frantically trying to wind up my affairs in the ministry and the constituency while keeping track of the construction on our new home. As soon as Parliament recessed for the summer, knowing that a new session would be preceded by an election, we chose to move to Vancouver Island, from where I would commute to Ottawa and the riding.

The long hours Joan and I spent on airplanes and in air terminals together did afford us time to hatch the most elaborate dreams for the nest that would house us for the rest of our lives. There would have to be a view of the ocean and some real mountains. There would have to be enough space to accommodate the entire family, 16 people by that time, for Christmas and other special occasions. A big lawn and garden and enough property for lots of shrubs and flowers were among the prerequisites. Of course, there would also be a sour-cherry tree for Joan, just like the one Emil had planted back home in Germany. I was aching to rediscover the joy and satisfaction one earns by creating something with one's hands, something real to stand back from at the end of a day and admire.

I would have preferred, perhaps, to buy an older house on a suitable property and then remodel it to our liking, but in the end we fell in love with Fairwinds, a new community development set in Nanoose Bay and featuring a golf course and marina. Jean Claude Mercier, my deputy minister, and his very able senior staff gave me a set of golf clubs and an instruction manual, suggesting that it might be a sport suited to my temperament and enjoyment during my retirement years.

Neither Joan nor I were particularly impressed when we first visited the site, to which Ursula had steered us on an earlier occasion. The place resembled a war zone, with monstrous-looking machines forcing the rugged terrain to yield fairways for the golf course. But now that it was finished and we could fully grasp the layout, we were ready to make our decision. To satisfy my own needs, we would order the house built only to local requirements for a "lock-up" stage. I would finish the rest, while Joan took care of the landscaping. The contract, signed in April, was to be completed by the end of July.

In order for Shakespeare's dictum "all's well that ends well" to prove itself true, something had to go wrong and it wasn't long before the wheels came off, just as they had on the utility trailer that carried all our worldly possessions on the move to Chetwynd 35 years earlier.

Although the contractor came highly recommended to us by the realty staff of the development, I did overlook a critical clue that should have indicated the need for caution. His office—the front seat of a pickup truck that had seen better days—reminded me of the experience at Bralorne with Charlie Cunningham, many years before. In this case the front passenger seat was occupied not by a filing cabinet, but by a rather large copy of the Holy Bible. Now, one should never pick up a Bible without opening it. Had I done so, God undoubtedly would have guided my thumb to the Book of Revelations to indicate what we were getting into. When finally the excavation phase neared completion, late in July, our highly regarded contractor confessed to a slight cost-overrun of $36,000 dollars, more than 10 times the original $3,500 estimate. This man clearly believed everything he read in the newspaper about the Ottawa way of doing business. God, as we all know, works in mysterious ways and sends his angels in the strangest disguises. In this particular instance, I decided that he had chosen a proper scoundrel to reacquaint us with the real world.

We had rented a small cabin at the bay in nearby Lantzville but our furniture, all our personal belongings, my computer, and important financial records, were all still in storage 5,000 kilometres away in Ottawa. Weeks of construction turned into months. By the end of the year we had discovered that even on Vancouver Island one must have proper clothing to be sheltered from the elements. Our clothing was in storage, together with the other stuff. When finally we managed to coax God's messenger into contributing enough to the project to let us recover most of our investment, I was most fortunate in being able to persuade Les Williams, the landlord of our oceanside cabin, to come to my aid in completing the work by ourselves.

Les is a man accustomed to the old-fashioned standards his namesake, my mentor Ed Williams, lived by when I worked with him in construction at 100 Mile House before moving to Chetwynd. Les brought with him a lifetime of experience and a commitment to excellence that made it an absolute joy to work with him. By the end of January, six months behind schedule, we were sufficiently advanced to order the delivery of our furniture and personal belongings. In the meantime, Joan took charge of the landscaping, giving free rein to her fertile imagination. The result of her effort is nothing less than spectacular and has earned her praise and adulation throughout the neighbourhood.

I firmly believe that a good measure of frustration in one's life is essential to keeping the mind active and stimulated. So, while Joan was telling everyone of her feeling that she'd died and gone to heaven, I chose to keep in touch with my humility by signing up for membership in the Fairwinds Golf Club the same day we were given the permit to occupy our new home. I needn't have worried about finding it difficult to adjust to a more normal way of life after such a tumultuous and stimulating career. Joan was never short of great ideas to put my multiple talents to work around the house.

My work as a managing director with Ensyn Technologies was never intended to be full-time, but it, together with a number of other interesting schemes I am involved with, keeps me in touch with the outside world, and I am satisfied and content to be part of something big, innovative, and important. As well, on those rare occasions when even the Fairwinds

Golf Course suffers a touch of frost or is just a bit too wet, Joan and I have rediscovered the sheer joy of cuddling up in front of the fireplace to read a good book just for the love of it. Finally, after discovering the miracle of the "spell-check" feature on my computer, I managed to overcome whatever reservations I might have had about writing and became an author myself.

The beauty and natural splendour that surrounds our new home is only exceeded by the genuine love, care, and respect the people who have discovered this little paradise show for one another. The waters of the Strait of Georgia are wide enough to afford Island dwellers the luxury of their own unique lifestyle. The city of Victoria, just two hours away, shows some ambition to become a metropolis, but still clings to its unique character and European flavour. Fairwinds is remote enough to be isolated from the hustle and bustle and invasion of contractors with their cranes and bulldozers and paving machines, all competing for every parcel of real estate so they can outfit it with yet another shopping mall and parking lot.

They seek to cater to people from all over the world who are attracted by the amenities and the lifestyle the Island has to offer. We are sufficiently far away from the traffic and noise that would irritate the birds, the deer, and the vast array of other wildlife that, a bit nervously at first, have graciously accepted these new neighbours who have chosen to share their space with them. Of course, the peace and harmony are interrupted from time to time by the occasional territorial conflicts that occur when it comes to protecting the vast variety of flowers and exotic plants the newcomers have introduced to the area, and which the deer in particular consider a special culinary delight. In fact, it is a constant battle of wits in which our four-legged friends continue to occupy the high ground and upper hoof.

After travelling huge distances to get here, the family and friends who come to visit us tend to stay a while, giving us ample time to renew the bonds that tie us together, to reflect on our life's experiences, and to celebrate what we have accomplished.

Joan and I have found our home now, and our peace. It was here that we gathered the family in 2004 and invited our many friends to help us celebrate the anniversary of Joan's arrival in Canada 50 years earlier. The occasion also coincided with our golden wedding anniversary. There are 17 of us now: Ursula and Gordon, Isabell and Gary, Frank and Debbie, Peter and Alex, and, making up the third generation, Mario, Jessica, Lisa, Jennifer, Kevin, Sadie, and Asia. Ursula still lives in Lantzville and has added massage therapy to her multi-faceted career in the literary world. Isabell, exceptionally gifted as a leader and organized and meticulous in her work, is a tireless volunteer in every community to which she moves with her husband. Gary has stayed loyal to West Fraser Timber all these years, requiring him to move from place to place, and in following him, Isabell has explored a series of professional careers, ranging from nursing to banking, and to accounting and business management.

Frank, after distinguishing himself as a management forester with one of Canada's highest-volume pulp mills in northern Alberta, has chosen to answer the call to serve in the political arena. (Who was I to dissuade him when he asked for my advice?) He was elected to the Alberta legislature in the 2004 election.

Peter only practises his profession peripherally. After completing his studies at York University, he wanted to take some time out to work in the public service in Ottawa. He has apparently chosen to make it his life's mission to use his training in psychology to unravel the complexity of the monster known as the Ottawa bureaucracy, and to dissect the peculiar psyches of the members that make Parliament work. His title with the Treasury Board is Director of Service Integration.

None of our children have ever given us cause to worry or to be anything less than immensely proud of them and their own impressive personal accomplishments. Joan and I derive our greatest pleasure and satisfaction by far from watching them and our grandchildren make their way in this complex world.

In August of 2004, we all managed to participate in another family reunion with our many relatives in Germany. It was an unforgettable experience. Close to a hundred people came together at one of the many events crowded into a 10-day period in the region of our ancestors. High in the Black Forest, there was a two-day event for the more immediate family, over 40 people. And then there was a special reception hosted by the mayor and council of the incorporated city of Rheinstetten, which now includes the old villages of Forchheim, Mörsch, and Neuburgweier.

What an honour it was for me, a member of a family with such humble beginnings, to learn that the city had acquired a bronze portrait of my image, sculpted by Martin Schliessler as an expression of our friendship, and that it now occupies a prominent place in Rheinstetten's hall of honour for native sons who have distinguished themselves in other parts of the world.

The sculpture of Frank in Rheinstetten's city hall.

Frank and Mayor Gerhard Dietz sign the "Golden Book," making Frank an honorary citizen of Rheinstetten.

Frank and Joan proudly show off their family, with the mayor, on the steps of Rheinstetten's city hall.

The event helped Joan and I to finally dispel the last vestiges of bitterness that we had carried with us from our early childhood and that had lingered in our consciousness. It gave us cause to renew our love and pride in our native country, feelings that had been tainted by its troubled past.

Our experiences in early life taught Joan and me to be very cautious about ever again becoming too absorbed in any excessive form of patriotism, but our hearts are filled to the brim with love for Canada. Politicians must be prepared to make great personal sacrifices, but they are also rewarded with certain unique benefits, not the least being the opportunity to travel the length and breadth of our great country. I have seen the sun rise off the coast of Labrador. I have been among the ice floes in the Arctic Ocean, and stood on the Queen Charlotte Islands to see the sun set over the Pacific. How inadequate even the most spectacular edifices created by the blood, sweat, and tears of man for the glory of God are against the special places he has allotted for us in his natural world, where we can be in touch with our inner beings and nourish our own personal spirituality. There are no people on earth more blessed than the people who are privileged to live their lives in this rich, generous, and beautiful land.

Despite all that, we feel no guilt in remaining loyal to the traditions of our ancestors. Joan delights everyone with her German culinary artistry. Here at Fairwinds, we still celebrate our traditional German Christmas. The prayers have not changed, nor have the hymns and the songs. Only the gifts have become a bit more elaborate and plentiful over the years. Yes, Joan and I never quite manage to suppress our emotions during these precious moments when our spirits are joined with those we love most. On one such occasion, it was Sadie as a little girl who asked her mommy: "Why is Grandma crying?"

Well, Sadie, your grandma is no doubt mourning her own lost childhood. She was crying perhaps for the children that live in places like Moccasin Flats; children we have visited in the slums of Rio de Janeiro, Manila, and in other places in the world, such as the homelands of South Africa. She would shed a tear no doubt for Mila Mulroney's hospital children and their parents we met one Christmas in Ottawa. But she would not like you to feel sad, because they are tears of joy as well: joy in being able to share in your happiness and in being blessed with the innocent, sweet, and genuine love you and our other grandchildren give us.

We are who we are because of our past. Reflecting on life in one's twilight years quickly leads to the discovery that without one's family and the friends acquired over the years, little else has much meaning. These pages are intended therefore mainly for our children and our many friends and benefactors—to give them a glimpse into our past, help them understand what has shaped our lives and the idiosyncrasies we've acquired, and perhaps allow them to pardon some of the indiscretions we committed, which may have offended others, in pursuit of our dreams.

I have some regrets, but I am not burdened with doubt about the righteousness of the path we chose to find happiness for ourselves and help promote a better world.

What Reviewers Have Said About *Finding Home*

"The story is an inspiration for youth. It is an inspiration for the immigrant. And it is evidence of the enduring quality of the human spirit."

—*Senior Living*, Victoria, B.C.

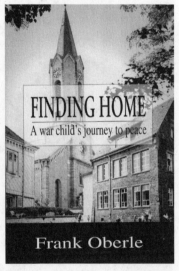

FINDING HOME
A war child's journey to peace

Frank Oberle

ISBN 1-894384-76-8 $22.95

"Autobiography is the ... strongest when it hits close to home. This searing, unsettling memoir is about ... nostalgia with the blinkers off. Oberle understands—and conveys—that in family life, everything is complicated, even a grown child's fear of abandonment ... Oberle's is the first book in recent memory that has the scope of a whole life arc with all of its nuances and unpredictability. The book is surprisingly readable and satisfying It's practically filmic."

—Chris DeVito, *CD Syndicated*, Richmond, B.C.

"If you ever have the chance to talk to Frank Oberle about his autobiography, *Finding Home*, bring a hankie ... *Finding Home* is about a time in his life he's rarely discussed ... a horrifying story ... he's spent a lifetime trying to forget."

—Diane Dakers, *Times Colonist*, Victoria, B.C.

Born in Forchheim, Germany, Frank Oberle survived the turmoil of Hitler's Germany and post-war chaos before immigrating to Canada in 1951. During his career he tried his hand at many jobs, including logger, gold miner, rancher, and town mayor, before serving six consecutive terms as a member of Parliament. In 1985 Frank became Canada's first German-born federal Cabinet member when Prime Minister Brian Mulroney made him Minister of State for Science and Technology. Four years later, as Minister of Forestry, his determination led him to confront the industry's clear-cutting practices and demand sustainable forest management. He received the Canadian Forestry Achievement Award in 1992 and was a founding member of the Canadian Institute for Advanced Research.

Frank lives near Nanoose, B.C., with his wife Joan. They have four children and seven grandchildren.